THE GOAL AND THE WAY

Prelude to the author's next book:
The Universe, God, and God-Realization

Works by Swami Satprakashananda

METHODS OF KNOWLEDGE: ACCORDING TO ADVAITA VEDANTA
HINDUISM AND CHRISTIANITY
SRI RAMAKRISHNA'S LIFE AND MESSAGE IN THE PRESENT AGE: WITH THE AUTHOR'S REMINISCENCES OF HOLY MOTHER AND SOME DIRECT DISCIPLES
MEDITATION: ITS PROCESS, PRACTICE, AND CULMINATION
THE GOAL AND THE WAY: THE VEDANTIC APPROACH TO LIFE'S PROBLEMS
THE UNIVERSE, GOD, AND GOD-REALIZATION
and other Vedantic treatises

THE GOAL AND THE WAY

The Vedantic Approach to Life's Problems

By

Swami Satprakashananda

THE VEDANTA SOCIETY OF ST. LOUIS

ISBN 0-916356-56-6
LC 77-075279 10/79

205 South Skinker Boulevard
St. Louis, Missouri 63105

Printed in the United States of America

ERRATUM

page	paragraph	line	for	read
205	4	2	868	686

CONTENTS

SYNOPSES OF CHAPTERS

PART ONE

WHAT IS MAN?

The Self and the Psychophysical Vehicle

C. The Causal Body

D. The Fivefold Sheath

III. THE MIND AND ITS WAYS: HOW TO WIELD IT

IV. PRĀNA, THE VITAL PRINCIPLE; ITS INDIVIDUAL AND COSMIC ASPECTS

A. THE INDIVIDUAL PRĀNA

B. THE COSMIC PRĀNA

PART TWO

THE MIGRATORY MAN

The Cycle of Birth and Rebirth and the Way Beyond

V. THE LAW OF KARMA AND FREEDOM OF ACTION

VI. MAN'S DAILY MIGRATION: WAKING, DREAM, AND DREAMLESS SLEEP STATES

PART THREE

MAN'S TWOFOLD JOURNEY OF LIFE
The Secular and the Spiritual Pursuit

IX. MAN IN QUEST OF THE ETERNAL

X. THE PATH OF PROSPERITY AND THE PATH OF SUPREME GOOD; THEIR NECESSITY

XI. THE SPIRITUAL OUTLOOK ON LIFE. HOW IT CONJOINS THE TWO WAYS

XII. THE ATTAINMENT OF THE HIGHEST GOOD THROUGH THE PERFORMANCE OF DUTY. *The Necessity for a Spiritual Outlook on Life*

PREFACE

The key to the solution of life's problems is the right determination of the goal and the way of life. Vedanta ascertains the goal and the way of life in view of what man really is. Man's plan of living depends on his idea of man. The search for the meaning of life ends with the finding of man's true nature and the process of its fulfillment.

The theme of the book is presented with arguments from the standpoint of common understanding and valid experience. I have also quoted the words of recognized authorities to corroborate the Vedantic view.

I am grateful to Mr. and Mrs. Richard L. Bergman, Mrs. Helen Smith (formerly teacher, Wagner College, Staten Island, N.Y.), and Dr. Huston Smith (Thomas J. Watson Professor of Religion and Adjunct Professor of Philosophy, Syracuse University, Syracuse, N.Y.) for reading the typescript of the book and making comments and emendations.

I am thankful to my Vedanta students who have helped me in different ways in bringing out the book. I very much appreciate the keen interest with which Mrs. Virginia Ward, a Vedanta student, has prepared the index.

I am indebted to all the authors and the publishers for permission to quote from their books. Their names with necessary information are given in the footnote under each quotation.

SATPRAKASHANANDA

The Vedanta Society
St. Louis, Missouri
March 21, 1974

NOTE ON THE PRONUNCIATION OF TRANSLITERATED SANSKRIT ALPHABET

a	as in all	ñ	n (palatal)
ā	as in far	ṭ	as in tool
i	as in tin	ṭh	as th in boat-house
ī	as ee in deep	ḍ	as in dog
u	as in full	ḍh	as in Godhood
ū	as oo in loop	ṇ	n (cerebral)
ō	as in note	th	as in thin
ṛ	as ri in prick	d	as th in then
ṁ	as ng in Hongkong	dh	as in Buddha
ḥ	as in oh!	n	(dental) as in noun
g	hard as in good	ph	as in loophole
ṅ	as ng in king	bh	as in abhor
c	as ch in church	v	as w
ch	as chh in thatch-hut	ś	as in short (palatal sibilant)
jh	as geh in hedge-hog	ṣ	(cerebral sibilant)

ABBREVIATIONS

AB	*Ātma-bōdha*
Ai.Br.	*Aitareya Brāhmaṇa*
Ai.U.	*Aitareya Upaniṣad*
ASS	*Ānandāśrama Sanskrit Series*, Poona, India
AV	*Ātmānātma-viveka*
BG	*Bhagavad-gītā*
BP	*Bhāṣā-pariccheda*
Br.U.	*Bṛhadāraṇyaka Upaniṣad*
BS	*Brahma-sūtras*
Ch.	Chapter
Ch.U.	*Chāndōgya Upaniṣad*
com.	commentary
CSS	*Chowkhamba Sanskrit Series*, Varanasi
CW	*The Complete Works of Swami Vivekananda*
GSR	*The Gospel of Sri Ramakrishna*
Is.U.	*Īśa Upaniṣad*
Jab.U.	*Jābāla Upaniṣad*
Ka.U.	*Kaṭha Upaniṣad*
Kai.U.	*Kaivalya Upaniṣad*
Kau.Br.	*Kauṣītaki Brāhmaṇa*
Kau.U.	*Kauṣītaki Upaniṣad*
Ken.U.	*Kena Upaniṣad*
Ma.U.	*Māṇḍūkya Upaniṣad*
Mbh.	*Mahābhārata*
MK	*Māṇḍūkya Upaniṣad Kārikā*
MS	*Manu-smṛti*
Mu.U.	*Muṇḍaka Upaniṣad*
NS	*Naiṣkarmya-siddhi*
NSP	Nirnaya Sagar Press, Bombay
Pd.	*Pañcadaśī*
Pr.U.	*Praśna Upaniṣad*
Rg.V.	*Ṛg-Veda*
Sat.Br.	*Śatapatha Brāhmaṇa*
SB	*Śrīmad-bhāgavatam*
S.com.	Śaṅkara's commentary
SD	*Sāṁkhya-darśanam*
sec.	section
SK	*Sāṁkhya-kārikā*
Sv.U.	*Śvetāśvatara Upaniṣad*
Tai.Ar.	*Taittirīya Āraṇyaka*
Tai.U.	*Taittirīya Upaniṣad*
trans.	translation
VC	*Viveka-cūḍāmaṇi*
VP	*Vedānta-paribhāṣā*
VS	*Vedānta-sāra*
VVP	Vani Vilas Press, Sri Rangam, Madras
YS	*Yōga-sūtras* of Patañjali

INTRODUCTION

The fundamental difference between man and what we call the lower orders of life is not in the physical form but in the psychical function. In human life the mind has reached a level at which it can think. Man not only sees, but reads and interprets things. He looks far beyond the senses. His knowledge is not confined within the domain of sense perception. The human mind has the capacity to probe the deepest secrets of nature and unravel the profound mysteries of life. Not only that, man can also regulate his life by his knowledge. The practical application of man's knowledge for the advancement of individual and social welfare is a characteristic feature of civilized life.

Much more important than sheer intellect is the moral sense of man. He is not a mere instrument of his instincts, as some psychologists hold. He can discriminate between right and wrong, true and false, noble and ignoble, good and pleasant. The instinctive urges are no doubt strong in man; but guided by reason, he can develop will power to control the natural impulses and pursue his chosen course. He has the choice of decision as well as the choice of action. He can dominate and direct the lower self by the higher self. This self-mastery constitutes the real nature of man. Man's advancement is proportionate to the development of this virtue.

Self-assertion and self-aggrandizement are the instinctive urges of animal life. Self-denial and self-sacrifice are the human attributes developed by moral culture. This distinguishes humanity from animality. Indeed, "humanity" is the distinctive mark of the human race as brutality is that of the beasts. In the animal kingdom life grows chiefly through rivalry and hostility in the struggle for existence. Those live who can subdue others. The fittest survive. On the human plane the scene changes. Mankind advances, as we see, through cooperation, self-abnegation, altruism. Man's worthiness rests on the fulfillment of his duties and obligations. Whenever this truth is forgotten, human society faces dissension and disaster, with attendant misery.

In human life there is an ideal, a regulative principle, a philosophy. Man's outlook on life determines his way of life. To man the art of life is more important than mere living. A life devoid of meaning and purpose is regarded as of little value. He who has no aim in life is like a breathing machine in human form. Man alone considers it glorious to sacrifice his life for the sake of the ideal. Such martyrdom immortalizes him. There have been martyrs in religion, in philosophy, in science, in nationalism. We revere them as heroes.

In man self-consciousness is much more developed than in other living beings. He is fully aware of himself as an individual distinct from the rest of the world. He can analyze his own being. He can distinguish the self from the not-self. He draws a distinction between the body and the mind, and knows that he has an outer as well as an inner life. He finds that his inner life is greater, deeper, and more glorious than the outer life. The physical body, however dominant and fascinating, forms but the exterior of his personality. The intellectual, moral, aesthetic, and spiritual aspects of life are the expressions of his inner consciousness.

One special privilege of human life is the power of self-expression. It has been rightly observed that nature begets, but man creates. Man not only has the ingenuity to invent but also the creative genius of the artist. He can give aesthetic expression to his ideas, thoughts, feelings, and imagination in varied fine arts, such as architecture, sculpture, painting, literature, music, and poetry. These works of art, more marvelous than the achievements of science, are the cherished treasures of man on earth. How poor mankind would have been without them! The cultural life of man begins with the development of the artistic ability. As long as man is concerned only with the bare necessities of life he cannot develop art. The production of art becomes possible when man emerges from the animal-like struggle for food and learns to idealize life.

However, there are human beings no better than animals. In fact, human brutes are worse than beasts. The practice of such devilry as duplicity, hypocrisy, treachery, conspiracy, and tyranny that so often marks man's dealings with man is unknown to the animal world. The quadrupeds are incapable of such wickedness and meanness. Indeed, the poet has every reason to lament: "What man has made of man." Nevertheless, in judging man we should take as our examples the true types of humanity and not the degenerate groups of individuals, just as an apple tree is to be judged not by the unripe, rotten, or worm-eaten fruits that the tree may bear but by those that are well-developed and typical. There have been among men such spiritual giants as Kṛṣṇa, Zoroaster, the Buddha, Lao Tzu, Christ; philosophers like Kapila, Vyāsa, Socrates, Plato, Plotinus, Kant, Schopenhauer; poets like Vālmīki, Homer, Virgil, Dante, Kālidās,

Shakespeare, Goethe, Wordsworth; artists like Leonardo da Vinci, Michelangelo, Raphael, Rembrandt; scientists like Archimedes, Āryabhatta, Galileo, Newton, Einstein; monarchs like Emperor Aśōka, Harun Al Rasid, Alfred the Great, Akbar; seers and saints like Śukadeva, Śaṅkarācārya, Saint Francis of Assisi, Meister Eckhart, Saint Rabia, Mirabai, and so forth — to mention just a few of the world's great personages known and unknown to history.

The crowning glory of human life is self-knowledge. Man can know himself as he really is. The body does not constitute his real self, nor the mind, nor the combination of the body and the mind. His real self, the very basis of his ego, is a self-intelligent principle. It is the knower of the body as well as of the mind. The mind cannot be self-intelligent, because the mind is known. There is something beyond that watches the mind. The mind falls into the category of the object. It should not be identified with the subject, the knower. Intelligence is the essence of the knower, and not of the known. The self-intelligent entity behind the mind, which watches all physical and mental events, is the only invariable factor in the human personality. It coordinates all physical and mental processes. It maintains the identity of man despite the incessant changefulness of the body and the mind. Unchanging, it witnesses all changes. Had it changed, it could not be the witness *per se*. We would have to posit another entity as the witness of this change. The witness cannot participate in the change it witnesses. The witness must be aloof from what is witnessed. The real witness, the ultimate knower, must therefore be changeless.

So the self of man is immutable. Being pure intelligence, it is self-evident. No one doubts his own existence. To him it is an axiomatic truth. "That he is" is an established fact for him. He may doubt or deny the existence of everything else, even of God, but not his own. Even in denying himself he has to affirm himself. Nothing can be affirmed or denied without presupposing the self-intelligent knower. The self must be the first thing real. The existence or nonexistence of everything else rests on the reality of the self. It is therefore self-existent. It existed before this body originated, it will continue to exist after the body drops and disintegrates.

The self is eternal. Anything that changes is a compound, that is, made up of parts. As the self is changeless, it cannot be composite: it must be simple and formless. Contrary to matter, it is self-shining, self-existent, immutable, free, pure, and blissful. It is the spiritual basis of the phenomenal existence. The body cannot hold it, nor can the mind. It must be one with the Supreme Being.

Such is the self of man. But through mysterious ignorance he gets identified with the body and the mind and ascribes to himself all that belong to them. Thus the unconditioned spirit becomes subject to all physical and mental conditions. As soon as man can realize his distinctness from the psychophysical adjuncts and his oneness with the Supreme Being, he becomes free from all bondages. The attainment of this Freedom is the highest goal of life. One can attain it even while living in the body. It is the ignorance of the true nature of the self which is the prime cause of bondage, and not the body nor the mind.

There have been great seers and saints in different climes and ages who have realized this Freedom and proclaimed it to be the Supreme End of life. So declares the Vedic seer of India, "I have realized this self-effulgent Supreme Being beyond darkness. By knowing Him alone one overcomes mortality. There is no other way out."[1] He who knows the Truth, becomes one with the Truth, because the Truth is his very self. You cannot objectify your own Self. You simply recognize the self. "The knower of Brahman becomes Brahman (the Supreme Being)," says the *Muṇḍaka Upaniṣad.*[2] Why? Because "That thou art."[3]

Self-realization and God-realization are not two different experiences. In realizing the self we realize God. In realizing God we realize the self. The self and God are subjective and objective views of the same Reality, which is beyond relativity and is neither the subject nor the object. In the relative plane it is the Eternal Subject, the Soul of all souls. The direct approach to It is, therefore, through the self. This is why we seek God with closed eyes in the inmost depth of our being. In the words of Jesus Christ, "The Kingdom of God cometh not with observation; neither shall they say, Lo here! or, Lo there! for behold, the Kingdom of God is within you."[4] Further, "God is a Spirit, and they that worship Him must worship Him in spirit and in truth."[5] To all worshipers the instruction of the Hindu Tantras is: "Worship the Divine, being divine [by evoking the divine spirit within]."

The same inner approach was taught by the great German mystic Meister Eckhart, who lived from 1260 to 1328 A.D.

[1]Sv.U. III:8.
[2]Mu.U. III:2.9.
[3]Ch.U. VI:8.7.
[4]Luke 17:20, 21.
[5]John 4:24.

> To get at the core of God at His greatest, one must first get into the core of oneself at his least, for no one can know God who has not first known himself. Go to the depth of the soul, the secret place of the Most High, to the roots, to the heights, for all that God can do is focussed there.[6]

The great Chinese sage Lao Tzu, in the sixth century B.C., spoke in a similar strain:

> Without going outside one's door, one understands [all that takes place] under the sky; without looking out from one's window, one sees the Tao of heaven. The farther one goes out [from oneself], the less one knows.
>
> Therefore the sages got their knowledge without traveling; gave the [right] names to things without seeing them and accomplished their ends without any purpose of doing so.[7]

Man's intrinsic divine nature and his relationship with God is the keystone of all theistic faiths. "Religion," as defined by Swami Vivekananda, "is the manifestation of the Divinity already in man."[8] In other words, it is the unfoldment of man's innate perfection. That the human soul is essentially pure and perfect is not only a fact of suprasensuous experience but also the basic principle of the process of evolution. If a human being can evolve into such a divine personality as Buddha or Christ, it necessarily follows that Buddhahood or Christhood must be involved in man. If, according to the theory of evolution, an amoeba is progressing towards perfection, then perfection must be latent in the amoeba.

A tiny seed grows into a giant oak tree because the tree exists in the seed in potential form. The growth of a living organism means the unfoldment of its latent potency. An oak tree never emerges from an apple seed. To hold that man evolves into a godlike being and at the same time deny that Godhood is involved in man is illogical. It is but a one-sided view of the evolutionary process. Evolution presupposes involution. If perfection or Divinity be man's goal, Divinity must be the origin of man. According to science man is a risen animal; according to religion, man is a fallen spirit. The acknowledgment of

[6]Raymond Blakney, *Meister Eckhart, A Modern Translation,* New York, Harper & Brothers, 1941, p. 246.

[7]Lao Tzu, *Tao Teh Ching,* in *The Texts of Taoism,* James Legge, trans., Sacred Books of the East, F. Max Muller, ed., Vol. XXXIX, 1891, reprint edn., New York, Dover Publications, 1962, Ch. 47, p. 89.

[8]CW IV, p. 304.

involution as antecedent to evolution harmonizes the seeming conflict between scientific and religious views.

To evaluate man we should take into account not merely his physical and mental stature but his spiritual nature as well. Those who think the body and the mind to be the principal factors of human personality naturally fail to see any truth in the conception of man's divine relationship. They may argue: "Imagine the immeasurable vastness of the universe as first revealed by Copernicus. Compared to that what is this puny man! Even this terrestrial globe appears to be something like a geometrical point. What relationship can man have with the omnipotent, omniscient Ruler of the universe if any such Being exists? It is an extreme case of human conceit to trace man's descent from God or to claim relationship with Him." But, in fact, man is ever united with God in spirit, though he fails to recognize this, being under a spell of amnesia, as it were.

In one of the monthly magazines of America I read the following interesting comment on the rude shock that man's pretensions to divine relationship have received from scientific discoveries:

> Three men have reduced us to our proper insignificance and put an end to the primitive dream that we are godlike or that there is any God for us to resemble. They are Copernicus, Darwin, and Freud. Copernicus began the revelation of the vastness of the universe and the consequent triviality of our poor molecule of a planet. Darwin showed man's ancestry reaching not up to the stars and their glory, but down to the mud and its fermentation. And Freud pushed our humiliation into the last pit by the knowledge that what we thought was the light of spirit is only the sickly gleams of funguses growing rank in the cellars of physiology.

It is needless to point out that these are only limited and distorted views of the human personality. If the very rudiments of human life be carnal, bestial, unholy, by no possible method of culture, by no alchemy, can they be transmuted into moral and spiritual virtues. But the truth is that there arise among men and women certain individuals who *do* realize their divine nature and whose life and conduct testify to their inner experience.

The same Supreme One is the indwelling spirit in all living creatures. "I am the Self existing in the hearts of all beings," says the Lord Kṛṣṇa.[9] Vedanta does not deny the soul, the spiritual self, to any sentient being, but acknowledges infinite variations in its manifesta-

[9]BG X:20.

tion according to the development of each individual mind. In the human life alone the realization of the self becomes possible. It is self-knowledge or God-vision that makes man free.

Devoid of supreme devotion to the Highest, one cannot attain this Freedom by meritorious deeds alone. Moral virtues, too, cannot take us beyond the relative existence. An individual may go to higher or lower planes of existence according to merits or demerits predominating in his nature. But he will come back to this human life after the effects of those deeds are exhausted. The human life alone is the sphere of action. Here you can undertake fresh karma, good or evil, and also cultivate self-knowledge. It is because of this blessed privilege that human life is considered to be the highest. The human life is short and frail, no doubt; but rightly lived it can serve even as the springboard to enter the Life Eternal.

PART ONE

WHAT IS MAN?

The Self and the Psychophysical Vehicle

CHAPTERS I-IV

CHAPTER I

MAN, REAL AND APPARENT

1. *The real man, the knower within, is the central principle of consciousness, distinct from the body, the organs, and the mind.*

It is a curious fact that man with all his pretensions to knowledge does not know himself. On the contrary, he has a mistaken notion of himself. Although an embodied being, he is not aware of the indwelling self, but is identified with the body, the dwelling. He thinks of himself and every other individual in terms of the physical tenement. It is not just a case of blissful ignorance. Man pays heavily for his misconception of himself. All his bondages and sufferings stem from this.

Ridden by the body-idea he ascribes to himself the attributes of the body. He thinks that he is born, that he grows, that he decays, that he dies; that he has hunger and thirst; that he is subject to heat and cold; that he is young or old, dark or fair, tall or short, slim or stout, well or ill; that he is a man distinct from woman. Consequently, to fulfill physical cravings and needs becomes the primary objective of his life. Being identified with the body, he identifies himself with the sense organs. He yearns for self-fulfillment on the sense-plane, fails to distinguish between pleasant and good, seeks security in the insecure, clutches at vanishing charms, and is swayed continuously by pleasure and pain, hope and despair, love and hate. Being preoccupied with the fleeting objects of experience, he can hardly turn his attention to the experiencer within, the unvarying light that manifests the varying facts of experience.

To all appearance, man is a physical or a psychophysical being, a changeful mortal creature. But really he is distinct from the physical body and the mind as well, because he is the knower of both. As he perceives external objects, so does he perceive his bodily conditions and mental states. The knower and the object known cannot be identical. They are ever distinct. While consciousness is intrinsic in the knower, the thing known is destitute of it. Neither the body nor the mind has consciousness inherent in it; otherwise neither could ever lose consciousness. For the same reason the real man, the knower within, is distinct from each of the ten organs: the five organs of perception and the five organs of action. He knows whether a particular organ is operative or inoperative, whether it is sound or unsound.

Thus, the real man, the knowing self, is other than the body, other than the organs, other than the mind, and other than their aggregate. As the central principle of consciousness in human personality the self is the ruler within. This is what integrates the heterogeneous physical and psychical factors into a coherent whole. This is what coordinates all physical, psychical, and vital processes in an individual. This is the only constant factor in human personality. This maintains one's identity despite all changes of the psychophysical constitution. The observer of all changing conditions undergoes no change. It relates the succeeding events to the preceding and notices the variation between the two. Otherwise changes could not be recognized.

The knower *per se* and the object known are of contrary nature like light and darkness. The one is self-manifest and manifests the other. Being in the category of the object, neither the body nor any of the organs is self-manifest. Even the mind is not self-manifest. It is the knowing self that manifests them all. As pointed out by Patañjali, "The mind is not self-luminous because it is perceivable."[1] That is self-luminous which has consciousness as its essence. Being of the nature of consciousness, the knower within, the real man, is self-luminous. As such this is self-evident. None requires any proof of his own existence. Every individual spontaneously knows that he *is*. He takes for granted his own existence as a cognizer. On the basis of this he determines the existence and nonexistence of all else. The existence of each and every object, known or unknown, presupposes the existence of the luminous self and the knower.

The luminous self shines *of* itself. It does not manifest itself. No reflex process is involved in the manifestation of the self. It is this self-luminosity that differentiates spirit (caitanya) from matter (jaḍa). Nothing material is self-aware or aware of anything else. Light is apparently self-luminous, but not self-aware. It is unaware of its own existence and the existence of all else. Anything destitute of consciousness, including the resplendent sun, belongs to the domain of matter. In this sense the mind as well as the physical body is

[1] YS IV:19. (The author of the *Yōga-sūtras,* Patañjali was the first great exponent of Yōga philosophy.)

material. But the mind belongs to a different order of matter than the body. It is constituted of the finest and the purest type of material substance. The luminous self is the sole spiritual entity in an individual. Man is essentially pure spirit ever shining. It is the radiance of the spiritual self that illuminates the psychophysical system, that is to say, endows the mind, the organs, and the body with a semblance of consciousness.

2. *The luminous self governs the whole psychophysical system by its radiance.*

Being composed of the purest and finest type of matter, the mind has the capacity to transmit the radiance of the luminous self to the organs and the body. It serves somewhat like a sheet of glass that transmits physical light to opaque objects. As the medium of transmission it becomes more or less permeated by the luster of consciousness. Just as a window-pane turns bright while transmitting sunlight, or just as an iron-ball becomes aglow being permeated by fire, even so does the mind shine with the borrowed light of consciousness. This is why the mind is very often confused with the luminous self. Western thinkers in general have often identified the spiritual self with the mind. Imbued with consciousness the mind serves as the primary instrument of knowledge. It is indispensable to every form of cognition. The ten organs and the physical body receive the light of consciousness through the mind, each according to its own nature. Being tinged with consciousness, more or less, the organs function and the body has sensation.

When a person dreams during sleep his sense organs lose the power of perception, the motor organs the power of action, the body the power of-sensation, and the mind the power of volition. This is because his consciousness recedes wholly from the body and partly from the mind. In dreamless sleep all his mental operations cease, because consciousness recedes from the mind altogether. No thought, no feeling, no memory, no imagination, no cognition of any kind stirs the mind. Even egoism drops. The incessant fluctuations of the mind become completely lulled.

Even then the involuntary bodily functions, such as respiration, digestion, and assimilation of food, which are associated with the autonomic nervous system, continue, being impelled by the vital principle, prāṇa, which keeps awake and guards the body like a sentinel while the mind and the organs are fully at rest. Undoubtedly, a glimmer of consciousness received from the luminous self keeps prāṇa operative in waking, dream, and deep sleep as well. As observed by Śaṅkara, "It is by being illumined by the light of consciousness of the ātman, its very self, that the vital principle functions."[2] The only source of life and light of a person is the luminous self. So says Śrī Kṛṣṇa to Arjuna: "Just as the one sun, O Bhārata, lights up the entire world, so the self abiding in the psychophysical system illumines the whole psychophysical domain."[3]

The knowing self is the sole ruler of the psychophysical organism. It is not that the ears hear, the eyes see, the mouth speaks, the hands work, the mind thinks, the vital principle animates. The fact is, it is the indwelling luminous self that hears through the ears, sees through the eyes, speaks through the mouth, works through the hands, thinks through the mind, and enlivens through the vital principle. So a person says: "I hear," "I see," "I speak," "I work," "I think," "I breathe," "I live," and so on. Basically, it is one and the same "I" that asserts itself through varying sense-perceptions, bodily activities, mental operations, and vital processes. Underlying the varying functions of the organs, the mind, and the vital principle, there is one constant entity, the knowing self. In fact, the organs, the mind, and the vital principle are his instruments. He directs and controls them. Says the *Chāndōgya Upaniṣad:* "He who [in this body] knows, 'I smell this,' is the self, for his smelling is the nose. He who knows, 'I say this,' is the self, for his speaking is the organ of speech. He who knows, 'I hear this,' is the self, for his hearing is the ear."[4] Indeed, the one central principle that unifies all bodily activities, all sense-perceptions, all mental operations, all vital processes in an individual is the self.

It is because the self is distinct from the organs that a person can have such experiences as "I see and hear the speaker," "I smell and touch the flower I see," "I taste the food I see and smell." From these instances it is evident that one and the same individual is the experiencer of sound, sight, touch, taste, and smell through the different organs. The experiencer that underlies the diverse organs cannot be identified with any one of them. Therefore, the self is distinct from the organs, which are his instruments of varied perception.

A person can visualize with the eyes closed what he sees with the

[2]Br.U. IV:4.18, S. com. (Śaṅkara was one of the greatest philosopher saints of India and the prime advocate of Advaita Vedanta. See pp. 205-6.)

[3]BG XIII:33. [4]Ch.U. VIII:12.4.

eyes open. This shows that the eyes are not the actual "seers." That which visualizes the sight with the eyes closed must have seen it with the eyes open. Had the sense organs (jñānendriyas) been the actual perceivers, then such acts of recognition, desire, etc., as "Here is the house I heard about," "I see the food that I tasted," "I want the garment I saw yesterday," would not have been possible. Says Śaṅkara:

> It is not proper to conceive each organ as an experiencer, for in that case it would be impossible to relate memory, perception, wish, etc., to one and the same subject in any individual. What one person has perceived another cannot recollect or know, or desire or recognize. Therefore none of the organs can be regarded as an experiencer.[5]

If the sense organs were the actual perceivers and the motor organs (karmendriyas) the actual doers, then there would have been a number of selves in an individual body, which is contrary to fact.

The *Kena Upaniṣad* opens with the questions:

> By whom willed and directed does the mind proceed to its object?
> By whom engaged does the vital principle (prāṇa), the foremost, perform its duty?
> At whose will do men utter speech?
> Who is the effulgent one that directs the eyes and the ears?

The answer is given:

> He [the luminous self] is the Ear of the ear, the Mind of mind, the Speech of [the organ of] speech, the Life of life, and the Eye of the eye.[6]

In the *Bṛhadāraṇyaka Upaniṣad* also, the luminous self is said to be "The Life of life, the Eye of the eye, the Ear of the ear, and the Mind of the mind."[7] The point is: the body, the organs, the mind, the vital principle, being devoid of consciousness, fall into the category of nonintelligent matter and cannot be self-operative. Their coordinate functions must be due to conscious spirit, the luminous self.

3. *The self, the witness of all changes, is changeless, and so birthless, growthless, decayless, deathless, and is inseparable from the Self of the universe.*

The self is invariable in the midst of the variable. What is cognized varies but not the cognizer. The external objects vary. The bodily

[5]Br.U. II:1.15, S. com. [6]Ken.U. I:1,2. [7]Br.U. IV:4.18.

conditions and the mental states vary. The functions of the organs and the mind vary. There are also variations in biological processes. It is the luminous self that cognizes them all. A change presupposes an unchanging observer who relates the succeeding event with the preceding one. In case the observer varies in the interim the change cannot be recognized. Being the observer of all variations, the self is beyond the variables. If any of the variables inhere in him, then he must be subject to variation. Therefore none of the changing factors of human personality can be regarded as intrinsic in the self.

In the Vedantic view the real man, the knower *per se*, is ever distinct from the psychophysical organism. He is not the unity of the physical and the psychical elements as some psychologists hold; nor is he the unity of the body, the mind, and the spirit, as some theologians maintain. If the present physical body be held as essential to the inner man, then death must mean the dissolution of human personality, and survival after death the revivification of the corpse, which is obviously absurd. Though appearing as a unity of diverse physical and psychical factors, man is essentially the central principle of consciousness that unifies them into a complex whole. It is in association with the mind, the organs, and the body that the luminous self plays the role of the knower and the doer.

As the simple spiritual substance, ever shining, changeless in the midst of the changeful, man is birthless, growthless, decayless, deathless, sorrowless, without hunger, without thirst, without the least trace of darkness, ever pure and free. In the words of the *Chāndōgya Upaniṣad:* "Free from sin, free from old age, free from death, free from grief, free from hunger, free from thirst is this ātman, whose desires prove true, whose will proves true."[8] Apparently man is mortal, but really he is immortal; apparently he is bound, but really he is free; apparently he is impure, but really he is pure; apparently he is ignorant, but really he is illumined.

It is by discovering the true nature of the self that man is reinstated in his innate freedom, purity, and blissfulness. Simultaneously he realizes his essential unity with the all-pervading Supreme Self, the Soul of all souls, who dwells within each and every individual as the inmost Self. This is how he attains complete self-fulfillment. As declared by the *Kaṭha Upaniṣad:*

> Eternal peace belongs to such wise persons — and not to others — as perceive Him, who is the inmost Self dwelling within, who is

[8]Ch.U. VIII:1.5.

Consciousness of all that are conscious, who is eternal in the midst of the noneternal, who, though One, dispenses the desired objects to many [being the all-knowing Supreme Lord].[9]

At the back of every finite center of consciousness is the all-pervading Consciousness, the Self of the universe. Just as the microcosm is held, sustained, and controlled by the individual self, so is the macrocosm by the universal Self. What is innermost in the universe is innermost in every individual. A wave is essentially one with the boundless mass of water that the ocean is, though apparently differentiated from it by name and form.

Similarly, the individual self is ever united with the Supreme Self, despite its apparent limitation due to ajñāna (ignorance).[10] Being associated with ajñāna, the finite self is seemingly limited and does not recognize its true nature as pure consciousness. Yet its intrinsic luminosity is not the least affected. This is why a person realizes himself as the knower of ajñāna and says, "I do not know myself." Just as fire enveloped by smoke does not lose its radiance, similarly the self shrouded with ajnana does not lose its innate luminosity. So says the *Śvetāśvatara Upaniṣad:*

As a lump of gold tarnished with dirt shines brightly when purified, so also the embodied being seeing the truth of ātman realizes oneness with Brahman, attains the Goal and becomes free from grief.[11]

As declared by Sri Ramakrishna in the present age: "To realize God is the supreme purpose of human life. Man can know God if he can know himself."

4. *The ego and the self. The one is the apparent man, the other the real man.*

The individualized self, being manifest through a particular mode of the mind characterized by "I-ness" and further identified with the mind, the organs, and the body, as the case may be, appears as the ego. Thus, the ego is the self identified with the not-self, neither of which undergoes actual change due to wrong identification. This is the apparent man. It is egoism that seemingly ties together spirit and

[9]Ka.U. II:2.13.

[10]Ajñāna is of the nature of a veil associated with the individual self (like smoke with fire), which causes inapprehension and misapprehension of its true nature.

[11]Sv.U. II:14.

matter, so that spirit seems to partake of the nature of matter and matter seems to partake of the nature of spirit.

Such expressions as "I am happy," "I am unhappy," "I am wise," "I am ignorant," "I am honest," "I am dishonest," "I am deaf," "I am silent," "I am active," "I am lazy," "I am young," "I am old," "I am tall," and "I am fair," indicate how the attributes of the mind, the organs and the body are ascribed to the knowing self. On the other hand, such expressions as "My mind cannot think," "My mind knows the truth," "I do as the mind decides," "These eyes can see," "These ears can hear," "These lips do not utter an untruth," "These hands are capable of work," and "The body feels weak," indicate how the cognizing and the motive power of the individual self are attributed to the mind, the organs, and the body.

Being identified with the body-mind complex, a person even ascribes to himself the external objects that concern it; for instance, property, family, profession, position, country, race. Hence such expressions as "I am wealthy," "I am a landlord," "I am a father," "I am a Rothschild," "I am a farmer," "I am a merchant," "I am a teacher," "I am the principal of the college," "I am an Arab," "I am an Italian," "I am an Aryan." Despite the identification of the self with the not-self in varied forms, every individual vaguely feels his distinction from the not-self. This is evident from such expressions as "my mind," "my eyes," "my family," "my position," "my clothes," "my house," "my country," "my race," "my religion." The owner distinguishes himself from what he owns or what he belongs to, even though imperceptibly.

The ego varies with the varying conditions of the body, the organs, the mind, and the external situation. It is the real man in disguise. The change of the guise does not mean the change of the inner man. So the basis of the ego, the conscious self, ever remains the same. This finds expression as the "I," or the unvaried cognizer of the variations. Invariable in the midst of the variable, the "I" maintains the identity of an individual despite all changeful experiences. The following statements illustrate the point: "I was a grandchild, now I am a grandfather." "I was a farmer, then I became a merchant, now I am a politician." "Yesterday I was unhappy, today I feel happy." "I had keen eyesight a year ago, now I have almost lost the power of vision." "I was a student of this college, now I am a dean here." "My ideas have been revolutionized: I was born a Roman Catholic, then I became a Protestant, now I am an agnostic." "I am a native of New Zealand, I was educated in England, now I am a citizen of the United

States." "In health and in sickness, in triumph and in defeat, my faith has suffered no change."

Just as the sun that appears to rise and set, to be bright and dim, to be large and small, is no other than the ever glorious, immense, stationary sun, similarly, the changeful ego is fundamentally the same as the ever pure, free, spiritual self shining with constant effulgence. The apparent man is but the real man appearing to be different from what he really is because of false identification with the psychophysical system. All movements, all changes, all development, all degeneration, pertain to the apparent man. The following expressions apply to the human being as he appears to be: "Man is mortal," "Man is born with potentialities," "Intellectual, aesthetic, moral, and spiritual attainments are the special privileges of man," "Man is a potential lover of God," "Man attains freedom from all bondages and sufferings." Virtue and vice, wisdom and folly, happiness and unhappiness, bondage and freedom, strength and weakness refer to the apparent man.

It is the apparent man, the ego, that performs righteous and unrighteous deeds and experiences their fruits, sweet and bitter; while the real man, the transcendental self, the witness of all changing conditions of the ego, ever shines in blissful glory and neither enjoys nor suffers. The luminous self reflected in the mind and apparently limited by it is the ego; the luminous self associated with the mind as the on-looker is the witness, which transcends the changing states of the mind and, consequently, of the organs and the body. The transcendental self is ever united with the all-pervading Self of the universe, the supreme object of love and devotion. Truly speaking, it is He who dwells within as the inmost self, the all-transcendent witness. By a beautiful imagery the *Muṇḍaka Upaniṣad* has depicted the respective position of the experiencing self — the ego, and the witness self ever united with the Supreme Self (Paramātmā):

> Two birds that are inseparable companions and have similar names [jīvātmā and Paramātmā] dwell in the self-same tree [the body]. One of the two eats fruits of varied tastes, the other looks on without eating. Clinging to the same tree the individual soul, the ego, becomes bewildered by his helplessness and laments. He becomes free from grief when he finds the other, adorable and all-free, and recognizes His glory [as inseparable from himself].[12]

[12]Mu.U. III:1.1,2. See also Sv.U. IV:6,7.

5. *The key to self-mastery leading to the highest Goal.*

It is in association with the psychophysical organism that man lives on different levels of life. He can turn to the spiritual self within; he can also turn to the gross physical body. The more he recognizes himself as pure, free, immortal spirit, the higher he rises in the scale of life. He attains more and more wisdom, more and more strength, more and more freedom, more and more peace and joy. Man's self-awareness is the key to his self-confidence, self-respect, and self-mastery. This is the access to the highest self-fulfillment.

Man fails to control the mind, the organs, and the body, particularly because he does not recognize himself to be distinct from them as their master. The self becomes identified with the not-self, and loses self-command. In the first place, it is to be understood that the body is the vehicle by which man can traverse the path of light or the path of darkness, the path of freedom or the path of bondage, the path of misery or the path of peace and blessedness, according to the way he directs it. This is not a prison-house to break away from. Nor is it a mass of flesh to torment, nor a pet to fondle. One should be neither antagonistic to the body nor enamoured of it. It must be taken care of and used as a vehicle for the journey to life's Goal.

An individual's position with regard to his body, the organs, and the mind is graphically depicted by the *Kaṭha Upaniṣad* with an apt simile, pointing out the way both to absolute peace and blessedness and to perpetual misery:

> Know the self to be the master of the chariot and the body to be the chariot. Know right understanding to be the charioteer and the mind (volitional and emotional) to be the reins. The sense-organs are said to be the horses and sense-objects the ways traversed by them. Discerning men say that the self, being united with the body, the organs, and the mind, is the experiencer.
>
> But he who has no right understanding is ever associated with an uncontrolled mind, his organs are unruly like the vicious horses of a charioteer; while he who has right understanding is ever associated with a restrained mind, his organs are under control like the good horses of a charioteer.
>
> Moreover, he who has no right understanding is ever associated with a distracted mind and remains impure, he cannot attain the Goal [supreme], but undergoes repeated births and rebirths; while he who has right understanding is ever associated with a restrained mind and remains pure, he attains that Goal wherefrom there is no rebirth.

> Indeed, the man who has right understanding for his charioteer, who holds the reins of the mind firmly, reaches the end of the road [the journey of life], and that is the supreme position of Viṣṇu [the all-pervading Being].[13]

It is evident that the body should be neither caressed nor despised, neither tortured nor disregarded, but should be judiciously used for reaching the ultimate Goal. One succeeds in giving the body, the senses, and the mind right direction only when one recognizes the self to be distinct from them as their master. This is the secret of self-mastery.

6. *The human personality is a graded organization.*

Broadly speaking man is capable of living on five different levels of life: spiritual, moral, intellectual, aesthetic, and physical. Of these the spiritual is the highest, the physical the lowest. Next below the spiritual is the moral level. There is no access to spiritual life but through the moral. Without inner purification by ethical discipline spiritual consciousness does not develop. This is why the Upaniṣad enjoins on a spiritual aspirant the practice of virtues, such as self-control, truthfulness, continence, sincerity, humility, kindness, charity. Above all, truthfulness has been emphasized by the Vedantic teachers. "One can reach God through truthfulness," says Sri Ramakrishna who taught from his own experience the essential unity of religions in this modern age. As declared by the *Muṇḍaka Upaniṣad:*

> This ātman, resplendent and pure, dwelling in the body, whom a person of strict self-discipline, free from all traces of iniquity, perceives, is attainable by constant practice of truthfulness, self-control, right knowledge, and continence.
>
> Truth alone triumphs, not untruth. By truth is spread out the path, Devayāna (lit. the way of the gods), by which the seers free from all desires, proceed thereto where is the supreme abode of Truth.[14]

[13]Ka.U. I:3.3-9. It is interesting to note that Socrates describes the soul under the image of two winged horses and a charioteer: "Now the winged horses and the charioteers of the gods are all of them noble and of noble descent, but those of other races are mixed; the human charioteer drives his in a pair; and one of them is noble and of noble breed, and the other is ignoble and of ignoble breed; and the driving of them of necessity gives a great deal of trouble to him." *Phaedrus, The Dialogues of Plato,* in *Great Books of the Western World,* Vol. 7, Chicago, Encyclopaedia Britannica, 1952, p.124.

[14]Mu.U. III:1.5,6.

With the growing awareness of the spiritual self, as a person recognizes his real nature to be pure, free, and immortal, he at the same time recognizes the real nature of every other individual to be pure, free, and immortal. Consequently he deals with his fellow-beings with due regard and consideration. His self-interest becomes naturally harmonized with social interests. Far from being conventional, his ethical life becomes an expression of his inner consciousness. Further, when he realizes his essential unity with the Supreme Self, he no longer finds himself confined within the psychophysical system; his self expands and enfolds all individual selves. Then he develops spontaneous love and compassion for one and all. He becomes occupied with doing good to all beings without any distinction. It is his very nature to abide by the ethical principle. "Thou shalt love thy neighbor as thyself," says Jesus Christ.[15]

That the basis of universal love is the realization of the oneness of the individual self with the Supreme Self is clearly indicated by the Vedantic literature:

> He who sees all beings in the very Self and the Self in all beings is averse to none because of that [experience].[16]

> Verily he sees who sees the Supreme Lord equally existent in all beings, Imperishable in the midst of the perishable. Since he sees the Lord equally existent everywhere, he injures not Self by self and so attains the highest Goal.[17]

> With a pure mind one should observe in all beings as well as in oneself only Me, the Ātman, who am both inside and out, and all-pervasive like space. O Uddhava [Śrī Kṛṣṇa addresses his disciple], he is considered a sage who, taking his stand on pure knowledge, thus regards and honors all beings as Myself, has the same attitude towards a scavenger as to a Brāhmaṇa, towards a thief as to a supporter of the Brāhmaṇas; towards a spark of fire as to the sun, towards a ruffian as to a kind man. Ideas of rivalry, jealousy, pity, and egoism readily leave a man who always thinks of Me in all men.[18]

Basically, morality is the attunement of the individual self to the Self of the universe. While a spiritual person practices this knowingly, a moral man practices the same unknowingly. Moral life is closest to the spiritual life. Fundamentally there is no difference between the two. Unselfishness is the prime moral virtue. It is the attunement of the individual self to the Self of the universe, the Soul of all souls.

[15]Matt. 22:39; Mark 12:31.
[16]Is.U. 6.
[17]BG XIII:27,28.
[18]SB XI:29,12-15.

It is through the moral life that the real self of man finds expression on other levels of life. The light of the spirit that conveys wisdom, freedom, strength, and joy shines upon the intellectual, aesthetic, and physical planes through the moral plane. Without moral purity intellect does not brighten, right understanding does not develop, insight does not grow. It is moral goodness that sustains aesthetic imagination and sensibility; otherwise they degenerate: sensuousness turns into sensuality. None can maintain physical health and strength unless he lives with self-restraint and moderation. It is through the cultivation of moral virtues that men can rise above the physical level and devote themselves to intellectual and aesthetic ideals. "Plain living and high thinking" becomes their motto.

7. *The ever pure, luminous self is not affected by the conditions of the psychophysical adjunct that are superimposed on it through ajñāna (wrong knowledge). (See footnote 10.)*

The more a person identifies himself with the gross physical body the more he degenerates. He finds himself in the grip of sense-desires, which are insatiable. Physical urges constantly goad him. Ridden by lust and greed he behaves like a brute. Yet the delusion of the body-idea, the root cause of all the evils he is attended with, does not in the least affect the real nature of the self — its pristine purity and glory.

There is an appropriate story in the Vedantic literature to illustrate this point: Once a lioness, roaming in search of prey, noticed a flock of sheep grazing in a meadow across a brook. She crept down to the brook and was eagerly watching the sheep on the other side, when a lamb strayed from the flock to the water's edge. Immediately the lioness jumped over the brook and fell upon the lamb, but at this moment she gave birth to a cub and died. From a distance a shepherd saw what had happened and cautiously proceeded to the spot. Having made sure that the lioness was dead, he took pity upon the offspring and carried it in his arms to the fold. There the cub was nurtured among the sheep.

In due course it grew up to be a fine young lion, but never recognized itself as such. Living with the sheep constantly and seeing sheep all around the young lion thought it too was a sheep. It grazed and lived on grass. No lion's roar ever reached its ears. Hearing only the bleating of sheep it learned to bleat as one of them. Though a lion, it never recognized itself as such and behaved in every respect like a sheep.

One day another lion was wandering nearby and saw much to his surprise what seemed to be a young lion, timidly moving with a flock of sheep, eating grass and bleating. "What a shame! I must reclaim him," muttered the lion. Slowly he proceeded to the brook, sprang to the other side and crouched under a bush, awaiting an opportunity to catch hold of the sheep-lion. At last he succeeded. The sheep-lion was frightened to death seeing his attacker's deadly face and finding itself in his grip.

"You are not a sheep, you are a lion; you have a face similar to mine." But the sheep-lion would not believe this. So the lion dragged it down to the brook and pointed to the reflection of their faces in the water. The lion said, "You see your face is exactly like mine. You are not a sheep. You are a lion. You can roar. You should not bleat and eat grass. Come away and live free in the forest as I do." With these words he roared lustily. As soon as the roar entered into the ears of the sheep-lion, it roared and roared and roared. With the lion-consciousness fully awakened it jumped the stream and proudly walked into the forest.

8. *It is man's idea of man that determines his view of life, and it is his view of life that determines his way of living.*

Man is said to be a born philosopher. An individual lives according to his own philosophy of life. His mode of living is sound or unsound, as his concept of man is sound or unsound. Without a right conception of human personality there cannot be a plan of right living. If the physical body is held to be the prime factor of human personality, then death must be the inevitable end of an individual, no matter what he does, what he achieves, what he aspires after. In such a case either dark pessimism or shallow optimism will prevail in human minds. In ancient India there was a school of materialists called the *Cārvākas,* whose slogan was: "As long as you live you should live happily. Live on butter even though you have to die a debtor. Once the body is reduced to ashes, what possibility is there of its coming back to life?" This view was known as *lōkāyatamata,* the common people's idea.

A similar view has prevailed in the Western world as well:

Let us eat and drink; for tomorrow we shall die.[19]

[19]*Isaiah* 22:13; I *Corinthians* 15:32.

Drink and dance and laugh and lie,
Love, the reeling midnight through,
For tomorrow we shall die!
(But, alas, we never do).[20]

As long as man is deluded by the body-idea, all human interests are bound to be subservient to the sense-life.

While the subhuman beings live solely on the physical plane, human beings can live not only on the physical but on other higher levels as well, such as aesthetic, intellectual, moral, and spiritual. Of these the spiritual is the highest. Life's fulfillment is in spiritual development, as we have noted; the lower must subserve the interest of the higher and not vice versa. A plan of right living must include all the levels of life. Not only that; it must assign to each its respective place. A right plan of living must be consistent as well as comprehensive. The relative positions of the different aspects of life have to be determined, otherwise the gradations of life-values cannot be ascertained, and a confusion of values is sure to result. And this is one of the major difficulties of modern man. For the effective solution of human problems it is essential that man must be viewed as a whole and in the right perspective.

9. *The pressing need of the right conception of human personality for right living is evidenced by history.*

It is a historical truth that man's idea of man has been the dominant force in the development of individuals and of nations as well. The social, political, cultural, ethical, and religious ideals and practices of a nation have their roots in its conception of human personality. Man's idea of man is at the core of every civilization that has grown in the world. It accounts for the strength and the weakness of each civilization. As observed by the historian Toynbee:

> The same Greek idea of man, which accounts for the Greek civilization's rise and culmination, is also the explanation of its strange and tragic fate. Hellenism was betrayed by what was false within it. . . . This weakness of the Greek idea of man, which was the ultimate cause of the breakdown of the Greek way of life in the fifth century B.C., was shown up when, later on, the Greek view encountered the Jewish view in Southwest Asia and the Ancient Asian view in India.

[20]Dorothy Parker, "The Flaw in Paganism," in *Not So Deep As A Well,* collected poems, New York, Viking Press, 1938, p.155.

> The Greeks met the Jews and the Indians as conquerors, and among the conquered peoples, the Greek way of life at first won great prestige. Asians and Egyptians took to talking, reading, and writing in the Greek language, to dressing in the Greek fashion, to taking Greek names, to imitating the Greek style in art and architecture.
>
> Yet, in the end, the Greek view was defeated by the Indian view in India and Central Asia and by the Jewish view in the Mediterranean world, including Greece itself; and these two competing ideas of man won their victory over the Greek idea on their merits. They won because they were found to answer better to human needs. They gave man greater help for living his life, and they also gave him more convincing answers to questions about the meaning of life by which man is always haunted. But though the Jewish and Indian views defeated the Greek view in the competition between them for the spiritual allegiance of mankind, they too were permanently affected by the encounter.[21]

10. *The right view of man is the key not only to right living but also to right knowledge of the universe.*

Man is the epitome of the cosmos. There is a striking correspondence between the microcosm and the macrocosm in every phase of existence from the grossest to the finest. "The microcosm and the macrocosm are built on exactly the same plan," observes Swami Vivekananda.[22] "Man is the measure of all things" is an old maxim attributed to the Greek Sophist philosopher, Protagoras (481-411 B.C.).[23] It has been well said, "The proper study of mankind is man."[24] Of all the pursuits of knowledge the study of man is the most interesting and illuminating. Not only does it acquaint the seeker with the intricacies of his psychophysical constitution but also opens unto him the direct approach to the Ultimate Reality.

Nevertheless, in his search for Truth man has been inclined to forget himself. From the earliest times, in most civilized countries, human beings have been interested in knowing the secrets of external nature. They have explored the world of experience in search for wealth, pleasure, power, and for knowledge as well. The sensible universe has so engaged man's attention as to make him believe that by investigating it he can know all about reality. However, as the

[21]Arnold J. Toynbee, "The Ancient Mediterranean View of Man" in *Man's Right to Knowledge,* New York, Columbia University Press, 1954, pp.3-4.

[22]CW II, p.447.

[23]See R. W. Livingstone, *The Greek Genius, and Its Meaning to Us,* Oxford, Clarendon Press, 1924, p.111.

[24]Alexander Pope, *Essay on Man,* in *The Works of Alexander Pope,* Vol. II, New York, Gordian Press, 1871, repr. 1967, Epis II, 1.1, p.375.

metaphysical inquiry into the realm of experience went deeper he became aware of the fact that the experienced presupposes the experiencer, and that the conscious self of man is more real than the unconscious nature.

This is the knowledge that dawned particularly on the minds of the seekers of Truth in ancient India. As a result, their focus of attention shifted from nonhuman nature to the human being. This does not mean, however, that the external world was left out of consideration. By studying the individual and the cosmos as an integral whole, the Indian sages recognized these important truths: (1) What is innermost in man is innermost in the universe. (2) The same Supreme Being interpenetrates the individuals and the cosmos. (3) The knowledge of man is the key to the knowledge of the universe.

We have found that man's inmost being is the central principle of consciousness, which illuminates the psychophysical organism and holds it as a coherent whole. This is invariable in the midst of the variable. It is the one presupposition of all human knowledge. It is the first thing real. What is self-luminous is self-existent. It cannot be different from the fundamental Reality. The ultimate one which is known by investigating into the objective universe as Pure Being or Existence is subjectively recognized as Pure Consciousness. Just as the microcosm is controlled and illuminated by the individual self, so is the macrocosm by the universal Self. The essential nondifference of the individual and the Supreme Self is the central theme of Vedanta.

The truth is: The same supreme Consciousness is the one Self of all. Says the sage Uddālaka to his son, Śvetaketu:

> Of all the created things and beings, my child, Pure Existence is the origin, Pure Existence is the support, Pure Existence is the end. . . . In that subtle essence all this has its being. That is Reality. That is the Self. That thou art, O Śvetaketu.[25]

A person can reach the Soul of the universe through his own soul. He can contact the Supreme Spirit through spirit. "Man is the most representative being in the universe, the microcosm, a small universe in himself," says Swami Vivekananda.[26] Corresponding to the physical body of the individual, there is the physical cosmos; corresponding to the individual subtle body, of which mind is the

[25]Ch.U. VI:8.6,7.
[26]CW IV, p.47.

principal component, there is the cosmic subtle body comprising the universal mind; corresponding to the individual causal body or ajñāna, there is the cosmic māyā, the primary cause of the world of phenomena. The Nondual Brahman, Pure Consciousness, ever calm and blissful, ensouls all individual and cosmic forms and yet transcends them all. As declared by the *Kaṭha Upaniṣad:*

> Just as one and the same fire, permeating the world, assumes different forms according to each and every object it burns, similarly, the one all-pervading Self, dwelling in each and every being, appears to have so many forms, and is also beyond them all.[27]

In human life consciousness has reached the level of definite self-consciousness. The central fact in human personality is the heightened self-awareness that distinguishes man from all other sentient beings. Not only does man realize himself as an individual distinct from all other things and beings, he has also the power of introspection, by which he can discriminate the real self, the knower within, from the psychophysical constitution. All difference between one jīva and another is in their psychophysical adjuncts. There is no difference whatsoever in the nature of the indwelling self, which is intrinsically pure, free, luminous, and united with Brahman. The same effulgent Being is the inmost Self of all jīvas, yet Its manifestation varies according to the psychophysical constitution of each. The same resplendent sun shines differently through different mediums.

Although Pure Consciousness is immanent in the whole universe as the Supreme Principle, yet its manifestation as varied forms of consciousness is to be found only in the animate beings. It is through the mental that consciousness finds expression on the physical plane. As observed by Śaṅkara:

> Although one and the same Ātman is hidden in all beings, moving and nonmoving, although It is perpetually immovable and immutable, yet on account of differences in the nature of the mind adhering to each as an adjunct, there is difference in Its manifestation as more and more capacity for talent, knowledge, joy, and so forth, as declared by the Śruti.[28]

[27]Ka.U. II:2.9.
[28]BS I:1.11, S.com.

CHAPTER II

THE THREEFOLD BODY AND THE FIVEFOLD SHEATH

The psychophysical vehicle of the self, the real man, can be comprehended in two different ways: (1) as the threefold body, and (2) as the fivefold sheath. We shall dwell at first on the threefold body and then on the fivefold sheath. Besides the physical body, the outstanding factor of human personality, every individual has two more bodies — the subtle and the causal, which are more potent, though invisible. The three bodies make up man's psychophysical constitution. While the physical body is the outermost, the causal body is the innermost of the three. It is through the physical body that we contact the external world. Indeed the three bodies serve respectively as the mediums of man's threefold daily experience — waking, dream, and dreamless sleep. Being composed of the same gross elements as the sensible universe, the physical body is perceptible by the sense organs and is called *the gross body* (sthūla śarīra). Though tangible it is far less durable than the two others. We shall delineate the three bodies one after another.

A. The Gross Body

1. *The physical body is man's temporary tenement and seat of waking experience.*

The physical body is so predominant in our consciousness that we assume it to be the only body that man has and ignore the other two, which cannot be perceived by the sense organs. An individual leaves the gross body at death and becomes reincarnate in another, but he retains the same subtle and the same causal body all along until he attains final Liberation in oneness with Brahman. Being identified with the physical body more or less, the individual soul, the experiencer within, experiences the external universe. This is his waking state. When he recedes from the physical body as in dream and deep sleep he loses all contact with the outside world, and does not miss it even. So says Śaṅkara: "Know this gross body to be like a house to the householder, on which rests man's entire dealing with the external world."[1] Just as the physical body serves as the medium of waking experience, so does the subtle body serve as the medium of dream experience and the causal body as the medium of dreamless sleep experience.

The five organs of perception (i.e., the ears, the skin, the eyes, the tongue, the nose) and the five organs of action (i.e., the organ of speech, the hands, the feet, the organs of evacuation and procreation), by which we deal with the external world, are evidently located in the physical body. But these bodily organs are not the real organs. The real organs are invisible and belong to the subtle body, but they operate through their physical counterparts, the bodily organs, which are their outer stations, so to speak. It is to be noted that the organ of touch extends all over the body, whereas every other sense organ has a particular location.

The physical body is thus defined by Śaṅkara: "Composed of the seven ingredients — marrow, bone, fat, flesh, blood, skin, and cuticle, and consisting of the following limbs and their parts — legs, thighs, the chest, arms, the back and the head, this body, the seat of delusion proclaimed as 'I and mine', is designated by the sages as the gross body."[2] Like any other object that comes into being the physical body is subject to six modifications (ṣaḍbhava-vikāra): origination, subsistence, growth, transformation, decay and destruction.

The physical body has been conceived as a city with a number of gates, within which dwells ātman, the self, its ruler. The gates are the orifices in the body. As the ruler is distinct from the city, so is ātman distinct from the body. Just as the ruler is responsible for the corporate life of the city, so is ātman responsible for the direction and the coordination of the different functions of the body and the organs. Just as the city collapses when its ruler deserts it, so the body corrupts when ātman departs from it. The *Kaṭha Upaniṣad* calls the gross body "the city with eleven gates":

> There is a city with eleven gates belonging to the unborn one of unwavering consciousness. He who meditates on Him grieves no more. Released [from the bonds of ignorance, desire, and karma] he becomes free. This is That.[3]

[1]VC 90.
[2]VC 72,73.
[3]Ka.U. II:2.1.

The eleven gates are the following openings: the two ears, the two eyes, the two nostrils, the mouth, the two organs of elimination, the navel, and the one in the crown of the head. In the *Bhagavad-gītā* the body is called "the city of nine gates," in which its master, who has self-knowledge, dwells happily.[4] The last two openings enumerated above are not included here.

2. *The materialistic position that man is but the body is not tenable.*

The materialistic position that man has no self other than the body and that consciousness originates from the bodily processes is untenable. It leaves the fundamental question regarding the origin and development of a living organism unanswered. The point is this: What is it that unifies the physical elements into a coherent system so as to make it live and grow according to a certain pattern? Surely, inert material elements cannot join together for concerted action, inasmuch as dull insentient physical objects cannot have any plan or purpose of their own. Purposiveness implies consciousness. The very existence of a living organism presupposes consciousness, explicit or implicit, as its guiding principle.

That which fashions the material form, develops, animates, and cognizes it too, must be something different from it. This is the non-material, luminous self, whose substance is consciousness. The initial need of the living processes is consciousness. It cannot be their by-product. As pointed out by the sage Kapila, the founder of the Sāṁkhya system, "The building of the body, the seat of experience, is due to the presence of the indwelling experiencer; otherwise its decomposition would result."[5]

From the fact that every individual regards himself or herself as the body, the materialists of ancient India, called the *Cārvākas*,[6] maintained like the materialists of modern times that the very body is the self and that consciousness derives from the body. They explained the origin of consciousness by an illustration: Just as the intoxicating property of liquor comes out of fermentation of rice, molasses, etc., even though it is not found in any of these ingredients, similarly, consciousness, though absent from all the four elements, i.e., air, fire,

[4]BG V:13.
[5]SD V:114.
[6]They are also called the *Lōkāyatikas,* that is, the followers of *lōkāyatamata,* the common people's view.

water, and earth,[7] yet emerges from their intermixture in the process of forming the body. They further contended that such manifestations of consciousness as knowledge, will, memory, etc., are not noticeable anywhere but in the physical body, so they must be its distinctive qualities.

Śaṅkara has refuted their view by the following argument: It is absurd to regard the body as the self, because consciousness is not its intrinsic quality like form, size, color, and so forth. These endure as long as the body lasts, whereas consciousness disappears at death. Then again, properties of the body, such as form, size, and color, are perceived by others, whereas manifestations of consciousness, such as knowledge, will, and memory, are not. Therefore, these cannot be classed with physical characteristics. Further, one may pertinently ask: What is the exact nature of that consciousness imagined by the materialists to be arising from the physical elements? It cannot be other than material, because the *Cārvākas* recognize only the existence of matter and its modifications. Now, if such consciousness be inherent in the body it cannot objectify the body, because a thing cannot operate on itself. Fire heat does not consume fire. Even the most expert dancer cannot climb his own shoulders.[8]

3. *Consciousness does not originate from the body nor from the mind. It is intrinsic in the self, the knower* per se.

The plain truth is that insentient material elements cannot produce consciousness, which is self-luminous and hence of contrary nature. The chemical actions or physical processes can generate physical glow like the flame of an oil lamp or the spark out of flint. Though radiant, neither has the self-luminosity of consciousness. Physical glow is not aware of itself or of anything else. It is stark blind. Being of the same nature as unintelligent matter it cannot objectify matter. No material product, howsoever refined or resplendent it may be, can lose its inherent materiality or unconsciousness. Devoid of consciousness it can by no means cognize anything. It can be only the object of cognition and never the subject, the cognizer. The source of consciousness must be something other than the bodily processes. This is ātman, the luminous self, the

[7]The *Cārvākas* do not recognize the fifth element, ether (ākāśa), since it is not apprehended by the sense-organs. According to them sense-perception is the only valid source of knowledge.

[8]See BS III:3.54, S.com.

cognizer of the psychophysical organism. It is ever the subject, and never the object. "He is never seen, but is the witness; He is never heard, but is the hearer; He is never thought, but is the thinker; He is never known, but is the knower," declares the *Bṛhadāraṇyaka Upaniṣad.*[9]

It is futile to trace the origin of consciousness to the heart or the brain. Nor does consciousness originate in the mind. Consciousness is the being of ātman, the knower *per se*, which is unborn. It is self-existent. Being composed of the purest type of matter, the mind has the capacity to transmit consciousness that belongs to ātman.

It is quite likely that from the mind the radiance of consciousness reaches the bodily organs through the heart and the brain, which are intimately connected with the nervous system. Both of them can be regarded as the physical mediums of mental functions. It is a universal belief that the heart is the seat of feelings and the head the seat of thought or intellect. From ancient times consciousness has been associated with these two physical organs in the East and the West as well. As observed by Dr. Seal:

> In Caraka and Suśruta[10] (as in Aristotle) the heart is the central organ and seat of consciousness; but in the Tantric writings[11] (as in Galen)[12] the seat of consciousness is transferred to the brain or rather the cerebro-spinal system.[13]

The close connection between the brain and the states of consciousness cannot be denied. Intelligence develops in children with the development of the brain. Disorders in the brain seriously affect one's thinking. The states of intoxication, anaesthesia, delirium, etc., also point to the close relation between the condition of the brain and the state of consciousness.

But although consciousness is closely associated with the brain, it does not originate there. Had consciousness been the outcome of the cerebral processes, as some scientists, psychologists, and

[9]Br.U. III:7.23.

[10]Caraka and Suśruta are the chief medical authorities of ancient India. The one is the originator of the Āyurvedic system of medicine, the other of surgery. Their works are still studied in India by the indigenous schools of medicine.

[11]The Yōga school holds the same view as the Tantras with regard to the seat of consciousness.

[12]The Greek physician, Galen, lived in Rome in the 2nd century A.D. His medical treatises, of which one hundred are extant, were accepted as authoritative for many centuries in Italy, Greece and Arabia.

[13]Brajendranath Seal, *The Positive Sciences of the Ancient Hindus,* London, Longmans, Green, 1915, pp.218-219.

philosophers maintain,[14] then all the thought processes including decision, determination, deliberation, volition, purpose, and so forth, could be explained in terms of mechanical forces governed by physical laws. In that case man would have been an automaton.

But, in fact, he is not. He has the choice of action as well as of decision. He is capable of volition; in other words, he has the freedom of will. There is a marked difference between conscious operations and mechanical processes. This must not be overlooked. According to Henri Bergson, there is infinitely more in a human consciousness than in the corresponding brain. The brain cannot secrete thought as liver secretes bile. Nor can it emit consciousness as the firefly emits light.

We have noted in the previous chapter that the self is distinct from the body and the mind, being their cognizer, and that consciousness is intrinsic in the cognizer. The mind and the body, although closely connected, are distinct; one does not derive from the other, nor does one form an integral part of the other. We shall discuss this point while dwelling on the mind (see Ch. III, sec. 2).

Thought is a function of the mind and not of the brain. It is an expression of consciousness through a particular modification of the mind. In the dream state during sleep a person can think, feel, imagine, even though he is not conscious of the body and the brain is almost inoperative. Whatever manifestation of consciousness is noticeable in the physical body and the organs in the waking state, is but a reflection of the luminous self. It is the mind that transmits the radiance of consciousness to the physical system. Neither the organ of perception nor the organ of action can function unless the mind joins with it. This is why no perception, no action is possible when a person is absent-minded.

In all probability the mind conveys the radiance of consciousness to the different organs through the brain. In this sense the brain can be regarded as the medium or the vehicle of consciousness, but not its source. According to William James the brain is the transmitter of thought to the body. Medical science testifies to the fact that a large

[14]Cf. Ernst Heinrich Haeckel, *The Riddle of the Universe,* 1901, included in *Outline of Great Books,* New York, Wise. 1937, p.476. "We no longer admit Descartes' theory that it [consciousness] is peculiar to man and resides in the pineal body. Personally, I admit consciousness wherever there is a centralized nervous system. . . . Recent research has shown that the development of consciousness in man is connected with the greater size and complexity of the rind of grey nerve matter which covers the brain. . . . When we further study the effect on mind of disease of the brain, or narcotics and anaesthetics, we are forced to conclude that consciousness is no more than a function of the brain."

portion of the brain can be damaged or even removed without destroying consciousness or seriously affecting thought processes.

4. *The location of the self in the physical body.*

According to the Upaniṣads the abode of the indwelling self is the heart. The *Chāndōgya Upaniṣad* calls the physical body *Brahmapuram* (the city of Brahman),[15] because Brahman dwells here as the internal ruler with a retinue of attendants, such as the ten organs and the mind. His abode is the small lotus of the heart. As immanent in the universe, nondual Brahman — which is Pure Consciousness, the finest of all existences — is the all-pervading Being (Puruṣa). But His direct manifestation in the phenomenal world is the innermost self of every individual, shining as the central principle of consciousness in the depth of the heart. Any expression of consciousness in man's psychophysical system is but a reflection of the luminous self. As defined by Śaṅkara: "The heart is a lump of flesh shaped like a lotus-bud facing downwards with the stalk upwards, in which are apertures for numerous arteries. It is the receptacle of life and is familiar, being observed when the body is dissected."[16]

Within the heart there is a tiny space about the size of the thumb,[17] where the mind (antaḥkaraṇa) is located. Being capable of expansion and contraction the mind can extend all over the body. Hindu psychology stresses the cognitive aspect of the mind with its two distinct phases — deliberative and determinative. The one is called *manas*,[18] the other *buddhi*. The term *buddhi* is also used to signify the entire cognitive mind. It is through the cognitive aspect that consciousness reaches the other levels of the mind, such as the conative and the affective. This is why the cognitive aspect is considered basic. Being the innermost of all the aspects of the mind, it is closest to the indwelling self. So the self is said to be "situated in buddhi (guhāhita)."[19] The Upaniṣads frequently refer to the self situated in buddhi located in the heart (guhā).[20] Though the self is often said to be situated in the space of the heart,[21] the meaning is that

[15]See Ch.U. VIII:1.1. The passage is quoted later. See also Br.U. II:5.18.
[16]Tai.U. I:6, S.com.
[17]Perhaps this space is in the right auricle of the heart.
[18]The term *manas* is also used for the mind as a whole (antaḥkaraṇa).
[19]Ka.U. I:2.12, S.com.
[20]See Ka.U. I:2.12; I:3.1; II:1.6,7; Mu.U. III:1.7; also S.com.
[21]See Mu.U. II:2.7; Tai.U. I:6.1; II:1.1; III:6.

the self is situated in buddhi located in the cavity of the heart (guhā).

It is the Supreme Self that dwells within the heart as the individual self. Being associated with buddhi, all-pervading consciousness becomes identified with it and seemingly limited like space inside a pot or sunlight manifest through a window-pane. The following description of the self bears out the point:

> Which is the self? This Omnipresent Being (Puruṣa) that is identified with buddhi and is in the midst of the organs, the (self-effulgent) light within the heart.[22]

The primary meaning of "the heart" is the lotus-shaped lump of flesh. Here it signifies *buddhi*, which is located in the heart. Buddhi is the most refined of all the modifications of prakṛti (the primordial nature) that constitute man's psychophysical system. It is but natural that it should have its seat in the heart, the central and most vital part of the body, and be a fit instrument for the manifestation of ātman. Indeed, the heart is the true abode of man's innermost self, the center of his personality. This is also evidenced by the fact that a person spontaneously points to the heart while referring to himself. He even firmly places his hand upon the chest while asserting himself.

Further, the seekers of Truth, free from worldly desires, with their senses withdrawn and their minds purified, realize Brahman as directly as a plum in the palm of the hand by constantly meditating on the luminous self within the heart as the all-pervading Supreme Self. So says the *Chāndōgya Upanisad:*

> In this city of Brahman there is a small lotus, an abode. Inside this there is a tiny space (ākāśa). That which is within this one should seek and yearn to know.[23]

The self is said to be identified with buddhi, because of man's failure to discriminate it from this limiting adjunct. Being mixed they seemingly partake of each other's nature. On the one hand, the self, which is intrinsically Pure Consciousness, appears to be endowed with the characteristics of buddhi, such as knowledge, determination, thought, in the same way as light shining through glass appears red, green, or blue according to the color of the glass. On the other hand, buddhi, which is material, appears as intelligent being permeated by

[22]Br.U. IV:3.7.
[23]Ch.U. VIII:1.1.

consciousness, just as glass appears radiant in association with light. The identification of the self with buddhi leads to its identification with all else. As declared by the *Bṛhadāraṇyaka Upaniṣad:*

> This self is indeed that Brahman identified with buddhi, with manas, with prāṇa (the vital principle), with the eyes, with the ears, with earth, with water, with air, with fire and what is other than fire, with desire and absence of desire, with virtue and absence of virtue, with everything, with this [what is perceived] with that [what is inferred].[24]

The individual self is said to be of the size of the thumb, because the space inside the heart, wherein it is manifest, is very tiny, like the thumb. Free from its limiting adjuncts the indwelling self is all-pervading Brahman, formless and featureless. As stated in the *Katha Upaniṣad:*

> The Omnipresent Being (Puruṣa) ever exists in the hearts of men as the innermost self of the size of the thumb. Him should man carefully distinguish from his [threefold body] as if separating the slender stalk from muñja grass. Him should man know as effulgent and immortal. Him should man know as effulgent and immortal.[25]

5. *Being illumined by the light of the self, the mind and the organs function.*

It is the light of the self shining through buddhi that reveals whatever we experience. In the words of Śaṅkara:

> Buddhi is the instrument for the perception of all objects like a lamp placed in front amid darkness. It has been said, "It is through the mind that one sees, that one hears."[26] Indeed, everything is perceived on being invested with the light of buddhi like an object in the dark illuminated by a lamp placed in front. The other organs are but the channels of buddhi.[27]

It is true that without external light nothing can be seen. But external light helps the eyes only when they are associated with consciousness. This is why a person cannot see things even in broad daylight in case he is absent-minded, or asleep with the eyes open. The

[24]Br.U. IV:4.5.
[25]Ka.U. II:3.17.
[26]Br.U. I:5.3.
[27]*Ibid.* IV:3.7, S.com.

inner light of consciousness proceeding through buddhi and the organ of vision first reveals the external light. Being illuminated by the radiance of consciousness, external light manifests things. It is to the conscious creatures that things are manifest (including light). Nothing is manifest to unconscious material objects, not even light.

Indeed, all perceptions and activities of man are due to the radiance of the luminous self permeating the mind, the organs, and the body. The process of permeation of the light of consciousness is thus described by Śaṅkara:

> Buddhi,[28] being transparent and nearest to the intelligent self, instantly receives the reflection of its radiance. This is why even a man of discrimination identifies himself with it first. Next to that is manas, which receives the radiance of consciousness being associated with buddhi. Then the organs receive the radiance of consciousness being connected with the mind, and then the body through contact with the organs.
>
> Thus the self successively illumines with the radiance of its effulgent being the whole aggregate of the body and the organs. It is because of this that every human being identifies himself with the body and the organs and their functions, in his own way, without any standard, according to his understanding.
>
> So the Lord has said in the *Bhagavad-gītā:* "As the one sun, O Bhārata, lights up the entire world, so the self, the knower of the body, illumines the whole body."[29] . . . Therefore, the self is the Light within buddhi located in the heart, the Omnipresent Being (Puruṣa) whose self-effulgence is utmost; because He is the illuminator of everything and not illumined by anything else.[30]

6. *The primacy of the human form.*

The all-pervading Being, Supreme Consciousness, is manifest as the innermost self in all living creatures (sarvabhūtāntarātmā).[31] But it is in human form that He shines most as distinct self-awareness. Of all the living beings man alone is capable of discriminating the self from the not-self. By recognizing the self as distinct from all its adjuncts, such as the body, the organs, and the mind, he can realize his unity with the Supreme Self and attain complete self-fulfillment. Man has the special capacity for the highest achievement, not to

[28] In this context *buddhi* represents the cognitive aspect of the mind (antaḥkaraṇa) and *manas* its volitional and emotional aspects.

[29] BG XIII:33.

[30] Br.U. IV:3.7, S.com.

[31] See Ka.U. II:2.10; Sv.U. VI:11.

speak of his high and higher attainments in many spheres of life.

The preeminence of the human body has been declared by the Śruti:

> [Man is] well formed, indeed. Man is truly fit for righteous deeds.[32]
>
> In the human body the self is most manifest. There being fully invested with insight, he speaks the truth known, he sees the truth known; he knows what is beneficial, he knows heaven and hell; he desires immortality through his mortal frame. Thus he is supremely gifted; while the lower animals have the knowledge of hunger and thirst only.[33]

To attain Liberation is the special privilege of human life. By rightly using his mortal body man can attain immortality. Having been born as a human being none should lose his chance for eternal life. It is suicidal. So the *Śrīmad-bhāgavatam* urges man to make the best use of the human body:

> The wise man having after many births obtained this extremely rare human body, which though frail is yet conducive to man's Supreme Good, should forthwith strive for Liberation before the body, which is always subject to death, chances to fall; for sense-enjoyment is obtainable in any body.[34]

Says Śrī Kṛṣṇa:

> Gaining the first and foremost requisite, namely, the human body, which is very difficult to attain and yet has been attained somehow, which can serve as a strong boat with the teacher as its helmsman and propelled by Me [God incarnate in human form] as by a favorable wind — with such means as these the man who does not strive to cross the death-bound ocean of repeated births and deaths verily commits suicide.[35]

Śaṅkara extols human birth:

> There are three things which are rare indeed and are due to the grace of God, namely, a human birth, the longing for Liberation and the protective care of a great sage.
>
> The man who having somehow attained a human birth and above all a male body and the mastery of the Vedas, is foolish enough not to strive after Liberation commits suicide, for he kills himself by clinging to things unreal.[36]

[32] Ai.U. I:2.3.
[33] Quoted by Śrīdhara Swāmī in his commentary on SB XI:7.21.
[34] SB XI:9.29. [35] *Ibid.* XI:20.17. [36] VC 3,4.

B. The Subtle Body

7. *The constitution of the subtle body (sūkṣma śarīra).*

Composed of the same five gross elements as the physical universe the physical body is perceptible by the sense-organs. But not so the subtle body, which is composed of the five subtle elements in their rudimentary, uncompounded state. It is the five subtle elements — ākāśa (ether), vāyu (air), tejas (fire), ap (water), and pṛthivī (earth), which by their fivefold combination called *pañcīkaraṇa* (quintuplication) produce the five gross elements. Naturally, the subtle body is too fine to be discerned by the microscope. It has seventeen component factors. As defined by Śaṅkara:

> The subtle body, the means of the jīva's experience [of the results of his karma] consists of the five prāṇas, the ten organs, the manas and buddhi — all formed from the rudimentary elements before the quintuplication (pañcīkaraṇa).[37]

The five prāṇas are the five phases of the vital principle. The one and the same vital principle, prāṇa, has, according to its five different functions, five different names — prāṇa, apāna, vyāna, udāna, and samāna. (See Ch. IV, sec. 3.) The ten organs located in the physical body are not the real organs according to Vedanta, as we have noted above. They are the outer stations of the real organs that belong to the subtle body. The five visible sense organs, viz. the ears, the skin, the eyes, the palate, and the nose, derive their power of hearing, touch, sight, taste, and smell from their counterparts in the subtle body. Similarly, the five visible motor organs, viz. the tongue, the hands, the feet, the anus, and the sex organs, derive their powers of speech, receiving and giving, walking, evacuation, and generation from their counterparts in the subtle body. Mind, the inner instrument (antaḥkaraṇa), has two distinct phases — manas and buddhi, according to its twofold function — deliberation and determination or decision. All these seventeen components of the subtle body are the products of the five subtle or rudimentary elements.

8. *The jīva retains the same subtle body here and hereafter.*

Being composed of the rudimentary elements the subtle body is extremely fine and durable. It is not destroyed with the destruction of

[37] *Ātma-bōdha,* 13. See also Pd. I:23.

the gross body.[38] At death only the gross body is left behind. Clothed with the subtle body the individual soul departs. It is the subtle body that conveys the individual soul, the jīva, in his migration to the other world; it endures until he attains final Liberation (mōkṣa).[39] So says the *Brahma-sūtras:*

> The subtle body continues until the final liberation [the realization of the jīva's oneness with Brahman through knowledge], because the scriptures declare the continuance of the transmigratory state till then.[40]

Throughout this period the jīva's gross body is renewed according to the fructification of his karma, but the same subtle body persists.

The bodily heat, being generated by prāṇa, remains in the body as long as life is there. It belongs to the subtle body and not to the gross body.[41] "The body is warm indeed as long as it lives and cold when it dies." In nirvikalpa samādhi, when all physical functions and mental operations cease, bodily heat (uṣma) serves as the only index of livingness. This has been demonstrated in the life of Sri Ramakrishna in the present age. Of the five prāṇas the udāna is responsible for the maintenance of heat in the body. "Fire, verily, is udāna."[42] It functions to the last. It attends on the departing soul. As it leaves, the body loses all heat.

The subtle body is the repository of all the subtle forces developed by the organs and the mind, which belong to it. Whatever capacity, whatever tendency, good or evil, a person acquires remain in the subtle body as potencies. It is because the impressions left on the mind by our actions, perceptions, thoughts, feelings, and desires are accumulated there in latent form. With all these contents the subtle body attends the soul as it passes out of the gross body. These subtle forces, being prevalent in due course, determine the individual's journey hereafter. He is reborn with them when some of them need concrete forms for their fructification. The psychophysical constitution of every individual is shaped primarily by the subtle forces conveyed by the subtle body from his previous incarnation or incarnations.

The subtle body is also called *liṅga-śarīra* (the index body), because it betokens the jīva's previous incarnation and also portends his future. A person is born with special capacities of the organs and

[38]See BS IV:2.10.
[39]See VP VII.
[40]BS IV:2.8.
[41]See BS IV:2.11.
[42]Pr.U. III:9.

the mind, such as a musical voice, a talent for painting, an aesthetic taste, a literary aptitude, a poetic genius, a bent for scientific study, a religious predilection, philosophic acumen, spiritual insight, because he cultivated such powers in his previous life or lives and did not lose them at death. They are conveyed beyond death by his subtle body to which they belong. Wrong tendencies and shortcomings are also conveyed the same way. Hereditary transmission is not a satisfactory explanation of man's inborn abilities, deficiencies, and proclivities; nor do environmental conditions account for the initial differences and inequalities among individuals. We shall discuss these points further when dwelling on reincarnation. (See Ch. VIII, sec. 8.)

9. *The subtle body as the seat of dream experience.*

Normally a person experiences three different states every day — waking, dream, and dreamless sleep. In the waking state the experiencer dwells especially on the physical body; in the dream state he dwells especially on the subtle body. When he falls asleep and dreams he recedes from the gross body to the subtle body. Out of the impressions stored in the subtle body from extensive waking experiences the experiencer creates dream-imagery. So he experiences the concretized impressions. Therefore, he is said to be *praviviktabhuk* (the experiencer of subtle objects).[43] As stated in the *Bṛhadāraṇyaka Upaniṣad:*

> When he dreams, he takes away a little [of the impressions of] this all-embracing world [the waking state], himself puts the [gross] body aside and creates [a dream body in its place], revealing his radiance by his own light — and dreams. In this state the man himself becomes the light.[44]

But the soul by itself does not experience waking or dream. It is in association with the mind that the soul functions as the experiencer. In the dream state it is the mind, the principal component of the subtle body, that serves as the sole instrument of experience. The agency of the mind in dream-experience is mentioned by the *Praśna Upaniṣad:*[45]

> In this dream state this deity [the mind] experiences greatness. Whatever was seen it sees again; whatever was heard it hears again; whatever was perceived in different places and directions it

[43]See Ma.U. 4. [44]Br.U. IV:3.9. [45]See also VC 99.

experiences again and again; it perceives all by becoming all that was seen or not seen, heard or not heard, perceived or not perceived, and whatever is real or unreal.[46]

Evidently, according to the sage Pippalāda, the expounder of the *Praśna Upaniṣad,* the dream-objects can be the replica of waking experiences and there can also be new construction, based on the impressions of the waking experiences. In other words, the dream-experience can be representative as well as presentative. We shall discuss this point later in the chapter on "Waking, Dream, and Dreamless Sleep" (Ch. VI).

C. The Causal Body

10. *The causal body is the medium of the experience of dreamless sleep.*

Just as the gross body is the seat of waking experience and the subtle body of dream experience, so is the causal body the seat of deep sleep experience. In profound or dreamless sleep all mental operations cease. No thought, no feeling, no imagination, no memory of any kind dwells in the mind. Neither pleasure nor pain, neither hope nor fear, neither love nor hate sways it any more. The ceaseless fluctuation of the mind gives way to utter stillness. Its diverse features and traits — its varied ideas, tendencies, merits, and demerits — merge in a state of complete passivity and uniformity. Just as the tree exists in the seed where all its diversities stay in potential form, so in deep sleep the mind enters into a causal state in which all its functions lie dormant and all its properties remain latent. So says the *Vedānta-paribhāṣā:* "Merit, demerit, and past latent impressions remain then [in deep sleep] in their causal form."[47] It is to be noted that in deep sleep the mind as possessed of the power of cognition subsides, but not the mind as possessed of the power of activation. Therefore the continuity of the vital processes is not contradictory. (See Ch.IV, sec. 2.)

In deep sleep the mind reaches the very base of the subtle body. This is the causal body underlying the subtle. From there the mind rises again in waking and dream states. In deep sleep even the ego that is ever ready to assert itself disappears; so a person loses self-

[46] Pr.U. IV:5. [47] VP VII, sec. on Cosmic Dissolution.

consciousness. He does not know whether he is a man or a woman, whether he is young or old, whether he is a teacher or a pupil, whether he is a farmer or a king, whether he is a saint or a sinner. As stated in the *Bṛhadāraṇyaka Upaniṣad:*

> In this state a father is no father, a mother no mother, the worlds are no worlds, the gods no gods, the Vedas no Vedas. In this state a thief is no thief, the killer of a noble Brāhmaṇa is no killer, an outcast no outcast, a hybrid no hybrid, a monk no monk, a hermit no hermit.[48]

11. *The causal body is of the nature of unspecified ignorance and emits bliss.*

Being enfolded by the causal body the experiencer of deep sleep faces a blank wall as it were. He is in a state of complete inapprehension. All that he is aware of is unspecified ignorance. So when a person wakes up from deep sleep, he says, "I slept happily; I did not know anything." This is a fact of universal experience. This shows that in deep sleep a person does not actually lose consciousness. He stays as the cognizer of the causal body, which is of the nature of ignorance, called avidyā or ajñāna, that veils him without affecting his self-luminosity and blissfulness. So he is vaguely aware of the existence of ajñāna and his innate bliss in deep sleep. In deep sleep only the veiling power of avidyā is operative, but not its projecting power. That the causal body is of the nature of avidyā (antiknowledge) is thus noted by Śaṅkara:

> This undifferentiated [avidyā] characterized as the equilibrium of the three guṇas [sattva, rajas, and tamas], is the causal body of the soul [ātman]. Profound sleep is its special state in which the functions of the mind and the organs are suspended.
>
> Profound sleep is the cessation of all kinds of specific cognition in which the mind remains in a subtle seed-like form. The test of this is the universal verdict, "I did not know anything then."[49]

Further,

> In dreamless sleep, when the mind is reduced to its causal state, there exists nothing [for the person asleep] as is evident from the universal experience.[50]

[48]Br.U. IV:3.22.
[49]VC 120,121.
[50]*Ibid.* 171.

As a person wakes up from deep sleep the mind and the organs with all their characteristics emerge from the causal body. The ego-consciousness is the first to rise, because the functions of the mind and the organs proceed from this. The causal body is designated *ānandamaya kōśa* (the blissful sheath) because it emits the blissfulness of the self and because it covers the self like a sheath. During deep sleep a person not only apprehends unspecified ignorance but also perceives indefinite happiness. This is evident from the fact that when he wakes up he reports on his deep experience: "I slept happily and did not know anything." The *Vedānta-sāra* thus delineates the causal body:

> Likewise, the ajñāna associated with the individual soul is known as the causal body because it is the causal state of egoism and the rest; it is also known as the blissful sheath because it veils the soul like a sheath and emits bliss; it is further known as profound sleep because into it everything subsides; and consequently it is also designated as the state of the dissolution of the gross and the subtle phenomena [that appear in the waking state and the dream state respectively].[51]

It is to be noted that the causal body is not intrinsically blissful. In deep sleep when all modifications of the subtle body subside, the absolute bliss of ātman finds expression, faintly though it may be, through the causal body. The bliss experienced in profound sleep is finer than that derived from the experience of agreeable objects in waking and dream states. Every form of delight is but the manifestation of the supreme bliss of ātman through a particular channel. The variations are due to the variations of the channels. As stated in the *Vedānta-paribhāṣā:*

> Happiness is also of two kinds — relative and absolute. Of these relative happiness is a particular manifestation of a modicum of bliss caused by differences in the mental mode generated by a contact with objects. . . . Absolute Bliss is Brahman alone.[52]

D. The Fivefold Sheath

12. *The threefold body constitutes the fivefold sheath or covering of the self, which is distinct from both.*

The five sheaths are the physical sheath, the vital sheath, the

[51] VS VII

[52] VP VIII, sec. 1.

mental sheath, the intelligent sheath, and the blissful sheath. They are successively finer and finer. The first one is the outermost and grossest and the last one the innermost and finest of them all. The preceding sheath is filled or permeated by the succeeding one. As stated by the *Taittirīya Upaniṣad,* the physical sheath is filled by the vital sheath, the vital sheath by the mental sheath, the mental sheath by the intelligent sheath, and the intelligent sheath by the blissful sheath.[53] These are called sheaths because they are like the coverings of the luminous self, the radiance of which, however, becomes manifest through them in the world of phenomena. The five sheaths do not exhaust human personality. Nor can they exist independently of the self, their witness, on which they are superimposed through avidyā or ajñāna. (See Ch. VI, sec. 6.) The physical body forms the physical sheath; the subtle body forms the next three — the vital, the mental, and the intelligent sheaths; the causal body the blissful sheath.

The luminous self, the unchanging basis of the ever changing ego, is distinct from them all, being their constant witness and sustainer.

Says Śaṅkara:

> There is some self-existent entity, which is the perpetual substratum of the ego-consciousness, and the witness of the three states [waking, dream, and dreamless sleep], and which is distinct from the five sheaths.[54]

As expressed by Vidyāraṇya:

> When the five sheaths are disowned [as not-self by discriminating the self from them] their witness-consciousness is all that remains. That is the real nature of the self. Its nonexistence cannot be proved.[55]

13. *The physical and the vital sheaths; their relation.*

The physical body is the physical sheath, which is called *annamaya kōśa* (the sheath consisting of food) because it is the product of food, lives on food, and dies without it. This is also said to be "filled with the essence of food (ānnarasamaya)."[56] This is animated by the vital sheath called *prāṇamaya kōśa* (the sheath of the vital principle).

The vital sheath is thus described by Śaṅkara:

[53]Tai.U. II:2-5.
[54]VC 125.
[55]Pd. III:22.
[56]See Tai.U. II:2.

The prāṇa [the vital principle with its five distinct functions — prāṇa, apāna, vyāna, samāna, udāna (see Ch. IV, sec. 3)]; which is familiar to us, conjoined with the five organs of action [the organ of speech, the hands, the legs, the organs of evacuation and generation] forms the vital sheath, permeated by which the physical sheath engages itself in all activities as if it were living.

Nor is the vital sheath the self, because it is a modification of the vital principle and like the vital principle it enters into, and comes out of, the body, and it never knows in the least either its own weal and woe or those of others, being ever dependent on the self.[57]

14. *The mental and the intelligent sheaths; their relation.*

A significant Sanskrit term for the mind is *antaḥkaraṇa* (the internal instrument). It defines the position of the mind in human personality. The term *manas,* which usually refers to the mind as a whole, is also used in a restricted sense. As we have noted above, the deliberative phase of the mind is distinguished from the determinative by the terms *manas* and *buddhi.* The volitional and the cognitive mind also are similarly distinguished. While *manas* refers to the volitional aspect, *buddhi* refers to the cognitive aspect of the mind. Cognition and volition are two distinctive powers of the mind. Being the finest of all the aspects of the mind and closest to the self, the cognitive mind (buddhi) reflects the radiance of consciousness. It is from the cognitive mind that other aspects of the mind (volitional and emotional) and the organs as well receive the light of consciousness more or less and operate.

The volitional mind with the five organs of perception (audition, touch, vision, taste, and smell) constitutes the mental sheath (manōmaya kōśa). The cognitive mind with the five organs of perception constitutes the intelligent sheath (vijñānamaya kōśa). Since it bears the reflection of the witness-self it appears to be self-luminous. Identified with the not-self the reflected self asserts itself as the agent. Impelled by self-consciousness in such forms as — "I am the knower," "I am the doer," "I am happy," "I am unhappy" — the intelligent sheath operates on the mental and the vital sheaths. It functions as the empirical self (vyavahārika jīva) that transmigrates.[58]

The relation of the intelligent sheath with the volitional and the vital is thus indicated by the *Vedānta-sāra:*

[57] VC 165, 166.
[58] See VS, sec. 13.

> Among these sheaths the intelligent sheath, which is possessed of the power of cognition, is the agent; the mental sheath, which is possessed of the power of volition, is the instrument; and the vital sheath, which is possessed of the power of activity, is the operation.[59]

15. *The intelligent sheath, which is endowed with the reflection of the witness self, functions as the jīva (the empirical self).*

Śaṅkara gives a graphic description of the intelligent sheath (vijñānamaya kōśa):

> Buddhi (the cognitive mind), with its modifications [such as egoism][60] combined with the organs of perception and having the characteristics of agent [the ideas of being a knower and doer], forms the vijñānamaya kōśa (the intelligent sheath), which is the cause of man's transmigration.
>
> The intelligent sheath, which is attended with the power of the reflection of consciousness, is a modification of prakṛti [insentient nature], is possessed of the power of knowledge and action and continually and intensely identifies itself with the body, the organs, and the rest.
>
> This is the jīva, which has no beginning,[61] which is characterized by egoism, which functions in countless ways on the relative plane. Owing to the impressions of previous incarnations it performs good and evil deeds and experiences their results.
>
> Being born in various bodies, high and low, it comes and goes. It is the intelligent sheath that has the waking, dream, and other states and experiences joy and grief.
>
> It always mistakes the duties, functions, and attributes of the different orders of life,[62] which belong to the body, as its own. The intelligent sheath is very effulgent owing to its close proximity to the transcendent self, on which it is superimposed and which being identified with it appears to transmigrate through delusion.[63]

The Vedantic view of the fivefold sheath reminds us of James Ward's conception of human personality as consisting of four concentric selves. In his *Principles of Psychology* he enumerates

[59] *Ibid.*

[60] The cognitive aspect of the mind, as distinct from the volitional and the emotional, has four distinct functions: deliberation, determination, egoism, and recollection. In a restricted sense the term *buddhi* refers to the function of determination. See Ch. III, sec. 6.

[61] According to Vedanta the creative process has no beginning. See Ch. X, sec.2.

[62] The four āśramas or the stages of the individual life. See Ch. XII, sec. 3.

[63] VC 184-188.

them: (1) the pure Ego or Self, (2) the thinking and willing self, (3) the imagining and desiring self, (4) the sensitive and appetitive self. The pure Ego is the subject. "This is central to all of them. It is the thinker of all our inmost thoughts, the doer of all our very deeds — no longer any presentation of self, but the self that has these and all other presentations."[64]

The intelligent sheath (vyavahārika jīva, the empirical self) operating on the mental, the vital, and the physical sheath can also be viewed as the four concentric selves. Beyond them all is the transcendental self, the witness of all thoughts and deeds. It is neither the thinker nor the doer. It is different from Ward's pure Ego or Self, which has some similarity to the intelligent sheath, the empirical self (vijñānamaya kōśa).

It is because of the reflection of the witness-self that the intelligent sheath functions as the knower and as the doer. But the soul of the intelligent sheath is not the reflection but the witness-self whose reflection it bears. The reflection has no existence independently of its basis, the witness-self, which is again nondifferent from the all-pervading Self, Brahman.

Says the *Muṇḍaka Upaniṣad:*

> In the highest golden sheath shines the stainless indivisible Brahman [as the luminous self]. It is pure; It is the Light of lights; It is That which the knowers of the self know.[65]

16. *The blissful sheath; its nature. The five sheaths endure as long as the individual endures.*

The intelligent sheath is permeated by the blissful sheath (ānandamaya kōśa), which is the finest and innermost of all the sheaths being their causal state. It is the causal body.

The blissful sheath is thus characterized by the *Taittirīya Upaniṣad:*

> Different from this very intelligent sheath and within it is the one consisting of bliss. By that (the blissful sheath) this is filled. This (the intelligent sheath) has the human form. According to the human form of this, that too, has the human form. Of that joy is verily the head,

[64]James Ward, *Principles of Psychology,* London, Cambridge University Press, 1933, p. 371.

[65]Mu.U. II:2.9.

delight the right wing, and great delight the left wing; bliss is the trunk; Brahman is the tail, the support.[66]

As described by Śaṅkara:

> The blissful sheath is that modification of ajñāna which manifests itself catching a reflection of the ātman that is Bliss Absolute; whose attributes are joy and the rest; and which appears in view when some object agreeable to oneself presents itself. It makes itself spontaneously felt to the fortunate during the fruition of their virtuous deeds; from which every corporeal being derives great joy without the least effort.
>
> The blissful sheath has its fullest play during profound sleep, while in the dreaming and wakeful states it has only a partial manifestation, occasioned by the sight of agreeable objects and so forth.[67]

The jīva retains the threefold body and consequently the fivefold sheath as long as he exists as an individual in the relative order. Even in Brahmalōka the free souls are not free from these adjuncts because of a touch of ajñāna in them. A person sheds them completely when he merges into Nondual Brahman by realizing the identity of the self with Brahman. But once a person realizes his unity or identity with Brahman he becomes free from all bondages and attains supreme beatitude, even though he may wear the threefold body or the fivefold sheath. By discriminating the self from the five sheaths, one should strive after the realization of its true nature and its essential unity or identity with the Supreme Self, even while living in the body.

Śaṅkara observes:

> This self-effulgent ātman, distinct from the five sheaths, the Witness of the three states [waking, dream, and dreamless sleep], the Real, the Changeless, the Untainted, the ever-lasting Bliss, is to be realized by the wise person as one's own Self.[68]

[66]Tai.U. II:5.
[67]VC 207,208.
[68]VC 211.

CHAPTER III

THE MIND AND ITS WAYS: HOW TO WIELD IT

1. *The imperative need of investigating into the nature of the mind.*

The importance of the human mind cannot be overrated. A person's happiness and unhappiness, knowledge and ignorance, strength and weakness, freedom and bondage, in short, his right and wrong mode of living, depend primarily on the state of his mind. The development of life truly means the development of the mind. Man's achievements in various fields are but the manifestations of his inner attainments. It is the superiority of the mind that makes man superior to all other living beings.

The one indispensable means of knowledge is the mind. From the grossest to the finest, from the lowest to the highest, whatever we want to know we have to know through the mind. The more the mind is concentrated on the object of knowledge, the clearer and deeper is the knowledge. Not only do we cognize and judge by the mind, we even work through the mind. Though well provided with necessary equipment, still hands cannot paint, write, or cook, unless the mind joins with them. Indeed, no methodical action is possible without calmness of the mind. Who can work when the mind is distracted or bewildered? Through the mind we see, through the mind we hear, through the mind we speak, through the mind we walk. Bodily organs can function only in association with the mind. There is a maxim: He who is master of his mind is a sage, who is slave to it is a fool. "The mind is the man, and the knowledge of the mind," says Francis Bacon.[1] Consequently, the questions arise: "What is mind?" "What is its position in human personality?" "How to manipulate it?"

Though the mind is not perceptible as a sense-object, yet its existence is acknowledged in natural course by men and women in general. This is evident from such common expressions as "I was

[1] *In Praise of Knowledge*, in *The Works of Lord Bacon*, Vol. I, Philadelphia, Carey and Hart, 1841, p.79.

absent-minded," "I have no peace of mind," "There is fear in my mind," "My mind wanders," "I have no control over my mind," "He is weak-minded," "I have a noble-minded friend," "The pure-minded are happy." Indeed, few deny the mind. There is, however, much disagreement as to its nature among the thinkers of the world. According to the Vedic philosophers the mind is distinct from the physical body and the knowing self as well, it is intermediate between the two; whereas it has been the prevailing tendency in Western thought to identify the mind either with the self or with the body. According to many Western philosophers mind is the subject that knows, thinks, feels, wills, remembers, imagines, and so forth; while according to many others the mind is but a bodily function. Some psychologists conceive the mind as a series of conscious states derived from the bodily processes.

2. *According to Vedanta the mind is a positive substance intermediate between the body and the organs on the one hand and the knowing self on the other.*

In the Vedantic view the mind is not a process; nor is it a function, or a state, or an attribute of something else. It is a positive substance, though not ultimately real. It has definite functions and states. It is one of the products of primordial nature, the potential cause of the universe, called prakṛti or māyā, which has no consciousness inherent in it. So the mind is characteristically nonconscious. Whatever is devoid of consciousness is considered by Vedanta as material. So prakṛti and its modifications, from the finest to the grossest, belong to the realm of matter. There are subtle and gross elements evolved from prakṛti. The combination of the sattva aspects of the five subtle elements produces the mind. So it is composed of the finest and purest type of matter. The mind is therefore stainless by nature and tranquil if unperturbed. It is the principal component of the subtle body. Not only is it distinct from the gross physical body but also from all other components of the subtle body, viz., the five organs of perception, the five organs of action, and the vital principle with its fivefold function. (See Ch. IV, sec. 3.)

The fundamental reality, nondual Brahman, Pure Being-Consciousness-Bliss, is the ground or the substratum of prakṛti. Being immanent in the manifold, Brahman is its all-pervading Self. He sustains the entire universe of endless variety and ceaseless change. He is the one source of consciousness of all sentient creatures.

He dwells in every human being as the inmost self, as the central principle of consciousness that functions as the knower and as the doer in association with the psychophysical system. More than in any other living form He is manifest within the human form as distinct self-awareness. Not only does man realize himself as an individual distinct from all other things and beings, he can discriminate the indwelling self, the knower within, from all that is known including the body, the organs, and the mind, which being observable fall into the category of the object. Just as a man can know the external facts, so he can know the bodily conditions and the mental states. The knower and the known are ever distinct, being of contrary nature. The knower has consciousness as its very essence and is changeless, while the known is devoid of consciousness and changeful.

Being identical with consciousness, the subject, the knower *per se,* is self-manifest, whereas the object, being devoid of consciousness is unaware of its own existence and the existence of all else. Since mind falls into the category of the object there is no consciousness inherent in it. So says Patañjali: "That [the mind] is not self-luminous, because it is visible [an object of inner perception]."[2] Thus, the mind is differentiated from the luminous self in the same way as the physical body, the organs, and the external objects are. According to Leibnitz and many other Western philosophers mind apprehends its own states. But Vedanta refutes this view. The one and the same thing cannot be both subject and object, which are of contrary nature. Light whose very nature is luminosity cannot be partly luminous and partly nonluminous. The subject is characteristically different from the object. The one cannot turn into the other. Moreover, something cannot operate on itself. Fire does not burn itself. Light does not shine itself but shines of itself.

It is to be noted that mind in itself is not perceivable. But the modes of the mind are invariably perceived by the luminous self as soon as they arise. Such mental modifications as cognition, deliberation, determination, volition, doubt, fear, hope, love, hate, joy, sorrow, memory, pride, anger, become facts of cognition inevitably. It is because the witnessing self is constant. Nothing escapes its watchful vision. Being changeless and ever present it is aware of the appearance and the disappearance of every mode of the mind. So there cannot be any function or state of the mind that is unperceived. As stated by Patañjali: "Since the self-intelligent ātman (the puruṣa), the lord of the mind, is changeless, the modifications of

[2]YS IV:19.

the mind are invariably known to it."[3] Of course, this refers to the contents of the mind in their manifest state and not in their potential or unmanifest state. As we have mentioned, it is in association with the mind and the organs that the immutable self appears to be the knower and the doer. In itself the self is unvarying consciousness. As such it is the ever steady witness of all mental happenings.

3. *Different views of the mind as an indriya (the organs of perception and the organs of action).*

According to Advaita Vedanta, mental modifications become manifest to the witness-self (sākṣī) directly without any intermediary; consequently, the mind does not serve as an instrumental cause of internal perception. But other Vedic schools, such as Nyāya, Sāṁkhya, Mīmāṁsā, regard the mind as the internal organ or *indriya* by which mental states are cognized. As the special cause of internal perception the mind is called by them *antarindriya* (internal organ). The term *indriya* strictly means a special cause of a specific type of perceptual knowledge or volitional action. While the mind is the general cause or means of external perception, each of the five sense-organs is the special cause of a distinctive type of sensory experience. For instance, the eyes are the special cause of visual perception, the ears the special cause of auditory perception. Therefore, the five sense-organs are called *jñānendriyas* (the organs of perceptual knowledge). Similarly, the hands, the legs, and the organs of speech, evacuation, and generation are called *karmendriyas* (the organs of action), each being a special cause of a specific volitional act. The mind is an instrument common to all these ten organs. Therefore, it cannot be counted an indriya.

The Advaitins of the Vivaraṇa school use the term *indriya* in this restricted sense. Therefore, they do not recognize the mind as an indriya. According to the author of the *Vedānta-paribhāṣā,* the mind is other than an indriya.[4] But Vācaspati Miśra and many other Advaitins regard the mind as an indriya. The author of the *Pañcadaśī* has mentioned the mind as the eleventh indriya.[5] Evidently, those Advaitins who are in favor of calling the mind an indriya, use the term in a wide sense. They include in it the general as well as the special cause of perceptual knowledge and volitional action. The Upaniṣads,

[3]YS IV:18.

[4]See VP I, Perception.

[5]See Pd. II:18. In his commentary on II:12 Rāmakṛṣṇa explains the mind as an *antarindriya* (internal organ).

as a rule, exclude the mind from the indriyas. "Higher than the indriyas is the mind," says the *Kaṭha Upaniṣad.*[6] But later scriptures, such as the *Bhagavad-gītā,*[7] the *Manu-smṛti,*[8] usually include the mind among the indriyas. Śaṅkara accepts both views.[9] That the mind is the internal instrument (antaḥkaraṇa) of inferential knowledge, and of such functions as deliberation, determination, reasoning, volition, recollection, doubt, imagination, is acknowledged by all Vedic schools.

4. *Proofs of the existence of the mind distinct from the sense organs and the physical body.*

That the mind is other than the sense-organs is thus proved by the Upaniṣad:

> [They say] "I was absent-minded, I did not see it." "I was absent-minded, I did not hear it." Obviously, through the mind one sees, through the mind one hears. Desire, deliberation, doubt, faith, want of faith, patience, impatience, shame, intelligence, and fear — all these are but [different modes of] the mind. Even if one is touched from behind, one knows it through the mind; therefore the mind exists.

Śaṅkara comments on this passage:

> Truly there is a mind apart from the external organs such as the ear. Because it is a well-known fact that even when there is a connection between the external organ, the object, and the self, a person does not perceive the object present before him, and when asked, "Have you heard what I have said?" a person says, "I was absent-minded, I could not hear. I have not heard it." Therefore, it is found that something else — the internal organ called the mind which joins with the objects of all the sense organs — exists, in the absence of which the eye and other organs, when connected with their respective objects, such as form and sound, fail to perceive them, although they have the capacity to do so, and in the presence of which they succeeded. . . . After the existence of the mind has been proved, the text proceeds to describe its nature.
>
> . . . Another reason for the existence of the mind is being stated. Because even if one is touched by somebody from behind invisibly, one knows it distinctly that this is a touch of the hand or that this is a touch of the knee; therefore, the internal organ called mind exists. If there is no mind to distinguish, how can the skin alone do this? That which helps to distinguish between perceptions is the mind.[10]

[6] Ka.U. II:3.7; see also Mu.U. II:1.3.
[7] See BG X:22, "Among the indriyas I am mind," says Śrī Kṛṣṇa.
[8] See MS II:92, "The mind is to be known as the eleventh organ."
[9] See BS II:4.17.
[10] Br.U. I:5.3 and S.com.

Sense-organs cannot perceive their respective objects unless the mind joins with them. Truly speaking, it is the self that perceives the objects through the mind and the sense-organs. In case the mind is not recognized as a requisite for perception then the following situation arises, as pointed out by the *Brahma-sūtras:*[11] When there is contiguity of the self, the sense-organ, and its object there will invariably be perception if these accessories are adequate for perception, or there will be no perception at any time if they are inadequate for perception. But neither of these two is the actual case. The fact is that sometimes there is perception and sometimes not. We cannot reasonably hold that the self, which is changeless, loses its power for the time being. Nor can we hold that the power of the sense-organ concerned is suspended for the time being. Therefore, it is to be admitted that the mind is an indispensable factor in sense-perception. Its presence and withdrawal account for the perception and the nonperception of the object when there is contiguity of the self, the sense-organ, and its object.

The Upaniṣad has given another reason for the existence of the mind distinct from the sense-organs. Not only does the mind enable the sense-organs to perceive their respective objects, it also judges the perceptions. As noted by Vidyāraṇya, the mind has the capacity to consider the merits and the demerits of things presented by the sense-organs with its aid.[12] It determines whether the object perceived is apparent or real, high or low, wholesome or unwholesome. The sight of a lake in a desert, howsoever agreeable to the eyes, the mind may disregard as false. Even the most melodious song it may reject as degrading. The mind may cherish some bitter herb as wholesome food, whereas a piece of delicious confection it may reject as disagreeable. The mind is capable of discriminating between what is pleasant and what is good, which appear identical to the sense-organ concerned. Further, sense-organs reveal the objects as they are in the immediate present, but the mind can ascertain their past and future as well.

Being composed of the purest and finest type of matter, the mind has the capacity to transmit consciousness, just as a glass-sheet has the power to transmit sunlight. Being permeated with the radiance of consciousness that belongs to the self, the mind appears to be conscious — somewhat like a crystal that looks lustrous when penetrated by light, or like an iron-ball that becomes aglow when

[11] BS II:3.32, S.com. [12] Pd. II:13.

penetrated by fire. It is because of this borrowed light of consciousness that mind proves to be the chief instrument of cognition and conation.

Consciousness is implicit in all such functions as thinking, willing, feeling, reasoning, doubting, remembering, rejoicing, sorrowing, imagining, fearing. These cannot be identified with mechanical processes. We cannot explain them as operations of the brain, which, being a part of the physical body, is devoid of consciousness; all brain processes must be physical. Nor can we ascribe those functions to any of the ten organs, each of which is fit only for some specific function. That there is a mind distinct from the physical body and the ten organs and that it is responsible for all these functions, is evident from the fact that without moving the body and without using any of the organs in the least, a person can vigorously think, feel, will, remember, imagine, and so forth.

It is true that the body and the mind are closely connected, and that one affects the other. Yet neither forms an integral part of the other. They are distinct entities. The body may be impaired without impairing the mind. By losing any of the bodily organs a person does not necessarily lose mental power. One can clearly distinguish between physical and mental ailment. When a person has heartache he can know whether it is in the physical heart or in the psychical heart. For physical distress — such as rheumatic fever, dyspepsia, cancer — one needs conventional medical treatment; whereas for mental distress — such as frustration, depression, anxiety, inferiority complex, sense of guilt, phobia — one needs psychotherapy or spiritual ministration. Then again, despite physical distress one can maintain inner poise and peace; and despite all physical comforts one can be extremely uneasy and unhappy. Further, one can give a severe blow to another's mind by whispering a few words into his ear without hurting the body in the least.

5. *The mind presides over the organs of perception and the organs of action. It is through them that it deals with the external objects. The Vedantic view differentiated from that of the advocates of extrasensory perception.*

The mind is the leader of the sense-organs and the motor organs as well. Without being directed by the mind none of them can operate. For action as well as for perception the light of consciousness is indispensable. It is the radiance of consciousness conveyed by the mind that enables the organs of perception and the organs of action to function. With perception there is cognition, with action there is conation; both of these are derived from the mind. Therefore by controlling the mind one can control all the ten organs.[13] The point is, the organs being inert by nature cannot be self-operative. They have to be driven by the mind bearing the radiance of consciousness borrowed from the self.

During sleep the body becomes motionless and the organs inoperative. It is because consciousness recedes from both with the withdrawal of the ego, the self identified with the mind and the body. A person is not aware of the body any more. Involuntary bodily functions, such as respiration, digestion, assimilation of food, continue because of the vigilant prāṇa, the vital principle, which is distinct from the mind. In the dream state all mental operations are involuntary because of the vagueness of ego-consciousness, which is disconnected from the body. In dreamless deep sleep the mental operations cease altogether, since the luminous self, the cognizer, recedes even from the mind.

It is worthy of note that the mind cannot deal with the physical objects independently of the organs.[14] It has no direct contact with external things and beings. It reaches them through the organs of perception and the organs of action, which belong to the subtle body but function through their outer stations in the physical body. So the mind is called *antarindriya* (internal organ) or *antaḥkaraṇa* (internal instrument), as distinct from the ten outer organs which are called *vahirindriya* (external organs) or *vāhyakaraṇa* (external instruments). One cannot hear a song just with the mind. Nor can one see, smell, touch, or taste a cake with the mind alone. The point is, the mind is responsible for perception in general, but the particularization of perception as auditory, visual, tactile, gustatory, olfactory is due to the sense-organs. This is why the association of the mind with the relevant sense-organ is an indispensable factor in each case of perception. Similarly, one cannot speak, write, or walk with the mind without using the relevant organ of action. It is in conjunction with the organs that mind deals with the physical objects.

The advocates of extrasensory perception hold that mind can go out of the body and contact the sense-objects directly. So says J. B. Rhine:

[13]See MS II:92.
[14]See Pd. II:12.

Clairvoyant perception is the awareness of objects or objective events without the use of the senses, whereas telepathy is the awareness of the the thoughts of another person, similarly, without sensory aid. The term *clairvoyance,* although it literally means "clear seeing," in reality has nothing to do with vision. Clairvoyant impressions may be in the form of visual imagery, but they may also be of other types as well. Any direct apprehension of external objects is clairvoyance if the senses are not involved.[15]

It is to be noted that Dr. Rhine means by "the senses" the organs of perception located in the physical body. But, according to Vedanta, the real organs are not the physical organs but their subtle counterparts which belong to the subtle body. In visual and auditory perception the mind goes out of the body attended by the pertinent sense-organ, which is as subtle as the mind. We have discussed the point of difference between Vedanta and the upholders of extrasensory perception elsewhere.[16]

6. *The fourfold function of cognition: deliberation, determination, egoism, and recollection.*

The mind is said to be *infinite* (ananta) because of its countless modifications.[17] Among the various functions of the mind[18] called antaḥkaraṇa-vṛtti (modes of the internal organ) Vedanta considers cognition basic. It underlies all other functions. None can feel or will, like or dislike, doubt or believe, think or guess, without any knowledge of the object concerned. Of the three aspects of the mind — the cognitive, the conative, and the affective — the cognitive (also called buddhi) is closest to the self. It has the predominance of sattva. It is radiant with the reflection of consciousness. Being identified with it the all-pervading Self becomes manifest as the individual self. So the self is said to be the knower (vijñānamaya puruṣa) shining among the senses with innate effulgence and dwelling within the heart, where the mind is located.[19] It is from the cognitive aspect that the radiance of consciousness reaches the conative and the affective aspect, and the organs as well.

[15]J.B. Rhine, *The Reach of the Mind,* New York, William Sloane Associates, 1947, pp.8-9.

[16]Swami Satprakashananda, *Methods of Knowledge (according to Advaita Vedanta)* London, George Allen and Unwin, 1965, Ch.I, sec.4,5, pp.42-46.

[17]See Br.U. III:1.9.

[18]See Br.U. I:5.3, "Desire, deliberation, doubt, faith, want of faith, endurance, want of endurance, shame, intelligence, fear — all these are but the mind."

[19]See Br.U. IV:3.7.

Cognition is a fourfold function consisting of deliberation (manas),[20] determination (buddhi),[21] I-ness or egoism (ahaṁkāra), and recollection (citta). When we see an object, say a chair, we do not know it all at once. At first we have a vague apprehension of it. As we cognize the object we cogitate, "What is it? Is it this or something else?" This deliberation is the function of manas. Then we search within for the impression of a cognate object to which the present object can be related. This search is the function of citta (recollection). This leads to the recognition of the object as a chair. Then we determine "This is a chair." This determination is the function of buddhi. It is decisive. With the ascertainment "This is a chair" arises the knowledge "I know the chair." Closely associated with buddhi is the function of "I-ness" or ahaṁkāra.

It is evident from the above illustration that cognition is a form of recognition. In order to know something new one has to relate it to something already known. The fourfold cognitive function represents the mind (antaḥkaraṇa). Other functions rest on this more or less. Of the four modes of cognition — manas (deliberation), buddhi (determination), ahaṁkāra (I-ness), and citta (recollection) — the first two are considered primary by the Vedantic teachers. The *Vedānta-sāra* includes citta in buddhi and ahaṁkāra in manas.[22] But the *Pañcadaśī* includes citta in manas and ahaṁkāra in buddhi.[23] We prefer the latter view.

7. *The magnitude of the mind. Though located in the heart it extends all over the body.*

As stated by Vidyāraṇya in his *Pañcadaśī,* the seat of the mind (antaḥkaraṇa) is in the heart.[24] Though located in the heart the mind is not confined there. Being composed of the finest elements, it has the enormous capacity for expansion and contraction. It extends throughout the body and can also move out to any distance with incredible speed. It can join with one or more of the organs at a time. So one can perceive things successively or simultaneously. The organs of action also can operate one after another or simultaneously. Not only that, the sense-organs and the motor organs can function together. An orator can speak, gesture, and see his audience at the same time. The audience can see the speaker, listen to his talk, and

[20]The term *manas* is also used for the entire mind (antaḥkaraṇa) and so is *citta.*
[21]The term *buddhi* is also applied to the cognitive mind as a whole.
[22]VS sec. 13. [23]Pd. VI:70. [24]*Ibid.* II:12.

applaud him. A person can see, smell, taste, and eat food while hearing his companion.

In the Vedantic view the mind is of medium magnitude (madhyama parimāṇa). It is neither *anu* (infinitesimal) as held by the Nyāya school, nor *vibhu* (all-pervading) as held by the Sāṁkhya school. According to Nyāya, the mind, being infinitesimal, cannot be connected with more than one organ at the same time. So a person cannot perceive more than one thing even when all the organs of perception have their respective objects presented to them. But Nyāya holds that in such a case the mind can move in a moment from one organ to another so as to make the perceptions appear simultaneous. The notion of simultaneity is false as in the case of instantaneous piercing by a needle of a hundred sheets of paper. The sheets are pierced one after another, howsoever fast it may be.[25]

8. *Importance of buddhi, the determinative faculty, which is the key to self-mastery.*

In Vedantic culture *buddhi* (the determinative faculty) has been given a very high place. It is of primary importance in the development of life. A well-developed buddhi serves as an unfailing guide in life. It can lead us to the ultimate Goal. Strictly, buddhi means right determination or decision without doubt or wavering. It carries conviction. It includes reason and understanding. It connotes the power of discrimination between the right and the wrong, between the real and the apparent, between the eternal and the noneternal, between the self and the not-self. It is by buddhi that one has to direct volition and emotion and control the organs. By a beautiful imagery the *Kaṭha Upaniṣad* has depicted buddhi as a charioteer driving the chariot of the body, of which the self is the master, towards the Goal Supreme, by holding the rein of the mind and guiding the organs, the horses, through the sensible world.[26] (See Ch. I, sec. 5.)

The following prayers in the *Śvetāśvatara Upaniṣad* for the attainment of true understanding indicate how highly buddhi was esteemed by the Vedic seers:

> He who is the origin of the gods and the source of their powers, who is the ruler of the universe, who is the all-seeing Rudra [the terror of the wrongdoers], who created Hiraṇyagarbha [the cosmic soul] in the beginning; may He endow us with salutary understanding!

[25]BP 85, *Siddhānta-muktāvalī.* [26]Ka.U. I:3.3-9.

> He who, though One and undifferentiated, created in the beginning, by the application of His manifold powers, various forms, having no purpose of His own, in whom the universe merges at the end, who is the luminous Supreme Self; may He endow us with salutary understanding.[27]

The key to self-mastery is the discrimination of the self from the not-self. The more a person is aware of the true nature of the self and its position as the ruler of the psychophysical organism, the greater is his self-control, that is, the control of the lower self by the higher self, of the apparent self by the real self. The aggregate of the body, the organs, and the mind, with which he is identified, is like the lower self. In order to direct the lower self by the higher self, he has to distinguish the higher from the lower by his buddhi, the discriminating reason. He has to realize himself as the sole master of the psychophysical system.

He has to recognize his distinction not only from the body and the organs, but also from the mind. It is through the mind that he must control the organs and the body. As long as he is identified with the mind he cannot have control over it. He is sure to be submerged in the mental waves, the incessant fluctuations of the mind caused by attachment and aversion (rāga-dveṣa) to sense-objects. He must hold himself above the mental waves and watch them before he can restrain them.

Broadly speaking, the emotions are of two distinct types: attraction and repulsion. Love, admiration, aspiration, sympathy, joy, veneration, pride, and the like, indicate attraction. Hate, anger, fear, sorrow, jealousy, disgust, shame, etc., are of the nature of repulsion. Buddhi serves as the most effective instrument of self-upliftment, that is, for raising the higher self from entanglement with the lower self. Says Śrī Kṛṣṇa:

> A person should lift the [lower] self by the [higher] self [through buddhi] and not degrade the self. For, verily, the self is the friend of the self and the self is the foe of the self.
>
> He who has controlled his [lower] self by the [higher] self, his [lower] self is the friend of the [higher] self. But for the man who has not controlled the [lower] self, his [lower] self behaves as a foe like an [external] enemy.
>
> The true self of him who is self-controlled and serene is ever steady [on the Supreme Self] in cold and heat, in pleasure and pain, and so in honor and dishonor.[28]

[27]Sv.U. III:4; IV:1. [28]BG VI:5-7.

9. *Reason, volition, and emotion; their relation. The way to the cultivation of willpower.*

A distinctive function of the human mind next to cognition is volition. It is closely allied with buddhi. Volition or will (saṁkalpa, kratu) carries out what buddhi decides. Buddhi has the capacity to judge the *pros* and *cons* of things and find what is most desirable. It can contemplate the possible courses of action in a certain situation and determine the one that is to be followed. To accomplish the purpose of buddhi is the role of will. In most individuals there is a cleavage between the rational and the emotional nature. By repeated efforts with firm will one can align the emotional with the rational nature and bridge the gap. Vedanta maintains the priority of reason (buddhi). Without right decision there cannot be right action. Will must be guided by reason.

But there are factors in man's psychophysical constitution, such as old habits, wrong tendencies, sense-desires, passions, and prejudices, that often vitiate his judgment and retard his power of action. Undesirable emotions prevail against the remonstrance of reason and the resistance of will. This is why it is necessary to develop both reason and will by all possible measures. By the exercise of his reason and will in every situation as far as possible a person can get rid of his weaknesses. There are positive courses by which one can cultivate the powers of reason and will. Persistent efforts in the right direction despite repeated failures is the secret of every great achievement. There is nothing man cannot accomplish by his indomitable will conjoined with clear and keen understanding. It is said in the *Chāndōgya Upaniṣad:*

> Now, verily a person consists of will. According to the will a person has in this world, so does he become on departing hence. Let him, therefore, form his will.[29]

Śrī Kṛṣṇa points to the imperative need of the exercise of will:

> With respect to each sense-organ there are attachment and aversion to its object. Yet one should not yield to them, because they are enemies on one's way.[30]

It is to be noted that subduing the senses does not mean the suppression of sense-desires but overcoming and outgrowing them by

[29]Ch.U. III:14.1.
[30]BG III:34.

legitimate experiences and by giving the mind a higher direction. This will be evident from the forthcoming discussion.

One has to develop willpower by its exercise. Any systematic course of self-development followed regularly for a certain length of time with firm resolve will develop the power of will. The special purpose of religious vows is the strengthening of will. By observing the vow of silence as a routine for a year or so a person can overcome his garrulousness and at the same time cultivate his will. Similarly, by carrying on some mode of worship according to a program from day to day the worshipper can develop his devotion to God while developing his power of will. Once the vow is made it should not be broken. Whatever plan a person will follow methodically for his physical, intellectual, aesthetic, moral, or spiritual culture for a specified period as a vow will enable him to develop correspondingly and promote his willpower.

10. *It is the freedom of will that distinguishes the human from the subhuman level. Man's moral responsibility is due to this. The importance of the waking state. No self-determination without self-awareness.*

In the human species will prevails, whereas in lower creatures instinct prevails. Man has the capacity to judge the alternative courses of action, make his choice, and follow the course he chooses. He may be wrong in his decision. Still he has the power to decide and to follow his decision more or less. He has the freedom of doing, or not doing, or doing otherwise, as he wants. It is true there are adverse factors in man's psychophysical constitution which can condition his freedom of judgment and his freedom of action. But this does not disprove his freedom of judgment and his freedom of action. Of course, freedom of will does not imply complete or absolute freedom. Will is as free as will can be. Indeed, volitional activity is the special privilege of human life.

This is altogether different from the involuntary functions, such as respiration, digestion and assimilation of food, circulation of blood, controlled by the autonomic nervous system. The motive power behind these functions is the vital principle (prāṇa), which is other than the mind. In dreamless deep sleep, when none of the ten organs function, when all mental operations cease, even then the involuntary bodily functions continue because of the ever active prāṇa, which knows no sleep.

Because of the freedom of will man has moral responsibility. He is accountable for his actions. As he sows, so he reaps. If he performs good deeds he derives benefit from them; they create a favorable situation for him here and hereafter. If he does wrong deeds, he suffers in consequence; they create an unfavorable situation for him here and hereafter. Such is the Divine Law. As declared by the *Mahābhārata,* virtue leads to happiness and vice to suffering. A wrongdoer may escape the man-made law but not the Divine Law. Moral rules and regulations are applicable in human life, because man has the power of choice between the right and the wrong course. He does not work mechanically like an automaton, nor instinctively like a brute. Volitional action is the characteristic mark of human life. It differentiates the human from the subhuman level. Moral instruction, which consists of directions and prohibitions, such as "Do this" and "Do not do this," would have been meaningless, in case man had no freedom of will. He has duties and obligations because of this. He can be entrusted with the responsibilities of a grave situation, inasmuch as he has the capacity for right judgment and right action.

Will implies self-determination. There cannot be self-determination without self-awareness. So unconscious will is a misnomer. Will functions in man's waking state, when his "I-consciousness" is pronounced. Being identified or associated with the psychophysical system, man has well-defined ego-consciousness. In the dream state, or in drunkenness, or in drowsiness, will does not function because of the vagueness of self-awareness. Only unrestrained emotion and imagination prevail in those states in which man has no self-control. Man progresses through volitional action directed by reasoning power. So all human progress is in the waking state. His intellectual, aesthetic, moral, and spiritual development is due to cultural operation carried on by will under the guidance of reason. No development is possible in the state of intoxication, when reason and will are benumbed more or less. In case a person wills as he desires, and acts accordingly without the guidance of reason, he may attain the desired object but no inner development is possible thereby.

11. *The conscious and the subconscious levels of the mind. Accumulation of impressions due to karma. Their four different states. The way to overcome them.*

Whatever thoughts, feelings, desires, memories, and imaginations prevail in the conscious mind do not dwell there steadily. They appear, disappear, and reappear. They dive below the surface, remain in the subconscious region as potencies, and in due course rise again as mental modes. We cannot see the entire mind. Most of it is hidden from our view. That part of the mind which is within the range of ego-consciousness in the waking state is the conscious plane. Below this is the subconscious region. The waking ego undergoes a change and dwells there in dream state. All our volitional actions in the waking state leave indelible impressions (saṁskāras) on the mind. The Sanskrit term for such actions is *karma,* which includes not only the bodily activities, but also the sensory experiences and the mental operations, that is to say, whatever we do with the body, or any of the organs, or the mind, knowingly, intentionally or deliberately. The greater the interest in the work, that is to say, karma, the deeper will be the impression. In a wide sense the term *karma* also applies to the impression created by it.

These impressions accumulate in the subconscious plane and stay there as subtle forces. We are constantly storing within us such impressions, good and evil, according to the nature of karma. From them our memories arise; from them we derive our tendencies, desires, emotions, and also our willpower, intellectual capabilities, aesthetic talents, moral character, and spiritual disposition, in conformity with their nature. Obviously, the subconscious mind is the receptacle of both good and evil factors. It is not to be dreaded as a dungeon of dark forces as represented by many modern psychologists. Judged from the moral standpoint our actions can be classified as righteous and unrighteous, bearing fruits sweet and bitter.

It is said in the *Bṛhadāraṇyaka Upaniṣad:*

> According as one acts, according as one behaves, so does one become. The doer of good becomes good, the doer of evil becomes evil. One becomes virtuous through virtuous action; one becomes sinful through sinful action.[31]

Consequently, the impressions come under two distinct heads — merit (puṇya), and demerit (pāpa) — which serve as retributive forces leading to a favorable or an unfavorable situation here and hereafter. Wherever a person goes his impressions go with him and fructify in due course. Time cannot erase them, distance cannot avert them,

[31]Br.U. IV:4.5.

death cannot annul them. Only our own actions can eliminate, diminish, or augment them; but this does not preclude others' help. At death a person leaves the gross body, but not the subtle body, where the impressions of karma are deposited. An individual's course of life is determined by the nature of the impressions (saṁskāras) acquired by his karma in the present and the past existence as well. What remains at death determines his journey beyond.

The impressions dwell within us in the manifest and in the unmanifest state, that is to say, in the conscious plane and in the subconscious plane. Most of the unmanifest impressions lie dormant. They cannot influence the conscious mind or behavior as long as they remain as such. For instance, even a ferocious animal cannot hurt us as long as it is asleep. Some impressions rise to the conscious plane from the subconscious and become manifest as thoughts, feelings, desires, tendencies, memories, capabilities, and so forth; this may or may not be due to external stimuli. It is they that usually motivate our active life.

Some impressions remain overpowered for the time being by circumstances. For instance, calamity, good association, social laws, family situation, and so forth, often restrain our propensities and prevent them from finding expression; the restraint may also be due to the prevalence of contrary tendencies in the conscious mind. These overpowered impressions often affect the conscious mind and create spontaneous fluctuations of attachment and aversion to things and beings, even though there be no external object or event to stimulate them. A person may repair to a peaceful retreat far from humanity's reach, yet he cannot get rid of these inner undulations.

Then there are other impressions which become attenuated or weakened by the cultivation of contrary virtues. For instance, selfishness can be overcome by the practice of unselfishness, anger by the practice of forgiveness, cowardice by the practice of courage. Sound education and right association are intended to weaken and eliminate the harmful and unwholesome elements within us and foster the salutary. Without systematic efforts with strong determination this cannot be achieved.

It is to be noted that whatever dark forces or unwholesome factors there may be in the subconscious mind, the battle against them has to be fought on the conscious plane in the waking state, when reason and will can predominate. This is the method that Vedanta stresses for self-development. It upholds the importance of the conscious mind, where alone is self-determination.

12. *Each individual is born with a particular psychophysical constitution in consequence of the residual impressions conveyed from the previous incarnation. Heredity does not explain the original differences in the inner nature of men and women.*

In consequence of the residual impressions due to his own karma in his past incarnation or incarnations each individual is born, strictly speaking reborn, in a favorable or in an unfavorable situation, with a particular psychophysical constitution and a stock of unfructified impressions. Thus, past karma is responsible for the original differences with which man starts life. While reaping the fruits of his past actions in the present life, he performs new actions and stores new impressions. None but he is responsible for his weaknesses and excellences.

Heredity does not explain the inequalities among human beings at birth. Hereditary transmission of mental characteristics is not possible. Body and mind being distinct, physical characteristics inhere in the physical body and mental characteristics in the mind. The child cannot inherit the mental characteristics of the parents, unless it is assumed that fractions of the parents' minds enter the zygote at conception. In that case the parents must lose tiny bits of their minds with the birth of each child. This is not however the fact. The child inherits from either parent only the particles of the physical body and some of its traits. The unborn child is led to the parents for the seed of the body it needs for the manifestation of its latent impressions. What physical traits are transmitted to the child must be merited by it. We shall discuss the question of heredity in further detail in the chapter on "How Is a Man Reborn?" (Ch. VII, sec. 8).

13. *The emotional nature of man becomes manifest earlier than the rational and the volitional, which await cultivation. Reason develops as the mind becomes purified through self-discipline.*

As a child grows into boyhood his emotions find expression naturally, long before he can develop his reason and will. His mind is swayed continually by joy, sorrow, love, hate, desire, hope, anger, fear, jealousy, and the like. He shows stubbornness rather than will. He is more impulsive than steady. He instinctively seeks pleasure. He is naturally drawn to what is attractive. Anything pleasant appears good to him. What food is palatable he will eat to his heart's content regardless of consequences. He is more anxious for play than for study. He wants to associate with anyone he likes. His intelligence is overpowered by his emotions. He cannot discriminate between the pleasant and the good, between the real and the false. For the power of discrimination he needs sound reason. This does not develop spontaneously like emotion. He has to cultivate it.

Reason is ever associated with moral goodness. Until the mind is purified by the practice of virtue no clear understanding or insight can develop there. It is the consensus of the Vedantic teachers that virtue brightens intellect, whereas vice darkens it. An immoral man with all his intelligence can be no better than a clever animal. Being deluded by such vices as greed, lust, pride, hatred, anger, fear, jealousy, he cannot distinguish between the pleasant and the beneficial, between the apparent and the real. In a fit of anger he may commit a heinous deed and reap the consequences all his life. With his mind distorted by passions and prejudices a man cannot use for his own good what power, what knowledge, what riches he has. He can abuse his technical and scientific knowledge as well. With the purification of the mind knowledge turns into wisdom. Therefore by all means one should overcome vices by the cultivation of virtues.

It is said in the *Maitreyī Upaniṣad:*

> By self-discipline purification of the mind is attained. Through purification of the mind clear understanding is reached. Through clear understanding self-knowledge is gained. He who gains self-knowledge does not return [to the moral plane].[32]

Śrī Kṛṣṇa speaks of threefold self-discipline: discipline of the body, discipline of speech, and discipline of the mind.[33] Discipline of the body and of speech are conducive to the discipline of the mind. Thought, word, and deed must be in accord. The term *tapas,* often translated as austerity, actually means the application of the body, the mind, and all the organs to the attainment of the single supreme purpose of life. This is *dharma* (upright living). By controlling the psychophysical self one realizes the spiritual self. Self-restraint is the way to self-unfoldment. It is not self-suppression, though often misunderstood as such.

14. *Moral observance becomes natural when a person develops sound reason. Until then he has to go through a compulsory moral course.*

As a person develops sound reason he realizes the importance of

[32]*Maitreyī Upaniṣad* IV:3. [33]BG XVII:14-16.

moral virtues. He sees clearly that man's material well-being is not secure unless he has the wisdom to make proper use of his external resources. There cannot be true understanding without the purification of the mind. It is man's moral nature that supports his physical, intellectual, and aesthetic life. It is also a prerequisite for spiritual awakening. Who can maintain good health unless he lives with moderation and self-restraint? Without moral goodness intellect does not develop into insight. Despite his erudition the man who is lax in moral principles cannot have clarity of vision. Unsupported by moral laws aesthetics tend to degenerate from sensuousness to sensuality. It is moral and ethical principles that harmonize the interests of the individual and of the collective life, and thus form a sound basis for social, political, national, and international organization.

As declared by the *Mahābhārata,* virtue is the sure source of happiness, while vice inevitably leads to unhappiness. Consequently, to a man of right understanding moral virtue is a value in itself, superior to any other temporal value. On no account will he sacrifice moral principles. Moral observance is natural with him. Righteousness is an expression of his inner consciousness. No laws, no commandments, no social convention is necessary to enforce morality on him. He can depend on his conscience, the voice of God within him.

But until a person can develop sound reason and qualify himself for voluntary moral observance, he has to go through a compulsory moral course, consisting of positive and negative rules of conduct. A general rule of moral conduct, as laid down by the *Mahābhārata,* is this: "Doing good to others is conducive to merit, while injuring others is contributive to demerit." In other words, unselfishness is a virtue, selfishness is a vice. In youth or adolescence, when sense-appetites invariably overcloud good sense, when the power of discrimination between the pleasant and the beneficial, between the undesirable and the desirable, is lacking, moral discipline is an essential prerequisite for self-unfoldment. It promotes the development of native potentiality by eliminating the adverse factors.

By examples and by precepts the parents, the teachers, and other seniors concerned should try to build the moral character of the youths in a twofold way — by persuading them to cultivate virtues (such as truthfulness, sincerity, honesty, obedience, humility, purity, endurance, and due consideration for fellow-beings), and by dissuading them from indulging in vices (such as falsehood, anger, hatred, jealousy, vanity, covetousness, deceitfulness). The importance of the moral ideals can be impressed upon their minds by setting forth the exemplary lives of the great men and women of the world. If early care is not taken of youths by indulgent parents and elders, if minors are allowed to be led astray by their sense desires, if their wrong notion of self-expression is not rectified by salutary teachings, then woe betide them! They will have to be disciplined by government laws when they are adults. In every country there are law courts, police force, military force, and social restrictions for the wicked, the undisciplined.

15. *Reason and emotion both are essential in human life. The one must guide the other. The mind becomes pure and calm when freed from emotional involvement.*

Emotions are not wrong in themselves. They need the guidance of reason. They are right or wrong according to the direction toward which they move. That very desire for the sense-object which causes delusion, bondage, and suffering, when turned Godward changes into divine love and leads to liberation, peace, and blessedness perpetual. So a devotee renowned in Hindu tradition prays to the Lord: "That undying love which the unwise have for the objects of the senses, may that love never leave my heart as I meditate on Thee." Reason has vision, but cannot move. Emotion can move, but has no vision. Reason is like a lame man that can see. Emotion is like a blind man that can walk. If the one rides on the shoulders of the other, conjointly they can get along very well.

Even wrong emotions have not to be crushed. They can be transformed or sublimated. As pointed out by Sri Ramakrishna they can be turned into good account by changing their course. As for illustrations: Instead of hating others one should hate one's own weaknesses. Instead of being angry with others' failings, one should be angry with one's own failings. Instead of being proud of transitory possessions one should be proud of one's divine heritage and refrain from doing anything unbecoming. Instead of being jealous of the worldly-minded one should be jealous of the devotees of God and make sincere efforts to emulate them.

Emotions make life zestful. Devoid of the flavor of love, or fellow-feeling, or regard, great achievements through reason and volition are like mechanical performances. Intellect can enlighten the way, but cannot give inspiration, which comes from the heart, from feeling. What man needs is the combination of head and heart. So says Swami Vivekananda:

> What we really want is head and heart combined. The heart is great indeed; it is through the heart that come the great inspirations of life. I would a hundred times rather have a little heart and no brain, than be all brain and no heart. Life is possible, progress is possible, for him who has heart, but he who has no heart and only brain, dies of dryness.
>
> At the same time we know that he who is carried along by his heart alone, has to undergo many ills, for now and then he is liable to tumble into pitfalls. The combination of heart and head is what we want. I do not mean that a man should compromise his heart for his brain or *vice versa,* but let everyone have an infinite amount of heart and feeling, and at the same time an infinite amount of reason.
>
> Is there any limit to what we want in this world? Is not the world infinite? There is room for an infinite amount of feeling, and so also for an infinite amount of culture and reason. Let them come together without limit, let them be running together, as it were, in parallel lines each with the other.[34]

When the mind becomes pure it tends to calmness, being free from emotional disturbance. The more the mind is purged of sense-desires the purer it becomes. It is attachment to sense-objects — in whatever form, things or beings — that causes emotional involvement. For instance, he who is attached to his wealth will naturally be proud of it; he will be envious of those who have more than he has and contemptuous of those who have less; he will be angry with those who stand in the way of his gaining more or try to deprive him of what he has; he will be fearful of losing his wealth and will worry about its security. Similarly, a person who is infatuated with the love for another becomes subject to all the wrong emotions. Hence, the pacification of mind is not possible without its purification. According to Patañjali, calmness of mind can be attained by cultivating friendliness toward the happy, compassion for the unhappy, delight in the virtuous, and indifference toward the wicked.[35] This shows that the cultivation of virtues is conducive to the tranquility of mind.

True happiness or pure delight of the self flows into the mind when it is calm. "How can he have happiness whose mind is not tranquil?" says Śrī Kṛṣṇa.[36] Just as kindliness tends to the calmness of

[34]CW II, p.145.
[35]YS I:33.
[36]BG II:66.

the mind, even so bitterness of feeling robs the mind of peace. Nothing is so distressing to the human mind as ill-will, in whatever form, viz., hatred, anger, jealousy, suspicion, vengeance, animosity. Whenever any of these hostile attitudes towards fellow beings prevail within a person he is victimized long before it reaches the target. His nerves become tense, his temper becomes sour, his vision gets blurred, and his judgment distorted. By forgiving an offense the person offended is more benefited than the offender. When Peter asked Jesus, "Lord, how oft shall my brother sin against me, and I forgive him? till seven times?" Jesus said, "I say not unto thee, until seven times: but, until seventy times seven."[37] He was not unreasonable.

Another disturbing factor is the habit of finding others' faults: instead, one should learn to look into others' virtues and emulate them. At the same time one should recognize one's own faults and rectify them. A critical, carping attitude towards our fellow-beings is a source of much unhappiness. "If you want peace of mind, do not find fault with others." This is the last recorded message of Sri Sarada Devi, the worthy consort of Sri Ramakrishna.[38] Swami Vivekananda told one of his disciples, "Judge men by their strong points rather than by their weak points." This does not mean that one should ignore others' faults. It only means one should not stress them. A positive and sympathetic attitude towards a person uplifts him, while the negative and antipathetic attitude depresses him. The great spiritual leaders have recognized this truth. With what encouraging and animating words Śrī Kṛṣṇa exhorts Arjuna on the eve of the battle of Kurukṣetra:

> Whence, O Arjuna, has this dejection not entertained by the noble-minded, not leading to heaven but to disgrace, come upon thee at this crisis? Yield not to unmanliness, O Pārtha, it does not become thee. Shake off this mean faint-heartedness and arise, O subduer of foes.[39]

16. *Inner purification is a prerequisite for the practice of concentration, which is a gateway to knowledge and energy.*

With the purification of the mind one gains the power to concentrate it on the desired object. The obstacle to concentration is

[37] Matt. 18:21,22.

[38] Swami Tapasyananda and Swami Nikhilananda, *Sri Sarada Devi, The Holy Mother,* (Her Life and Conversations), Madras, Sri Ramakrishna Math, 1958, p.292.

[39] BG II:2,3.

distraction caused by sense-attachment. The concentration of the mind is indispensable to knowledge. Without the intense application of the mind to the subject of investigation one cannot gain adequate knowledge of it. Says Swami Vivekananda:

> How has all the knowledge in the world been gained but by the concentration of the powers of the mind? The world is ready to give up its secrets if we only know how to knock, how to give it the necessary blow. The strength and force of the blow come through concentration. There is no limit to the power of the human mind. The more concentrated it is, the more power is brought to bear on one point; that is the secret.[40]

What obstructs concentration obstructs the acquisition of knowledge. The obstructing distractions, as stated by Patañjali, are illness, mental laziness, doubt, lack of enthusiasm, lethargy, clinging to sense-pleasures, false perception, failure to attain concentration, unsteadiness in concentration. These are accompanied by grief, despondency, tremor of the body, and irregular breathing. They can be removed by the practice of concentration on a single object.[41]

A general method of concentration of the mind for spiritual aspirants is the practice of meditation on God as the inmost self ever shining within the heart. "Though all-pervading, God becomes gracious on being worshipped there [in the heart]," observes Śaṅkara.[42] "The kingdom of God is within you," says Jesus Christ.[43] Generally speaking, one can gain the power of concentration by practicing meditation on anything that appeals to one as good.[44] But one has to continue the practice of meditation steadily from day to day. If a person succeeds in concentrating the mind on one particular object, he will be able to concentrate it on any other object as he wills. This means that he will have the power of both attachment and detachment at his command. He will be able to fix his thoughts on the object of his choice and to withdraw them from there as he wants.

Until a person develops this power his mind will be inclined to get stuck on something or other and to leave it at its own sweet will. Through the practice of concentration one gains the capacity to gather up the scattered forces of the mind and direct them into whatever channel he chooses. When the mind becomes pure and calm

[40]CW I, pp.130-31.
[41]YS I:30-32.
[42]BS I:2.7, S.com.
[43]Luke 17:21.
[44]YS I:39.

it hardly rambles. There is no knowing how much mental energy a person loses every day in vagaries. Swami Brahmananda made the remark: If a person loses a little money he regrets it, but he hardly notices how much energy of the mind he wastes daily in vain thoughts and idle dreams.

17. *The cure of mental troubles lies in strengthening the mind by positive courses. The need of a central ideal in life.*

At the same time Swami Brahmananda encouraged pupils to develop the mind by regular spiritual practice, holy association, scriptural study, and high thinking. He gave this illustration: Just as a cow being well taken care of and well fed gives plenty of rich milk, similarly, the mind, when properly trained and enriched with noble ideas, thoughts, and sentiments bears abundant wholesome fruits. The point is, for the effective solution of its problems the mind has to be strengthened by positive courses, such as the cultivation of virtues, the development of will and understanding, practice of concentration, receiving inspiration from the lives and the teachings of the great personages.

As the mind gets strong it yields clear vision, equanimity, hopefulness, courage, cheerfulness, kindliness, endurance, and other blessed qualities. All such ailments as depression, despondency, anxiety, unsteadiness, impatience, fearfulness, selfishness are but the symptoms of a weak mind. When the mind is weak it is easily affected by adverse conditions. In case the mental trouble originates from, or is aggravated by, some adverse condition, it can be remedied for the time being by the removal of the cause. In order to have a sound body one has to take care of it in health as well as in sickness. Similarly, in order to have a sound mind one has to take care of the mind even though there be no ailment.

Further, a person should cultivate single-mindedness by holding firmly to a central ideal of life. He must direct all his activities, sensory experiences, thoughts, feelings, will, and imagination to the attainment of the primary objective. This will lead to the coordination of all his resources, external and internal. This is the most effective way of checking the vagaries of the mind and the consequent frittering of energies. "The mind," says Sri Ramakrishna "is like a package of mustard seeds. Unless you hold it firmly it will be extremely difficult to gather the seeds once they are scattered." Holding to a central ideal is the key to the integration of personality.

This also makes life meaningful and removes all inner conflict. None can be at peace with himself until he can find, according to his aptitude and situation in life, a worthy cause to live for. The nobler the ideal, the higher is the life.

But it is to be noted, whatever ideal a seeker of secular values may hold — be it prosperity, social or political leadership, scientific or philosophic knowledge, aesthetic genius, honor, or fame — he should on no account deviate from the moral course. In all his dealings with his fellow-beings he should be honest and kindhearted. He must know for certain that no level of life is sound or secure without a moral basis, and that he cannot deviate from the path of virtue without risking his own interest.

18. *The development of the power of introspection. Its efficacy. Being directed to higher values the mind becomes detached from the lower.*

With the purification of the mind its outgoing tendencies diminish. It develops inwardness. Thus a person gains the competence for self-introspection. He can observe the deeper levels of life — emotional, volitional, rational, aesthetic, moral, and spiritual — which belong to his inner being. He can closely watch the workings of the mind. The more he can know the mind the greater will be his power to manipulate it. None can solve his problems effectively until he can know his own mind. Human problems are basically psychological and not biological. Life's blessings consist not of the external, but the internal resources. It is said that each man has his own peculiar cast of mind. None can know a person more intimately than he himself. No external diagnosis can reveal a man's inner nature as clearly as internal perception. To know another's internal life through his behavior is an indirect approach, whereas introspection is the direct way.

A man's joy and sorrow, love and hatred, hope and fear are known to him directly through inner experience. He is happy not because he is surrounded with comforts, but because he feels so within himself. Despite all hardships and privations one can be happy; despite all honors and luxuries one can be unhappy. One is happy or unhappy according as one feels within oneself. It is through her inner experience that a woman knows whether she loves her husband or not, rather than through her behavior towards him. She may smile on seeing the husband, speak sweet words to him, kiss him and embrace him, and yet in the depth of her heart she will know that she has no love for him. Similarly, in spite of all external expressions of love a person may not have any love for his wife. By inner perception he can know immediately whether he loves her or not. A man's external behavior is not a sure index of his internal states.

By actual observation a person can find his own attitudes and aptitudes, his own excellences and weaknesses, and map out a life for the development of his potentialities. He can also gain the insight, the penetrating vision, by which he can recognize the transcendental self beyond the empirical. As observed by Swami Vivekananda:

> The powers of the mind should be concentrated and turned back upon itself, and as the darkest places reveal their secrets before the penetrating rays of the sun, so will this concentrated mind penetrate its own innermost secrets. Thus will we come to the basis of belief, the real genuine religion. We will perceive for ourselves whether we have souls, whether life is of five minutes, or of eternity, whether there is a God in the universe or none. It will all be revealed to us.[45]

A key to life's development is to train the mind to be interested in higher and higher values. A direct contact with right types of persons and their guidance is a very effective means. As the mind turns to higher values it becomes detached from the lower. A philosopher or a scientist whose principal purpose is the cultivation of knowledge will not be interested in pleasures and possessions in the way a seeker of prosperity is likely to be. Such a person will accept in natural course plain living and high thinking as the motto of his life. Similarly, an artist whose aesthetic imagination can comprehend the beauty of truth, goodness, selfless love — and can dwell on the same — will have no difficulty in rising above the sense-plane. A seeker of eternal verities naturally becomes disinterested in temporal values. For those who cherish and pursue lofty ideals the observance of moral and ethical principles is no problem. But others can follow the course with sincere effort once they are convinced that it is in their own interest to do so.

19. *How righteousness leads to spiritual awakening. The close relation between morality and spirituality.*

Men of good sense who in their search for wealth, or pleasure, or power, or fame, do not deviate from the path of righteousness, whose

[45]CW I, p.131.

minds become purged of all dross by the practice of virtue, gain the most out of this life. From actual experience they apprehend the inherent limitation of the world of dualities. Not only do they realize the bitterness of misery but also the futility of pleasures. They become convinced that their inmost longing for immortality, for light beyond all darkness and delusion, for supreme bliss beyond all bondages and sufferings, cannot be satisfied in the relative order. Thus disenchanted of the diversified manifold marked by interdependence they look beyond, recognize the all-free, all-pure, Divine Being underlying the order of phenomena, and accept Him as the supreme goal and ideal of life and worship Him with single-hearted devotion as the innermost Self.

Says Śrī Kṛṣṇa:

> But the men of virtuous deeds, whose demerits are exhausted, become free from the delusion of dualities and worship Me with firm resolve.
>
> Those who strive for freedom from old age and death taking refuge in Me come to know Brahman [the Supreme Being], all about the individual self, and all about action.
>
> Those who know Me as the One sustainer of natural phenomena, their presiding deities,[46] and all sacrifices, know Me even in the hour of death steadfast in mind.[47]

Because of the fundamental unity between morality and spirituality, moral observance invariably leads to spiritual awakening; in other words, moral sense develops into spiritual consciousness. The basic moral virtue, as we have indicated above, is unselfishness. It is selfishness that incites a man to wrong deeds. None but a lunatic will hurt another unselfishly. Unselfishness signifies self-expansion, that is to say, widening the self by doing away with the limitations of egoism. This tends to the recognition of the apparent self as it really is. Awareness of the true nature of the self leads to the awareness of its unity with the Supreme Self. The basic principle underlying the moral and the spiritual life is the same. It is the attunement of the individual soul to the Supreme Self, the one Self of all. A moral man practices this unknowingly, a spiritual man practices this knowingly, deliberately. None can attain spiritual enlightenment without mastery over the organs and the mind. As stated in the *Kaṭha Upaniṣad:* "He who has not desisted from evil ways, whose senses are not under control, whose mind is not

[46]The intelligent forces guiding the working of nature. [47]BG VII:28-30.

concentrated, whose mind is not composed, cannot attain this [the self] through right knowledge."[48]

20. *Inner purification through self-discipline transforms the subjective and the objective vision of the aspirant and paves the way to supreme peace and freedom.*

With the development of clear understanding and insight the aspirant gains the power of discriminating the self from the not-self. As he becomes aware of the true nature of the self he naturally rises above the psychophysical plane. Sense-attachment loses its hold on him. With the knowledge of the self as distinct from the psychophysical system, the knowledge of the Supreme Being underlying the order of phenomena and distinct from it dawns upon him.

As long as a person identifies himself with the body, the organs, and the mind he is bound to be interested in all that concerns them. He cannot but react favorably to what is agreeable to them and unfavorably to what is disagreeable to them. Because of this twofold reaction he is subject to being constantly swayed by attraction and repulsion. Whoever lives on the psychophysical plane and is attached to the variegated world of experience cannot attain serenity of the mind.

On the other hand, the man of self-knowledge who discovers the supreme Unity underlying the diversified universe of ceaseless change ever reposes in Immutable Brahman. So declares the Upaniṣad:

> The One who dwells in every origin, in whom all this dissolves [at the end] and appears in various forms [at the time of creation], who is the Ruler, the Bestower of blessings, the Adorable Lord, by discerning Him one attains the supreme peace.[49]

How to quiet the mind is a problem common to all human beings. Overcoming the vices by the cultivation of virtues is a partial solution of the problem. The complete cure of the restlessness of the mind and the attainment of inner serenity, are not possible unless the mind is detached from the ephemeral and set on the Eternal. Thus it is a twofold course: (1) steady practice of concentration of the mind on God, the Supreme Self, and (2) making the mind free from all

[48]Ka.U. I:2.24.
[49]Sv.U. IV:11.

attachment to the temporal. This is patent from the following dialogue between Arjuna and Śrī Kṛṣṇa:

> This yōga, O Madhusūdana [an epithet of Śrī Kṛṣṇa], which you have declared to be characterized by evenness — I do not see how it can long endure because of the restlessness of the mind. For the mind, O Kṛṣṇa, is restless, turbulent, strong, and obstinate. To me it seems as hard to control as the wind.
>
> Undoubtedly, O mighty Arjuna, the mind is restless and hard to control. Yet, O Son of Kuntī, it can be controlled by practice [persistent effort to fix the thoughts on the Supreme Self] and detachment [dispassion for sense-objects]. I consider yōga is hard to attain by one who is not self-controlled, but by the self-controlled it is attainable by striving through proper means.[50]

Similarly, in his *Yōga-sūtras* Patañjali prescribes a twofold method for the attainment of perfect serenity of the mind: (1) Persistent efforts to make the mind calm, that is to say, to reinstate it in its innate serenity. (2) Complete mastery over all attraction of sense-objects in this world and the worlds beyond.[51]

While impure mind causes bondage, pure mind leads to freedom. In the words of the Upaniṣad:

> The mind is well spoken of as of two kinds — pure and impure. The impure mind is that which is possessed of desire and the pure is that which is free from desire.
>
> It is indeed the mind which is the cause of men's bondage and liberation. The mind that is attached to sense-objects leads to bondage. Being dissociated from sense-objects it leads to liberation. So think the wise.[52]

By turning the mind from the search of the temporal to the search of the eternal, one moves from the path of mortality to the path of immortality, from the way of bondage to the way of liberation.

"Bondage and liberation are of the mind alone," says Sri Ramakrishna.[53] Purification of the self means the purification of the mind. The pure mind is ever imbued with the light of the spirit, that is, with God-consciousness. There is hardly any difference between the pure self and the pure mind, as expressed by Sri Ramakrishna. The Supreme Self is ever manifest to the pure-minded. "It is through the purified mind that Brahman has to be perceived as It is," says the

[50]BG VI:33-36.
[51]YS I:12-15.
[52]*Amṛtabindu Upaniṣad* 1,2. Cf. Pd. VI:68.
[53]GSR, p.138.

Bṛhadāraṇyaka Upaniṣad.[54] "Blessed are the pure in heart: for they shall see God," says Jesus Christ.[55]

We have found the imperative need of investigating into the true nature of the mind in order to know how to manipulate it. No human progress is possible without the discipline of the mind. From coarse material achievement to the highest spiritual attainment every advancement in life requires corresponding mental training.

We conclude with the pertinent words of Śrī Kṛṣṇa on the attainment of the highest Goal through the mind:

> But those whose ignorance is destroyed by the knowledge of the self—their knowledge, like the sun, manifests that Supreme Being.
>
> Those who are convinced of That, whose mind is set on That, who are devoted to That, whose last resort is That, reach a state from which there is no return, their sins being washed off by knowledge.
>
> The wise look with equal eye on a Brāhmaṇa possessed of learning and humility, an outcaste, a cow, an elephant, and a dog.
>
> Even here [in this very life] is the relative existence conquered by those whose minds rest on equality; for Brahman is the same in all and flawless; therefore they are established in Brahman.
>
> The knower of Brahman who is established in Brahman with the mind steady and undeluded, rejoiceth not on getting what is pleasant nor grieveth on receiving what is unpleasant.
>
> He whose mind is unattached to external sense-objects attains to the bliss that is in the Self; he with his mind absorbed in Brahman through meditation enjoys undying bliss.
>
> Pleasures born of contact of the senses with the objects are indeed the sources of suffering; they have, O son of Kuntī, a beginning and an end; no wise man revels in them.
>
> He who is able to overcome the urge of passion and anger in this very life before the body drops is steadfast [in yōga] and a happy man.
>
> He whose happiness is within, whose delight is within, whose light is within, that yōgī established in Brahman, attains the Bliss of Brahman.
>
> The sages whose demerits are destroyed, whose doubts are dispelled, whose minds are disciplined, who are devoted to the welfare of all beings, attain freedom in Brahman.[56]

[54] Br.U. IV:4.19.
[55] Matt. 5:8.
[56] BG V:16-25.

CHAPTER IV

PRĀṆA, THE VITAL PRINCIPLE; ITS INDIVIDUAL AND COSMIC ASPECTS

Prāṇa can be viewed as functioning in living individuals and also as sustaining the cosmic order. The individual prāṇa is the life principle that distinguishes the animate from the inanimate. It has a cosmic counterpart. The cosmic prāṇa is the universal potent energy that holds the living and the nonliving as a complex, as a coordinated whole. While it is all-pervading as potential energy, its manifestation differs in the diversified universe. Prāṇa is manifest as the life principle only in the animate. We shall at first dwell on the individual prāṇa, that is, the life principle that animates the psychophysical structure of an organism. Later on, we shall dwell on its cosmic counterpart and the correlation of the two.

A. The Individual Prāṇa

1. *Prāṇa, the vital principle, is distinct from both the physical and the psychical factors in an individual. The mainspring of a living organism is the self-intelligent ātman.*

The life principle is neither physical nor psychical, but vital. It is of its own kind. It vivifies the physical body, and is not derived from, nor dependent on, it. Conjointly with the ten organs and the mind (antaḥkaraṇa) prāṇa constitutes the subtle body, which endures even after the physical body drops and disintegrates. Though inseparable, these component factors are distinct from one another. They perform their respective functions being invested with the radiance of consciousness by the luminous self (ātman), which holds them as a unity. In none of them is consciousness intrinsic. "Divested of the light of ātman, which is Pure Consciousness, they are in themselves like wood or clods of earth," remarks Śaṅkara.[1] Any gleam of consciousness noticeable in them is received from the self (ātman), directly or indirectly. Being borrowed, the radiance is bright or dim according to the nature and condition of the receptacle.

Without being endued with the light of ātman, none of the organs, nor the mind, nor prāṇa can function. So the self (ātman) is said to be "the Prāṇa of prāṇa, the Eye of the eye, the Ear of the ear, and the Mind of the mind."[2] In fact, the organs, the mind, and prāṇa are like so many attendants of the self (ātman) to carry out specific functions. Being closely allied with the self, its master, prāṇa stays in the physical body as long as the self stays and accompanies it when it departs. So it is said: "When it [the self] departs, prāṇa follows; when prāṇa departs all the organs follow."[3]

We have noted that in the Vedantic view the self-luminous ātman is the sole spiritual entity; all else belongs to the realm of matter, gross and fine, being devoid of intrinsic consciousness. Therefore, prakṛti (primordial nature) and all its modifications, from the grossest earth to the cosmic mind (mahat), which constitute the world of phenomena, physical and psychical, come under the category of matter (jaḍa). None of them is self-intelligent; none of them has consciousness as its essence. Although material by nature, the ten organs, the mind, and prāṇa belong to a much finer order of matter than the physical body.[4] They arise from the sattva and the rajas aspect of the subtle elements, whereas the physical body is composed of the gross elements that originate from the subtle elements with tamas preponderant in each. Just as the sattva aspect of each of the five subtle elements being combined produces the mind (antaḥkaraṇa), so their rajas aspect being combined produces prāṇa.

It is through the mind that prāṇa receives the light of the self-luminous ātman. Purposiveness is implicit in livingness because of this light, howsoever faint it may be. An innate plan of self-development and self-preservation is noticeable in all living things. The behavior of a living being is characteristically different from that of a self-moving machine. Biological functions are other than

[1]Br.U. IV:4.18, S.com.

[2]Br.U. IV:4.18.

[3]*Ibid.* IV:4.2.

[4]Cf. Brajendranath Seal, *The Positive Sciences of the Ancient Hindus,* Longman, Green & Co., London 1915; reprint edn., Moti Lal Banarsi Dass, Delhi, 1958, pp.242-43. "The Vedantists are believers in an independent vital principle. . . . Life is a sort of subtle rarefied *ether-principle* (adhyātma-vāyu) pervasive of the organism — which is not gross *vāyu* (air), but is all the same subtilized matter, like the manas (mind) itself, for, in the Vedanta, everything other than the Self (Ātman) is *material* (jaḍa)."

mechanical processes. They differ from psychical functions as well. The way of prāṇa is not the way of the mind, or of the physical body.

2. *It is prāṇa that animates the body in the waking, dream, and dreamless sleep states.*

Being composed of subtilized or rarefied matter, prāṇa has a tendency to expand. It pervades the entire physical body made of the essence of food.[5] Prāṇa is subtler than the nerves. It operates on the nervous system, the central and the autonomic as well. It is wholly responsible for the functions of the autonomic system, which is not controlled by will. It penetrates the nails, the hairs, and the bones, where the nervous system does not extend. Being endowed with life all these grow. Prāṇa vitalizes the whole body. "Prāṇa is indeed, the essence of the members [of the body]. Truly, it is their essence. Hence, from whichsoever member prāṇa departs forthwith it withers."[6] Prāṇa is responsible for all the physiological functions.

None of the ten organs, nor the mind, animates the body. They have their specific functions. A person may lose one or more of the organs, such as the power of hearing, the power of speech, the power of vision, and so on, without losing life, or liveliness. Mental powers may be impaired without impairing vitality. It is a fact of common knowledge that the feebleminded, such as idiots and morons, do not necessarily lack the vigor of life. In animals and plants there is still less manifestation of mental powers, yet they are found to be vigorous. So says the Upaniṣad:

> One lives deprived of speech for we see the dumb; one lives deprived of eyes for we see the blind; one lives deprived of ears for we see the deaf; one lives deprived of mind for we see the infants; one lives deprived of arms; one lives deprived of legs; for thus we see. But now it is prāṇa that being allied with the knowing self seizes hold of this body and makes it rise. . . . What is prāṇa, that is the knowing self [being allied with it]; what is the knowing self, that is prāṇa; for together they live in this body and together they go out of it.[7]

Like the organs prāṇa is subordinate to the self. It performs everything for the self as a minister does for the king.[8]

During deep sleep, when the organs and the mind cease to function, the vital processes continue. The respiration becomes

[5] Cf. Tai.U. II:2.
[6] Br.U. I:3.19.
[7] Kau.U. III:3.
[8] See BS II:4.10, S.com.

slower and the heart beat softer, but neither stops. The act of digestion, consisting in the secretion of bile, pancreatic juice, etc., in the movements of the gastrointestinal tracts and the absorption of the food substances, proceeds. In the dream state the mind, though inwardly active, is not conscious of the body. "The immortal radiant self, the lone wanderer [being unrelated], preserves the unclean nest [of the body] with the help of prāṇa and roams out of the nest."[9] The self does not actually go out of the body in dream. "Though he dreams staying in the body, yet having no connection with it like the ākāśa [etherial substance] in the body he is said to be roaming out," remarks Śaṅkara.[10]

In dreamless sleep all mental operations stop, yet prāṇa keeps on functioning. "[When all the organs sleep] it is the fires of prāṇa that keep watch in this city [of nine gates, the gross body]."[11] Even then prāṇa is not dissociated from the mind or the self.

> The mind (antaḥkaraṇa) has two distinct powers — the power of cognition and the power of activation. In deep sleep the mind as possessed of the power of cognition subsides, but not the mind as possessed of the power of activation; therefore continuity of the vital processes is not contradictory.[12]

The fact that the mind (antaḥkaraṇa) controls the organs of action and the organs of perception as well, testifies to its two distinct powers, motive and cognitive. The less the light of consciousness transmitted by the mind, the deeper is the sleep. Even the faintest reflection of consciousness serves as the motive power for prāṇa.

3. *The fivefold function of prāṇa.*

The same life principle, prāṇa, has five different names according to its five different functions. These are *prāṇa, apāna, samāna, vyāna,* and *udāna.* It is to be noted that the term *prāṇa* is used to signify the life principle as operative in the body as a whole and also as carrying on a specific function. *Prāṇa,* in the latter sense, is the life principle operative in the lungs and the heart, and responsible for respiration. It tends to move upward to the mouth and the nostrils. It is the principal vital force (mukhya prāṇa); it functioning, others

[9]Br.U. IV:3.12.
[10]*Ibid.,* S.com.
[11]Pr.U. IV:3.
[12]VP VII, Cosmic Dissolution, sec. 2.

function.[13] *Apāna* functions below the heart down to the navel and helps elimination. *Samāna* (lit. the equalizer) is located in the stomach; it digests and assimilates food and drink.

Vyāna (lit. the pervading one) is so called because it pervades the whole body and operates on the nerves. It regulates *prāṇa* and *apāna* as their nexus. It is responsible for the utterance of speech and actions of great effort, such as lifting a weight, jumping over a fence, and so forth. Śaṅkara remarks:

> *Vyāna* is so-called because it exists all over the body through the nāḍīs [cords][14] that extend from the heart in all directions like the heat rays from the sun. It functions especially in the joints, the shoulders, and the vital parts. It manifests itself in the performance of deeds requiring great strength, while both prāṇa and apāna stop functioning.[15]

Udāna functions upward from the sole of the feet to the head. It promotes growth and helps in rising up, etc. It also conveys the soul in passing out of the body. As we have noted, it maintains bodily heat; as it leaves, the body loses all heat.

It is to be noted that *prāṇa, apāna,* and *samāna* are responsible for the functions of the autonomic nervous system, such as the

[13]Cf. Perry D. Strausbaugh and Bernal K. Weimer, *General Biology,* John Wiley and Sons, New York, 1938, p.13. "Respiration is constantly taking place in all organisms. Its cessation means death, and thus it is one constant invariable characteristic of living matter."

[14]The term *nāḍī* has been variously translated — as nerve, artery, vein, duct. Perhaps, the word has these different meanings in different contexts. Generally speaking, *nāḍī* means a vital channel of transportation or communication in the psychophysical system. According to Surendranath Dasgupta, ". . . they (nāḍīs) are some kind of ducts, through which blood and other secretions flow, and many of these are extremely fine, being about the thousandth part of a hair in breadth." (S. Dasgupta, *A History of Indian Philosophy,* Vol.II, London, Cambridge University Press, 1952, p.345).

But the term has also been used definitely in the sense of *nerve* in ancient Indian Literature. As noted by Brajendranath Seal, "The writers of Yōga and Tantra schools use the term *nāḍī,* by preference, for nerves." (Seal, *The Positive Sciences of the Ancient Hindus,* p. 219.) We find such expressions as "manōvahā nāḍī (sensori-motor nerves)," "ājñāvahā nāḍī (volitional-motor nerves)," "prāṇavahā nāḍī (automatic-motor nerves)."

It may be noted that the analysis of the human system by the medical authorities of ancient India is rather psycho-physiological than anatomical. This may be one of the reasons why their physiological or anatomical terms do not always correspond with those of modern medical science. However, in a number of cases identification is possible; for example, *snāyu* signifies "nerve," *śirā* "artery," *dhamanī* "vein," *srōta* "duct or channel," and so forth. I have used the word "cord" for *nāḍī* instead of "nerve" or "duct," because it has a wider meaning and is appropriate in the present context.

[15]Pr.U. III:6, S.com.

movement of the lungs, beating of the heart, secretion of bile, etc., and peristalsis of the alimentary canal; *vyāna* and *udāna* are associated with the cerebro-spinal system. Though operating on the physical body, the five prāṇas belong to the subtle body as we have noted before (Ch. III, sec. 7).

4. *Vedanta refutes the Sāṁkhya view of prāṇa as the conjoint operation of the ten organs and the mind.*

In the Sāṁkhya view prāṇa is not a distinct entity, but the resultant of the coordinated functions of the eleven organs (including the mind as the internal organ).[16] This is illustrated by an analogy. Just as a cage moves in consequence of the simultaneous activities of a number of birds inside it, similarly, the vital process is the natural outcome of the concurrent operations of the organs and the mind.

Vedanta refutes this position.[17] In the first place, the ten organs and the mind cannot have any conjoint action. Each of them has its peculiar way of operation. They do not all function together. Besides, had the vital process been the effect of their united actions, then it would have been extinct in the absence of any one or more of them. Secondly, the analogy is not to the point. The activities of the birds are characterized by a common feature — movement, which is similar to the movement of the cage and, therefore, conducive to it. In the operations of the ten organs and the mind there is no such common factor resembling the vital process as can contribute to it. Moreover, prāṇa, which is the foremost of them all, cannot be regarded as a mere function of one or more of them.

5. *Prāṇa is a basic principle in the psychophysical system, and not its product. Modern theory of biogenesis confirms the Upaniṣadic view.*

The Upaniṣad distinguishes prāṇa from the five material elements, the ten organs, and the mind. "From this [the Supreme Self] originates prāṇa, mind, all the organs, ākāśa, air, fire, water, and earth, which supports all."[18] That a distinct vital principle vivifies the body has been illustrated by a parable in the *Praśna Upaniṣad.*[19] Once the five material elements, the ten organs, and the mind were bragging among themselves, "We hold this organism intact and

[16]See SK 29 and Vācaspati's com.
[17]See BS II:4.9.
[18]Mu.U. II:1.3.
[19]Pr.U. II:2-4.

sustain it," each maintaining its predominance. To them prāṇa, the vital principle, said, "Do not be deluded. I alone, having divided myself fivefold,[20] hold this organism intact and sustain it." But they would not believe him. Then prāṇa out of indignation acted as if he were leaving the body. As he arose all others arose with him; as he stayed all others stayed. Just as the bees fly up when their monarch flies and settle down when it settles down. so did the organs and the mind. Then, being pleased, they extolled prāṇa. Indeed, none but prāṇa is responsible for the building and the upkeep of the body with all the organs.

But prāṇa does not originate from the material constituents of the body, nor from the organs, nor from the mind, nor from their combination. It is not a function of any of the ten organs, nor is it their conjoint operation. "Prāṇa functioning, the organs function."[21]

It is not a mere process, but a principle. It is an original, determining factor in the psychophysical system of a living being. It cannot be characterized as physical, psychical, psychophysical, or biophysical. It is a type in itself. It is *vital.* It can be conceived as vivifying, substantive energy with an inherent tendency to move.

The activities of a living being — its ways of self-development, self-preservation, and reproduction — cannot be explained without postulating a subtle, stable, dynamic, animating principle that pervades the entire system, vitalizes all its parts, and integrates them into a self-sustaining, self-regenerating complex whole. This must be distinct from the material components of the body. Nor can it be identified with the mind. Prāṇa is unique, but not "mysterious." Its conception is corroborated by facts. The life-history of an animate being — the record of its birth, growth, decay, and death — is not that of self-moving machine. Its ways are far more significant than the involuntary operations of an automaton. No machine is begotten, nor does it grow, nor does it reproduce, nor does it putrefy.

The modern theory of biogenesis that all life must come from preexisting life also points to the uniqueness of life as a distinct principle. The former theory of abiogenesis or spontaneous generation, that living things or life can come from inanimate matter, has long been rejected. About the middle of the eighteenth century it was the French chemist, Louis Pasteur, who finally disproved the theory of spontaneous generation by his classic experiment. "So far as any biological doctrine can be said to be firmly established it is the

[20]Fivefold life principle — prāṇa, apāna, vyāna, udāna, and samāna (see sec. 3).
[21]Tai.U. II:3.1.

doctrine that all living things are the product of living things."[22] It is life that begets life. The theory of biogenesis, has however, suffered a change in recent years. A tendency to support spontaneous generation in a modified form has developed. But no conclusive evidence has yet been found.[23]

It is to be noted that the physical and the chemical processes in the material structure of an organism do not enliven it. It is life that makes it alive. We live not because we breathe; but we breathe because we live. One can live without breathing as some yōgīs do despite the suspension of breath; but one cannot breathe without living. We live not because we eat; but we eat because we live. One can live a number of days without eating, but one cannot eat a single morsel of food without living. In fact, it is prāṇa that consumes food to sustain itself and the organs. So it is said, "Whatever food is eaten is eaten by the life principle alone, and it rests on that. . . . Whatever food one eats through the life principle satisfies these [the organs]."[24] All activities of a living organism cease as soon as prāṇa leaves it. Prāṇa initiates the vital processes; it cannot be their resultant. It is existent at the inception of the living organism. It animates inanimate matter.

To hold that the material components of a living organism generate life some way or other is to fall back on the theory of abiogenesis. The materialists of ancient India, the Cārvākas,[25] maintained that consciousness as well as life originated from the chemical combination of the physical elements in the composition of the body. In their view living things could arise spontaneously from lifeless and inorganic matter. They pointed out as representative cases of spontaneous generation, the growth of mosquitoes and the like in moisture and of maggots and other worms in stale curd during the rainy season. The upholders of the theory of abiogenesis in the West similarly believed that "under the influence of the sun's rays the

[22] *Encyclopaedia Britannica,* 1948 edn., s.v. "Biology," by Charles Singer. Since then, experiments have been made to produce life out of lifeless matter; but the results so far have been inconclusive. As noted in a recent book on biology: "Despite the exciting research now going on, biologists are still a very long way from creating cells from nonliving matter." (William L. Smallwood and Edna R. Green, *Biology,* Morristown, New Jersey, Silver Burdett, 1968, p.235.) Further, "But no evidence of plausible hypothesis for the transition from molecule to organism was yet presented." (1972 Britannica Book of the Year, The University of Chicago, Encyclopaedia Britannica, Inc., 1972, p. 418.)

[23] See William T. Keeton, *Biological Science,* New York, W. W. Norton, 1967, pp.765-6.

[24] Br.U. I:3.17,18.

[25] See Ch.II, sec.2.

mud and slime of ponds and streams transformed into frogs, toads, and eels."

6. *The modern view that the livingness of an organism is due to a typical organization of its material constituents is not tenable.*

That a living organism is controlled by a vital principle distinct from its material components is evidenced by its peculiar constitution. What distinguishes a living being from a nonliving thing is not, according to modern biologists and other scientists, the nature of its material constituents, but their special organization. In their view this is the distinctive mark of every protoplast or cell, the structural unit of plant and animal life; there is no fundamental difference between organic and inorganic matter. On the difference between living and nonliving matter Schrödinger, the great German physicist, remarks:

> The arrangements of the atoms in the most vital parts of an organism and the interplay of these arrangements differ in a fundamental way from all those arrangements of atoms which physicists and chemists have hitherto made the objects of their experimental and theoretical research.
> From all we have learnt about the structure of living matter, we must be prepared to find it working in a manner that cannot be reduced to the ordinary laws of physics. And that not on the ground that there is any "new force" or what not, directing the behavior of the single atoms within a living organism, but because the construction is different from anything we have yet tested in the physical laboratory.[26]

The biologists give a similar account of the difference:

> Whether matter is alive or not depends upon the peculiar, intricate combinations of atoms and compounds such as the proteins, carbohydrates, fats, salts, and the like, of which it is composed. It will be readily understood that living protoplasm is constantly changing, taking in materials from the environment, working them over, using them, and finally discarding them as wastes. Yet, in the process of material change, the living protoplasm usually in the form of an organism, maintains its individuality until death. The living organism is like a whirlpool in a stream. It retains its identity even though its constituents are constantly shifting and changing.[27]

It is a well recognized biological fact that a living organism is

[26]Erwin Schrödinger, *What is Life?*, New York, Cambridge University Press, 1946, pp.2,76.

[27]Perry D. Strausbaugh and Bernal K. Weimer, *Elements of Biology*, New York, John Wiley and Sons, 1944, p.27.

invariably characterized by peculiar, intricate combinations of the material elements of which it is composed. So the question arises, do these arrangements of its material constituents make the organism alive? If its livingness depends wholly on these arrangements, then it has to be acknowledged that nonliving matter, somehow or other, develops into the living. But the actual fact, as observed by the biologists, is that life invariably comes out of life and never out of lifeless matter. How can one account for this without the recognition of life as a distinct principle or force directing and vivifying the material constituents of a living organism? Further, every living organism is "like a whirlpool in a stream" of matter, so one may pertinently ask: Can the ever-shifting and changing material constituents of the organism maintain the pattern of its structure and behavior without a distinct, stable, basic principle to sustain them and work on them? Some biologists and other scientists may not recognize any "new force" in a living organism, as is evident from Schrödinger's remarks, but without its acceptance the question "What makes a living thing alive?" finds no adequate answer. A new force that is neither physico-chemical nor mechanical, but *vital,* must be there; otherwise the living organism would not behave as it does, in a way characteristically different from a self-operative machine.

Natural philosophers have tried to prove that forms of life can originate from the transformations and the new combinations of lifeless matter and energy in the process of evolution of the physical world. Says Osborn, the paleontologist:

> Living matter does follow the old evolutionary order, but represents a new assemblage of energies and new types of action, reaction, and interaction — to use the terms of thermodynamics — between those chemical elements which may be as old as the cosmos itself, unless they prove to represent an evolution from still simpler elements. Such evolution, we repeat with emphasis, is not like that of the chemical elements or of the stars; the evolutionary process now takes an entirely new and different direction. . . . The central theory which is developed in our speculation on the Origin of Life is that every physico-chemical action and reaction concerned in the transformation, conservation, and dissipation of energy, *produces also, either as a direct result or as a by-product, a physico-chemical agent of inter-action which permeates and affects the organism as a whole or affects only some special part.* Through such interaction the organism is made a unit and acts as one, because the activities of all its parts are correlated.[28]

[28] Henry Fairfield Osborn, *The Origin and Evolution of Life,* New York, Charles Scribner's Sons, 1921, intro.

Even so, a living thing cannot result from the correlation of the material ingredients and forces. A mechanical process of evolution can produce at best a self-operative machine. The enormous gap between a living organism and an automaton remains unbridgeable. Johnston aptly remarks: "From the point of view of mathematical physics all that we can say about the origin of a living organism is that it must have been *an enormously improbable occurrence.*"[29] So says Haldane, "Though the physico-chemical, or mechanistic, conception of life is still very much alive in the minds of popular writers, I think it is now far from being so among serious students of biology."[30]

7. *The living and the nonliving are fundamentally different despite their interaction.*

As far as we can see, the living and the nonliving are the two primary types of existence in the diversified world. The one does not originate from the other. The living differ from the nonliving in their essential nature, their composition, and characteristics. There is, however, an interrelation between the two as we have noted. Before their manifestation both remain latent in the undifferentiated primordial nature, from which they emerge in due course. The animate beings arise in the order in which the physical universe, their habitat, is formed.

From the very beginning every animate creature, unicellular or multicellular, is vested with a potential material structure, of which it is the indwelling controller. The central principle within every living thing is responsible for the coordination of the material components of the physical vesture, its functions, its development according to a definite plan, and its correlation with the environment. A living organism has also the capacity for self-reproduction, self-preservation, and self-restoration, which are not noticeable in any nonliving thing. All these characteristics betoken consciousness, implicit or explicit, in every living being from the lowest to the highest order. The higher a living creature in the scale of evolution, the greater is the manifestation of consciousness in it.

It is a fact worthy of note that a living being alone develops consciousness and never does a nonliving material thing, be it large or

[29]James Johnston, *The Essentials of Biology,* New York, Longmans Green, 1932, p.302.

[30]J.S. Haldane, *The Philosophical Basis of Biology,* New York, Doubleday, 1931, p. 11.

small, luminous or nonluminous, steady or unsteady. Even the immense, resplendent sun, the mighty ruler of the entire solar universe, is totally devoid of consciousness. It has not the least self-awareness or the awareness of anything else whatsoever, which are the two characteristic marks of consciousness. This universal fact — that a living being alone develops consciousness — points to the intimate relation between livingness and consciousness. The higher a being the greater is the manifestation of consciousness in it. The greatest manifestation of consciousness is noticeable in man. This is what makes man the highest of all living creatures.

The evolution of a protoplast into a human being is not possible unless man is involved there. Something cannot come out of nothing. As is the cause so is the effect. This is the universal law. Evolution is invariably preceded by involution. A seed can develop into the tree that already exists there in potential state. The evolution of a living thing depends primarily on its potentiality and secondarily on the external factors. A nonliving thing can grow by accretion or the addition of external materials; but a living thing, howsoever small it may be, grows by the inner capacity for assimilation of materials of its own choice.

Inside the cell, the fundamental unit of life, there is the nucleus: its control center, which is responsible for its livingness and for any development whatsoever. The cell functions as a system because of its potentiality indicative of intrinsic consciousness. According to biologist William T. Keeton, the nucleus plays the central role in cellular reproduction.[31] It has also been found that if the nucleus is removed by expert surgery the cell cannot live any longer. Indeed, purposiveness is immanent in the cell. As noted by Schubert-Soldern:

> When Schwann (1839) and Schleiden (1833) enunciated the cell theory, they thought the cell was the physical unit of life. This was a mistake because the cell itself manifests all the qualities possessed by a complete organism. Nevertheless, it seems abundantly clear that the cell is the unit of the living form. The cell behaves then in many ways like an organism. This is particularly evident in the case of unicellular organisms.[32]

In every multicellular organism, be it a plant, an animal, or a human being, there is a control center; otherwise the coordination of

[31]See William T. Keeton, *Biological Science*, p.72.

[32]Rainer Schubert-Soldern, *Mechanism and Vitalism*, London, Burns and Oates, 1962, p.91.

its multifarious factors and their functions would not have been possible. The ways of a living being, insignificant though it may be, are different from those of an automaton, or any other mechanical device. No human ingenuity can create life out of lifeless matter. A living being belongs to a different category of existence. It has the threefold body and the fivefold sheath. It is the self that holds the psychophysical vehicle. It is more than "a psychophysical unity."[33]

But livingness is not identical with consciousness. The vital principle (prāṇa) itself is not self-aware, as we shall see. It is man's inmost self that is of the nature of pure consciousness. Because of this man is self-aware and is aware of all else within its scope. The luminous self is self-evident, real to itself. It requires no proof. This is why each man is sure of his own existence and certifies the existence of all else including lifeless matter. Being associated with the luminous self, the vital principle as well as the mind receives the radiance of consciousness more or less, which enables them to function. The inner controller, consisting of the luminous self, the mind, the vital principle, and the ten organs in subtle forms, is the living being, the jīva, in the true sense.

The physical body is but a temporary abode or a vehicle. Although the physical garb varies beyond recognition in the course of evolution, the indwelling jīva remains identical throughout its progression and retrogression. The gross material elements provide the jīva's conveyance, the physical body, suitable for the journey of life here and hereafter. So we see, prāṇa is not self-operative. The question is raised in the *Kena Upaniṣad:* "At whose command does prana, the foremost, do its part?" The answer is given: "Being directed by the luminous self does prāṇa operate."

Not only prāṇa, but also the mind, and the ten organs, as we have noted, derive their power of action from the same spiritual source. Indeed, the luminous self is responsible for all psychological, biological, and physiological processes in an individual. It is the real man and the sole agent. With regard to this the same Upaniṣad says: "He is the Ear of the ear, the Mind of the mind, the Speech indeed of the [organ of] speech, the Life of life, and the Eye of the eye. The wise giving up identification with the not-self and going beyond this world [rising above the temporal order] become immortal."[34]

[33]"Each living organism is to be regarded as a psychophysical unity," says Ralph Stayner Lillie, *General Biology and Philosophy of Organisms,* University of Chicago Press, 1945, preface.

[34]Ken.U. I:1,2.

Evidently the Upaniṣad rejects both the Vitalist and the Mechanistic view of the living being.

8. *Prāṇa exists at the very inception of an organism. "It is the oldest and greatest," says the Upaniṣad.*

Prāṇa is not a "new force" in a living organism. It prevails at its origin. According to the Upaniṣads prāṇa is "the oldest and greatest."[35] Why? Śaṅkara explains:

> How is it known that prāṇa is the oldest and greatest, since at the very conception prāṇa and the organs are likewise connected with the germ cell formed by sperm and ovum? The answer is: nevertheless, the seed, unanimated by life, does not germinate; therefore, prāṇa must operate earlier than the eyes and the organs. Hence it is the oldest in age. Prāṇa fosters the embryo from the moment of conception. After it has started functioning then only the eyes[36] and other organs begin to grow.
>
> Therefore, it is reasonable that prāṇa is the oldest among them. But one may be the oldest member in a family and yet not be the greatest for lack of qualities; then again, the second or the youngest member may be the greatest, being rich in qualities, though not the oldest. Neither of these is the case with prāṇa. It is, indeed, the oldest and the greatest. How is it known to be the greatest? This will be illustrated by a story.[37]

The story in short is this.[38] The ten organs and the mind, disputing over their respective greatness, went to Brahmā (Prajāpati) and said to him, "Which of us is the greatest?" He said, "That one of you will be the greatest — who departing from among yourselves — the body will be considered still more unclean."

At first the organ of speech went out of the body. After staying away a whole year it came back and said, "How did you manage to live without me?" They said that they lived just as dumb people do, without speaking through the organ of speech, but living through prana, seeing through the eyes, hearing through the ears, and knowing through the mind, and having children through the organ of generation. So the organ of speech entered the body.

In this way, the eye, the ear, the mind, and the organ of generation went out and came back, one at a time. It is to be noted that by "mind" the mental capacity of understanding or intellect is meant here, not

[35]Br.U. VI:1.1; Ch.U. V:1.1.
[36]Among the organs the eyes are formed first in the embryo (Sat.Br. IV:2.1.28).
[37]Br.U. VI:1.1, S.com. [38]See Br.U. VI:1.7-13; Ch.U. V:1.6-12.

the mind stuff (antaḥkaraṇa). Each of them found that others had managed to live without him and the body had been intact. Then came the turn of prāṇa.

As prāṇa was about to go out, he uprooted all of them, like a big, fine horse of Sind pulling out the pegs to which its legs were tied.

"Please do not go out, sir, we cannot live without you," they cried out.

"Then give me tribute," said prāṇa.

"Let it be so." With these words the organs and the mind offered him tribute.

9. *Other than prāṇa is the knowing self, the ruler within.*

Even this all-important prāṇa is not the self, because it is not its own master. In fact, prāṇa does not sustain the body; it is the self that sustains it by the agency of prāṇa. So it is said in the Upaniṣad: "Neither by prāṇa nor by apāna does any mortal live; but he lives by something else on which both these rest."[39] Indeed, the self is the sole support of prāṇa, the mind, and the ten organs. It integrates them all and correlates their functions. Nay, it is their prime mover. None of them is self-intelligent. As we have noted, it is the radiance of the luminous self that enables them to function. The self operates in these various forms, so to speak. As the Śruti says,

> People do not see the self, for viewed in its aspects it is incomplete. When it performs the function of living, it is called prāṇa; when it speaks, the organ of speech; when it sees, the eye; when it hears, the ear; when it thinks, the mind. These are merely its names according to functions. He who meditates on one or another of its aspects does not know, for it is then incomplete, being limited to a particular aspect.[40]

The fact that prāṇa is not the knowing self on account of being devoid of consciousness, has been illustrated by a story in the *Bṛhadāraṇyaka Upaniṣad.*[41] Once a proud Brāhmaṇa, Bālāki Gārgya by name, came to Ajātaśatru, the King of Varanasi (Banaras), and said to him, "I will teach you about Brahman [the Supreme Being]." The King said, "For this proposal I give you a thousand cows." But all that Gārgya said indicated only the conditioned Brahman, and not the Unconditioned, the Absolute. Ajātaśatru rejected one by one

[39]Ka.U. II:2.5.
[40]Br.U. I:4.7.
[41]*Ibid.* II:1.1-15 (adapted).

Gārgya's conceptions of Brahman, which were well-known to him. Then Gārgya with his knowledge of Brahman exhausted had nothing more to say and remained silent with his head bent down.

Ajātaśatru:	Is this all?
Gārgya:	Yes, this is all.
Ajātaśatru:	By knowing this much one cannot claim to have the knowledge of Brahman.
Gārgya:	I approach you as a student.
Ajātaśatru:	It is contrary to custom that a Brāhmaṇa should approach a Kṣatriya for the knowledge of Brahman.[42] However, I will instruct you.

So saying, the King took Gārgya by the hand and stood up. They walked together to a part of the palace where a man was asleep. The King addressed the sleeping man by the special and characteristic names of prāṇa several times. But prāṇa, though functioning in his body at the time, did not respond to the call. The man did not wake up. Then the King pushed him until he awoke. Had the power of perception been inherent in prāṇa, then it would have readily responded to the sound within its reach, when called by its distinctive names.

It is a fact of common observance that fire, whose very nature is to burn and shine, invariably burns whatever combustible thing is within its reach, and shines. The fact that prāṇa did not respond, when addressed by its own name, proves its lack of innate power of perception. The point is, prāṇa is not the experiencer. Other than prāṇa is the experiencer, the self.

It often happens, however, that a person, when fast asleep, does not respond even though addressed by his own name. From this should it be assumed that he is not the experiencer? No. The reason is this. During sleep, the self, the experiencer within, is dissociated from the body and the organs and is not related to them in the same way as in the waking state. Had this very aggregate of the body and the organs been the actual experiencer, then it would remain the same when lying down, so it would invariably respond to a touch or call; pushing and not pushing would make no difference in its waking. But, since the experiencer is something other than the body and the organs, it — being differently related to them during sleep — does not readily respond to a mere touch or call and has to be awakened by

[42]For the fourfold social order see Ch. XII, sec. 2.

pushing; so pushing and not pushing makes a difference in this case.

Ajātaśatru roused the sleeping man by repeatedly pushing him with his hand, since he could not be awakened otherwise. Pushing was necessary because of the fact that something other than the aggregate of the body and the organs is the experiencer. Śaṅkara comments:

> Therefore, it is proved, that that which awoke through pushing — blazing forth as it were, flashing, as it were, coming from somewhere, as it were, and rendering the body different from what it was, by endowing it with consciousness, activity, a new look and so forth, is an entity other than the body and different from the types of Brahman advocated by Gārgya.[43]

B. The Cosmic Prāṇa

10. *The individual and the cosmic prāṇa.*

Fundamentally, prāṇa is very subtle, potent, all-embracing sustaining energy. It is mobile by nature. It is formless and ubiquitous. It permeates whatever physical body it animates. Being manifest as life force in an animate being it is said to be individual prāṇa. So individual prāṇa is a phase of the cosmic prāṇa, which unites the animate and the inanimate. Prāṇa penetrates gross matter and subtle mind as well. But its manifestation in the multiform universe, physical and psychical, differs according to the nature of the medium through which it finds expression. It is noticeable as vital force only in a living organism. In a machine it becomes manifest as mechanical power. In the psychophysical constitution of a human being its threefold expression as physical, vital, and psychical power is to be found. Indeed, cosmic prāṇa is the one universal source of each and every kind of energy. Says Swami Vivekananda:

> Out of this prāṇa is evolved everything that we call energy, everything that we call force. It is the prāṇa that is manifesting as motion; it is the prāṇa that is manifesting as gravitation, as magnetism. It is the prāṇa that is as gravitation, as magnetism. It is the prāṇa that is manifesting as the actions of the body, as the nerve currents, as thought force. From thought down to the lowest force, everything is but the manifestation of prāṇa. The sum total of all forces in the universe, mental and physical, when resolved back to their original state, is called *prāṇa.*[44]

[43]Br.U. II:1.15, S.com. [44]*Raja-Yoga,* CW I, pp.147-8.

Cosmic prāṇa is uniform. It assumes the forms, so to speak, of different material bodies, large and small, animate and inanimate, through which it becomes manifest. It is said in the Upaniṣad:

> It [prāṇa] is equal to a white ant, equal to a mosquito, equal to an elephant, equal to these three worlds [the earth, the heaven, and the interspace — the body of Virāt, the world-soul], equal to this entire universe [the body of Hiraṇyagarbha, the cosmic soul].[45]

Śaṅkara observes:

> Prāṇa is equal to all these bodies, such as that of a white ant, etc., in the sense that it fully abides in each of them, just as the essential characteristics of the cow [that is, cowhood] abide in each individual cow. It cannot be merely of the size of these bodies, for it is formless and all-pervading. Nor does the equality mean just filling up those bodies by contraction and expansion like lamp-light in a jar, a mansion, and so forth. For the Śruti says, "these are all equal, and all infinite."[46] And there is nothing inconsistent in an all-pervading principle assuming in different bodies their particular size.[47]

As a matter of fact the universe is one continuous existence — physically, vitally, psychically, spiritually. There is no break anywhere, nor the least gap in the sense of a void. The gross is pervaded by the fine, the fine by the finer, the finer by the still finer. The finest is the Supreme Self, Pure Consciousness, which penetrates everything and is not penetrated by anything. An individual is a part and parcel of the cosmos in all its aspects. His prāṇa coexists with the cosmic prāṇa, wherever he may be, until he attains final Liberation in oneness with Brahman, Pure Being-Consciousness-Bliss.

The cosmic prāṇa is associated with the cosmic soul (Hiraṇyagarbha) as a limiting adjunct, in the same way as the individual prāṇa is associated with the individual soul (jīvātmā). It is nondifferent from the universal mind (mahat) with will predominant in it. Rajas prevails there as the fundamental principle of motivity. Here is the first manifestation of rajas from prakṛti (primordial nature). It is the fountainhead of all energy. It is to be noted that the mind has the potency of action as well as the potency of knowledge. The potency of action becomes manifest through will and the potency of knowledge through intellect. The motive force of the organs of action in an individual is his volitional mind, and the motive force of the organs of perception is the cognitive mind.

[45]Br.U. I:3.22. [46]*Ibid.* I:5.13. [47]*Ibid.* I:3.22, S.com.

The cosmic mind (mahat, lit. the great principle) is the common ground of all individual minds. As such it is pure mind, being free from the specific qualities of every individual mind. To give an illustration, the common basis of all particular bodies of water, such as the well, the lake, the river, the sea, is but water pure and simple. Swami Vivekananda remarks on *mahat,* one of the twenty-four principles of Sāṁkhya philosophy: "Mahat is universal. It covers all the grounds of sub-consciousness, consciousness and super-consciousness; so any one state of consciousness, as applied to this Mahat, would not be sufficient."[48]

The cosmic prāṇa functions as the creative energy of Hiraṇyagarbha (the cosmic soul) in moulding the diversified physical universe out of the gross material elements (mahābhūtas) created by the Supreme Lord, Īśvara. It is also called *Sūtra* (the Thread), on which are strung all things and beings from the highest to the lowest that the universe is composed of. The Upaniṣad praises the meditation on the Sūtra and the Internal Ruler (the Supreme Self) within it:

> He who knows that Sūtra and the Internal Ruler who is within the Sūtra and governs it . . . indeed knows Brahman or the Supreme Self, the worlds such as the earth controlled by the Internal Ruler, the gods such as Fire presiding over those worlds, the Vedas, which are the authority for all, the being such as the Virāt (the world-soul) and the rest held together by the Sūtra and controlled by the Internal Ruler who is within it. He knows as well the self, which is the agent and experiencer and is controlled by the same Internal Ruler, and all the worlds similarly controlled.[49]

The Sūtra is also called *Vāyu* (lit. the Air), by which the whole world is pervaded. "Vāyu is that Sūtra. Through this Sūtra or Vāyu this and the next life and all beings are held together. Therefore . . . when a man dies, they say that his limbs have been loosened, for they are held together by the Sūtra or Vāyu."[50] Śaṅkara remarks:

> Vāyu is that subtle entity, which like the ether supports earth, etc. [the five subtle elements], which is the substance of the subtle body consisting of seventeen parts, the receptacle of the impressions of past actions,[51] which is collective as well as individual, and whose external

[48]CW II, p.441.
[49]Br.U. III:7.1.
[50]*Ibid.* III:7.2.
[51]See Ch. II, sec. 7.

forms, like the waves of an ocean, are the forty-nine Maruts.[52] That principle of Vāyu is called the Sūtra.

So it is said in the *Bhāgavatam:*

> He [the Supreme Lord] through His transcendent power stirs into activity His māyā consisting of the three guṇas and through that projects first the Sūtra.
> This [the Sūtra], the manifestation of prakṛti, is described by the sages as projecting the manifold, and in which the universe is strung and through which the jīva [individual soul] transmigrates.[53]

As explained by the commentator Śrīdhara, "The Sūtra is the principle of mahat [the universal mind] with the power of action predominant." This implies that there is the prevalence of rajas in the Sūtra. So it is the source of all energy.

11. *The different meanings of prāṇa.*

Thus, the term *prāṇa* is used to denote the cosmic as well as the individual aspect of the vital principle. The cosmic prāṇa has different names, such as *mahat, sūtra, vāyu.* It also signifies Hiraṇyagarbha or Brahmā, the cosmic soul, with whom it is associated as a limiting adjunct. In the following passages *prāṇa* (the cosmic prāṇa) refers to Hiraṇyagarbha:

> All that exists in the three worlds is under the control of prāṇa [Brahmā].[54]
> He [the Supreme Lord] created prāṇa [Hiraṇyagarbha].[55]
> With the thought of creation Brahman [the Supreme Lord] expands, so to speak. From Him arises prakṛti, from prakṛti prāṇa [Hiraṇyagarbha].[56]

In some cases *prāṇa* is indicative of Saguṇa Brahman:[57]

> It is into Prāṇa that all these beings go; and it is from Prāṇa that they come.[58]
> This whole world — whatever there is — vibrates having originated from Prāṇa.[59]
> This same Prāṇa is verily the intelligent self, blissful, ageless, immortal. . . . He is the Protector of the world, He is the Sovereign of the world; He is the Lord of all. "He is my self," this one should know. "He is my self," this one should know.[60]

[52]These are the personifications of intelligence underlying various manifestations of air as their presiding deities or conscious guides.

[53]SB XI:9.19,20. [55]*Ibid.* VI:4. [57]See BS I:1.23. [59]Ka.U. II:3.2.

[54]Pr.U. II:13. [56]Mu.U. I:1.8. [58]Ch.U. I:11.5. [60]Kau.U. III:8.

In several instances in the Upaniṣads the organs are meant by the term *prāṇa,* because the vital principle functions through each of them, assumes the form of each, so to speak. As stated in the *Bṛhadāraṇyaka Upaniṣad:*

> Death [in the form of fatigue] did not overcome this prāṇa (the vital principle) in the body. The organs resolved to know it. "This is the greatest among us that, whether it moves or does not move, it feels no pain nor is injured. Well, let us all be of its form." They all assumed its form. Therefore they are called by the name of *prāṇa.*[61]

In the *Chāndōgya Upaniṣad* we find a similar expression:

> Prāṇa (the vital principle) indeed is the absorber. When one sleeps speech merges in prāṇa, the eye merges in prāṇa, the ear merges in prāṇa, the mind merges in prāṇa; for prāṇa, indeed, absorbs all these.
>
> These, indeed, are the two absorbers: Air among the gods [the forces of nature] and prāṇa (the vital principle) among the prāṇas [the organs].[62]

12. *Prāṇa, as a cosmic principle, correlates the microcosm and the macrocosm.*

The cosmic prāṇa maintains the animate and the inanimate world as a unity. It is the unison of the forces functioning in them that keeps up the cosmic order. There is constant interaction and intermingling of the living and the nonliving. On the one hand, inanimate nature acts upon the organism; on the other, the organism reacts to and acts upon inanimate nature. An incessant interchange of their material components is going on. This continuous coordination, or the dynamic relation, of the two orders is the very basis of the process of living.

There is no fixed line of demarcation between the living and the nonliving world so far as their material aspect is concerned. The circulation of physical elements from one to the other does not stop even for a moment. In view of the intricate, dynamic correlation of the animate and the inanimate, the two counterparts of the world-system, one can rightly conceive a living organism as a vehicle of an all-embracing, potential, sustaining energy. "Like spokes in the nave of a wheel all are set in prāṇa," declares the Upaniṣad.[63]

[61] Br.U. I:5.21.
[62] Ch.U. IV:3.3,4.
[63] Pr.U. II:6.

Corresponding to the fivefold vital force that operates in an individual there are outer forces that sustain the sun, the earth, ākāśa, air, and fire. The following description of prāṇa in its individual and cosmic aspect points to their correlation:

> From the Supreme Self arises this prāṇa, which is associated with the self as the shadow with the body. For karma due to the tendencies of the mind prāṇa comes into the gross body.
>
> Just as a monarch appoints his officers with the command — "You govern these dominions, you govern those" — similarly, prāṇa employs the subordinate prāṇas in their respective places.
>
> He engages the apāna in the organs of evacuation and procreation. He himself operates in the eyes and the ears and through the mouth and the nose. Between these two [at the navel] is the samāna [equalizer], who assimilates food and drink offered as oblation to the fire in the stomach. From this [combustion] rise seven flames [the functions of the two eyes, the two ears, the two nostrils, and the organ of speech].
>
> The individual self dwells in the heart, where there are one hundred and one nāḍīs [cords]. Each of them has one hundred branches. Each branch again has seventy-two thousand subbranches. The vyāna moves in them.
>
> By one of these that is upward [the susumnā] ascends the udāna. It conducts the departing soul to the realm of the virtuous as a result of his virtuous deeds, to the region of the sinful as a result of his sinful deeds, or to the world of men as a result of his mixed deeds.
>
> The sun, indeed, is the external prāṇa, for it rises favoring the prāṇa in the eye. The prāṇa controlling the earth controls man's apāna to make the body stable. The prāṇa in ākāśa [the outer space] between the heaven and the earth is the counterpart of the samāna [in the inner space]. The [surrounding] air [that is, the prāṇa there] is the counterpart of vyāna.
>
> Fire [the ubiquitous energy of heat], indeed, is the udāna. So when a person leaves the body it loses all heat. With the organs absorbed in the mind he departs for rebirth.
>
> Whatever thought prevails in a dying person, with that he resorts to prāṇa. United with the udāna and the soul, prāṇa leads him to the world of his thought.
>
> The wise person who thus knows prāṇa becomes immortal and his progeny will never be extinct. So there is the following verse:
>
> He who knows the origin of prāṇa, its entrance [into the body], its presence, its fivefold operation, its individual and cosmic aspect, attains immortality;[64] Yea; he attains immortality.[65]

[64]This, of course, is relative immortality. The absolute immortality is attainable only through Self-knowledge, the realization of Nondual Brahman.

[65]Pr.U. III:3-12.

13. *The cosmic prāṇa is not the fundamental Reality.*

The Upaniṣad extols prāṇa, but does not view it as ultimate or immortal. It is evident from Sanatkumāra's final instruction to Nārada in the *Chāndōgya Upaniṣad:*

> Prāṇa, is, verily, greater than aspiration. Just as the spokes of a wheel are fastened to the nave, so are all objects including name, speech, mind and its powers fastened to this prāṇa. Prāṇa moves by prāṇa [that is, by its own strength]. Prāṇa gives prāṇa; prāṇa gives to prāṇa [because the giver, the gift, and the recipient are manifestations of prāṇa]. Prāṇa is the father; prāṇa is the mother; prāṇa is the brother; prāṇa is the sister; prāṇa is the teacher; prāṇa is the brāhmaṇa.
>
> If a person speaks insolently to his father, mother, brother, sister, teacher, or a brāhmaṇa, then others say to him, "Shame on thee! Thou art the killer of thy father; thou art the killer of thy mother; thou art the killer of thy brother; thou art the killer of thy sister; thou art the killer of thy teacher; thou art the killer of a brāhmaṇa."
>
> On the contrary, after prāṇa has departed from the body, even if a person were to burn them together in a pile, piercing them with a poker, still others would not say to him, "Thou hast killed thy father, thou hast killed thy mother, thou hast killed thy brother, thou hast killed thy sister, thou hast killed thy teacher, thou hast killed a brāhmaṇa."
>
> Prāṇa is verily all these. He who knows prāṇa as such, reflects on it, and perceives it, becomes the declarer of the transcendental reality. If he is asked, "Are you a declarer of the transcendental reality?" He will say, "I am." He will not deny.
>
> But the declarer of the transcendental reality in the true sense is he who is such by the knowledge of the Truth.[66]

Thus, according to Vedanta, the fundamental Reality is not the all-embracing prāṇa, but the all-knowing, all-transcending Self. From this arise prāṇa and all else. No unintelligent principle can be the ultimate cause, because it is not self-existent. Its existence presupposes the Supreme Self, Pure Being-Consciousness-Bliss. That is the Infinite. "The Infinite is immortal, the finite mortal," says Sanatkumāra. "The Self, indeed, is below. The Self is above. The Self is behind. The Self is before. The Self is to the south. The Self is to the north. The Self, indeed, is all this."[67]

[66]Ch.U. VII:15.1-4; 16.1.
[67]*Ibid.* VII:24.1; 25.2.

14. *The Vedantic view of the cosmic prāṇa is different from the Western Theory of Vitalism.*

Some leading Western philosophers, such as Schopenhauer, Nietzsche, Eucken, Bergson, Driesch, have conceived vital energy as a cosmic principle. They recognize the supreme importance of life, though they disagree as to its meaning. In their view the vital principle is the dynamic self-regulating, self-developing fundamental cause. "It evolves by means of its own inherent and spontaneous creative power." But it is after all a blind force, full of animation without illumination. Like Schopenhauer's unconscious will-to-be, Henri Bergson's *elan vital* (the vital impulse) is the basic principle of the creative evolution.

But, according to Vedanta, no blind potentiality, let alone material entity, can bring into being the cosmic order. Not being self-evident, *elan vital* cannot be the fundamental Reality. Nor can it move of itself, being characteristically inert. It needs the quickening touch of consciousness. Unconscious will is a misnomer. Will implies self-determination. It is invariably preceded by consciousness.

What is devoid of consciousness is also destitute of the power of self-movement. Only a sentient being is found to be self-acting in the true sense. An insentient thing is impelled to act. A machine does not move without a driving power. A seed does not germinate or grow without the stimulation of light or heat. Thus, in the last resort, one has to say that all movements in the material universe have their primary source somewhere beyond it. Anything that is devoid of consciousness, be it solid matter, or energy, or mind, moves because of its direct or indirect contact with conscious spirit.

Prāṇa, being inherently unconscious, cannot be self-acting. It functions only in contact with the luminous Self. Animation is ever associated with consciousness, howsoever faint it may be. Pure Consciousness is at the root of life. It does not derive from life.

15. *A mortal becomes immortal by relinquishing all limiting adjuncts including prāṇa. Immortality is beyond life and death.*

Pure Being-Consciousness-Bliss, the finest of all existences, underlies the phenomenal world, as the all-pervading, all-knowing, all-transcending Self. All diversities, all transformations are in the apparent manifold, the product of māyā, its potential cause, which serves as the creative power of the Omnipresent Being. He is the

Reality in all finite forms, individual or cosmic. He is manifest as the experiencer in every living being. As associated with the cosmic prāṇa and the cosmic mind, He is apparently limited as the Cosmic Soul (Sūtrātmā or Hiraṇyagarbha). Being associated with the individual prāṇa as well as the individual mind He is apparently limited as the individual soul (jīvātmā).

Allied with the individual prāṇa as well as the mind, the individual soul (jīvātmā) becomes incarnate in physical form. It is through prāṇa that he enters into the body, stays in it, and passes out of it. He lives and dies, he is born and reborn, as long as he clings to life. Eventually he attains self-knowledge and realizes his identity with Brahman. Being released in due course from all limiting adjuncts, including prāṇa, he becomes unified with Nirguṇa Brahman. "Being but Brahman he is merged in Brahman."[68] "He who knows that Supreme Brahman becomes Brahman indeed."[69]

The *Praśna Upaniṣad* gives a graphic description of the attainment of the Ultimate Goal:

> As these flowing rivers, bound for the ocean, disappear into the ocean after having reached it, their names and forms being destroyed, and are called simply the ocean — even so, these sixteen parts[70] of the seer, whose goal is the Puruṣa [the all-pervading, all-knowing, all-transcending Self], disappear into the Puruṣa after having reached Him, their names and forms being destroyed, and are called simply the Puruṣa. He becomes free of parts and immortal.[71]

A knower of Saguṇa Brahman retains his individuality and attains approximate immortality. He dwells in Brahmalōka till the end of the cosmic cycle, when he reaches the Ultimate Goal, being merged in Nirguṇa Brahman.

[68]Br.U. IV:4.6.

[69]Mu.U. III:2.9.

[70]The sixteen parts, as stated in the previous verse, are prāṇa (the limiting adjunct through which the Self appears to be individualized), faith, space, air, fire, water, earth, the organs (of perception and of action), mind, food, vigor, self-discipline, mantras (directions of work), karma, the worlds (the results of work — merits and demerits), and name.

[71]Pr.U. VI:5.

PART TWO

THE MIGRATORY MAN

The Cycle of Birth and Rebirth and the Way Beyond

CHAPTERS V-VIII

CHAPTER V

THE LAW OF KARMA AND FREEDOM OF ACTION

1. *It is his ignorance of the true nature of the self that ties man to the mortal plane.*

To all appearance the common background of human life is the same old drama of smile and tear, hope and fear, love and hate, success and failure, enacted in the four consecutive stages of birth, growth, decay, and death. This underlies all the varying conditions of life — social, political, economic, cultural, and racial. The theory of life may change, the pattern of living may vary, yet the panorama of dualities persists. In spite of his heart's longing for unalloyed joy man cannot avoid suffering; in spite of his severe struggle for freedom he cannot escape bondage; in spite of his constant striving after good he cannot get rid of evil.

This is the human situation that has prevailed throughout the past. And this prevails in the present age despite unprecedented material progress due to the advancement of scientific knowledge and technology. This is so in the East and in the West as well, notwithstanding economic and cultural divergences. None can evade dual experience, no matter where he lives. Whether he lives in a farmer's hut or in a royal palace, whether in a solitary cell or in a crowded city, whether among barbarians or in a highly civilized society, he will inevitably face the pairs of opposites.

Is this all that man has to live for? Is this the final fact of life? Is this the ultimate destiny of man? If it be so, then why is it that the human mind refuses to be reconciled to the situation? Why does mortal man seek immortality? Why does the bound man seek complete freedom? Why has the imperfect man the vision of perfection? The truth is, man is not really mortal or bound, or imperfect, yet he misapprehends himself as such through deep-seated ignorance, while his real nature asserts itself continuously.

In fact, it is the ever shifting phenomenal universe that is characterized by pairs of opposites, such as light and darkness, life and death, construction and destruction, prosperity and adversity, good and evil. Beyond the panorama of dualities, beyond the flux of relativity, is the All-good, All-free, All-pervading Self which sustains the passing scene. Being tied to the order of phenomena by his ignorance of the true nature of the self and of its unity with the Supreme Self, man moves up and down here and hereafter in vain search for life beyond death, for light beyond darkness, for joy beyond sorrow, for freedom beyond bondage. So says the *Śvetāśvatara Upaniṣad:*

> In this vast wheel of Brahman, which enlivens all beings and in which all things rest, the migratory soul turns round and round thinking that the self in him and the Mover of the wheel are different. When blessed with the knowledge of his unity with the Mover, then he attains immortality.[1]

The cosmic process continuing endlessly in the cyclic order of the projection, the preservation, and the dissolution of the universe is conceived as the wheel of Brahman, its unmoved Mover.

The root cause of the jīva's transmigration is his ignorance of the true nature of the self. Under the spell of this ignorance (avidyā) not only does he fail to recognize the self, but even identifies the self with its adjuncts — the body, the organs, and the mind. The self identified with the not-self is the ego, the apparent man, as we have explained (Ch. I, sec.4). Being identified with the body, the organs, and the mind an individual becomes attached to them and interested in all that concerns them. Consequently, he feels an urge to secure what is agreeable to them and shun what is disagreeable to them. Thus, from the root cause ajñāna (avidyā) proceeds man's desire for the diverse objects of the sense world and from this desire (kāma) proceeds action with a will.

The Sanskrit term for volitional action is *karma.* It inevitably produces a result according to its nature. Good karma leads to good consequences, evil karma to evil consequences here and hereafter. As a man sows, so he reaps. As stated in the *Bṛhadāraṇyaka Upaniṣad:*

> Man is indeed filled with desire. As is his desire, so is his resolution. As is his resolution, so is his action. As is his action, so is the result he reaps.[2]

[1]Sv.U. I:6. [2]Br.U. IV:4.5.

Hence, avidyā, kāma, and karma form the chain that ties the individual soul to the wheel of repeated birth and death in the variegated universe marked by origination and destruction, growth and decay. Patañjali notices the fivefold root of karma — avidyā (ignorance), asmitā (egoism or I-ness), rāga (attachment), dveṣa (aversion), and abhiniveśa (clinging to life).[3] The tap-root is avidyā.

2. *The significance of karma and the impressions created by it.*

The Sanskrit term *karma* often used synonymously with *work* has a special significance which the English word does not have. Indeed, the two terms cannot be used interchangeably. As we have noted, karma is strictly volitional action. It is based on the recognition of man's power of judgment and his capacity to choose his course of action. Not only does man experience sense-objects, but he also evaluates them. He can distinguish between the high and the low, between the true and the false, between the wholesome and the unwholesome, between the good and the pleasant, between the right and the wrong. With the senses he perceives the objects; with the mind he judges them.

Karma is distinguished from instinctive action, which is unintentional; from reflex action, such as sneezing; and from all involuntary functions, such as respiration, digestion and assimilation of food, controlled by the autonomic nervous system. It includes, as we have noted (Ch. III, sec. 11), all voluntary bodily activities, sensory experiences, and mental operations; that is to say, whatever we do with the body, or with any of the five organs of action, or with any of the five organs of perception, or with the mind, knowingly, intentionally, or deliberately.

The following instances clearly distinguish karma from work. If a person lies still in bed pretending to be sick in order to avoid work, obviously he does not do any work, but he "does" karma. He can thus evade work, but he cannot evade karma and its consequences. Suppose a person after having had his dinner at the end of the day's labor reclines and rests, while watching television with emotional reactions to the varying scenes; obviously he performs no work, but he performs karma and shall reap its fruits sooner or later. Similarly, when a person sits quietly and intensely thinks of a problem, he fervidly does karma, even though to all appearance he does no work.

Usually, an action is of short duration; it begins and ends at the

[3]See YS II:3ff.

present time. How can it produce an effect in the future? The explanation is this. Each karma produces a twofold result: the one is immediate and cognizable, the other is remote and not noticeable in its present form. For example, a person rescues a drowning man at the risk of his own life. The drowning man's life is saved; the rescuer derives great satisfaction out of the noble deed and perhaps wins the applause of the bystanders. These are the immediate and visible results of his karma.

Over and above, the same karma leaves on the mind of the rescuer a cognate impression[4] which will incline him to similar self-sacrifice in the future and will also be conducive to the development of a favorable situation for him here or hereafter. Thus, whatever karma a person performs — physical, verbal, or mental, be it good or evil — apart from producing the immediate and visible result, also leaves on the subconscious mind a relevant impression, which dwells there as a potency and inevitably fructifies in due course. Evidently, the nature of the impression depends on the nature of the karma; the greater the interest of the doer in the karma, the deeper the impression.

Thus every individual is constantly accumulating within himself the subtle impressions of the diverse karma he performs. These are the factors that build his inner nature and also serve as retributive forces leading to a favorable or an unfavorable situation here and hereafter. We shall not enlarge on this point as we have already dwelt on it (Ch.III, sec. 11).

In the same context we have explained how the impressions stay within us in four different states: (1) manifest, (2) dormant, (3) overpowered, and (4) attenuated. A man's inner nature and outer condition are determined mainly by the impressions acquired by his own karma. From the moral standpoint a man's diverse karma can be classified under two distinct heads: righteous and unrighteous. Consequently, the impressions of karma are in a wide sense of two kinds: merit and demerit, capable of producing results — favorable and unfavorable situations in the doer's life here and hereafter.

3. *The law of karma is the logical sequence of man's moral responsibility due to freedom of action. It counters predestination, fatalism, accidentalism, and naturalism.*

Freedom of action is a special privilege of human life. It

[4] The Sanskrit terms for the impression of karma are saṁskāra, āśaya, anuśaya, adṛṣta, apūrva, dharma-adharma. The term *karma* is also used for its impression.

demarcates the human from the subhuman level. While in lower beings instinct prevails, in human beings volitional action prevails. So the human life is said to be "the field of karma (karma-kṣetra)." Man's inner development awaits cultivation, that is, deliberate effort. Even his physical development is not adequate without physical culture. While lower beings are confined to the physical level, man can rise above the physical to the higher levels of life, i.e., intellectual, aesthetic, moral, and spiritual, which are accessible only through systematic volitional action, that is to say, karma. Without cultivation, without repeated efforts in the right direction, none can attain them. It is a noteworthy fact that evolution in the subhuman plane is a natural process, whereas in the human plane evolution is mainly the result of cultural operation.

Man is accountable for his own deeds inasmuch as he has the freedom of choosing his course of action. The penalty of the privilege is moral responsibility. He has to use the privilege judiciously. His joys and sorrows, his excellences and weaknesses, depend on this. "By virtuous deed one verily becomes virtuous, as by sinful deed one becomes sinful," declares the Upaniṣad.[5] Just as a man's conduct molds his character, so does his character determine his conduct. As he sows so does he reap.[6] This is the law of karma. It is the universal law of cause and effect in relation to human life.

On the human plane it is an inviolable moral law. There is no effect without a cause. As is the cause, so is the effect. Righteousness is the sure source of happiness, as unrighteousness is of unhappiness; the one inevitably leads to a favorable situation and the other to an unfavorable situation here and hereafter. There is no unmerited gain or loss according to the law of karma. None can elude it. It is said in the *Mahābhārata,* "As a calf recognizes and approaches its mother in the midst of a thousand cows, even so the effects of past deeds do not fail to recognize and visit the doer in his new life."[7]

As explained by Swami Vivekananda:

> Every thought that we think, every deed that we do, after a certain time becomes fine, goes into seed form, so to speak, and lives in the fine body in a potential form and after a time it emerges again and bears its results. These results condition the life of man. Thus he moulds his own life. Man is not bound by any other laws excepting those which he

[5]Br.U. III:2.13.

[6]Cf. St. Paul, Gal. 6:7, "Be not deceived; God is not mocked: for whatsoever a man soweth, that shall he also reap."

[7]Mbh. (Śānti-parva) XII:181.16.

makes for himself. Our thoughts, our words, and deeds, are the threads of the net which we throw round ourselves, for good or for evil. Once we set in motion a certain power, we have to take the full consequences of it. This is the law of karma.[8]

According to this law every individual is responsible for his prosperity and adversity, for his elevation and degradation, for his enjoyment and suffering. There can be other factors contributing to these conditions, but they must be subsidiary. "One should lift the self by the self [by his own power of discrimination]," says Śrī Kṛṣṇa.[9] The law of karma rules out fatalism, accidentalism, and naturalism in human affairs. No supernatural power determines the events of man's life. There is no scope for chance in human existence. It is not blind nature that motivates human actions. Karma is ever associated with self-determination. No volitional action is possible without self-awareness. The doctrine of predestination is a dogmatic version of fatalism. According to this all that happens to human beings is predetermined by God; some are foreordained to everlasting happiness and some to everlasting misery. It makes God responsible for man's vices and sufferings. How can God be conceived as all-just and all-merciful in such a case?

But the law of karma lays the whole responsibility on man. So says Swami Vivekananda:

> Each one of us is the maker of his own fate. This law knocks on the head at once all doctrines of predestination and fate, and gives us the only means of reconciliation between God and man. We, we, and none else, are responsible for what we suffer. We are the effects, and we are the causes. We are free therefore. If I am unhappy, it has been of my own making, and that very thing shows that I can be happy if I will. If I am impure, that is also of my own making, and that very thing shows that I can be pure if I will. The human will stands beyond all circumstance. Before it — the strong, gigantic, infinite will and freedom in man — all the powers, even of nature, must bow down, succumb, and become its servants. This is the result of the law of karma.[10]

4. *God's sovereignty does not contradict individual freedom.*

But the freedom of man does not counter God's existence as the Supreme ruler. It is His paramountcy that maintains order and harmony throughout the universe and makes the operation of laws

[8]CW II, p.346. [9]BG VI:5. [10]CW III, p.125.

possible. Law means the uniform way in which things happen in the world. It is an interpretation of the pre-existent order. It does not establish order. It is because of the rulership of the almighty Lord that all things and beings are held in their respective positions. Under His overall control everything functions in its own way. "From fear of Him the wind blows, from fear of Him the sun rises, from fear of Him fire burns, rain falls and death, the fifth, moves fast."[11]

That the overlordship of God does not interfere with the individual freedom can be elucidated by illustrations. The sun fosters the growth of vegetation. Without the sun nothing can grow. Yet each plant grows according to its type and potency under the sun. Or, take the case of a manufacturing plant run by electricity. With electricity as the prime mover, each part of the machinery operates in its own way. Similarly, God enlivens all beings; He is the sole sustainer of the universe; it is because of Him that individuals function each according to his inherent potentiality.[12]

The sovereignty of God and man's freedom of action go together. He is the prime Mover, but does not play the role of the absolute dictator with regard to the jīvas. Under his supreme control each individual has freedom in his limited sphere.

It is said in the *Kauṣītakī Brāhmaṇa Upaniṣad:*

> It is He indeed who makes him perform virtuous deeds whom He would raise high above these worlds; and it is He indeed who makes him perform vicious deeds whom He would cast below these worlds. He is the Protector of the world. He is the Sovereign of the world. He is the Lord of all.[13]

From this it may be assumed that man has no freedom of action since God directs all his activities. But the intention of the text is not to deny man personal freedom, but to point out God's supremacy. Whatever power man has is derived from Him. None can work independently of Him. Yet each person has the freedom to use the power in his own way. To give an illustration: None can see without light. Yet every individual can use the light in his own way, to perform whatever deed he chooses. The more a man recognizes the Source of

[11]Tai.U. II:8.1.

[12]It is worthy of note that according to Vedanta there is no absolute beginning of creation. There cannot be any creation out of nothing. Creation means the development of a potential cause. Similarly, destruction means reversion to the causal state. Something cannot be reduced to nothing, or annihilated, infinitesimal though it may be.

[13]Kau.U. III:8.

power, and curbs his ego, the better is the flow of power in him.

God is the dispenser of the fruits of actions of all (karmādhyakṣa).[14] Says the *Bṛhadāraṇyaka Upaniṣad:* "That great birthless Self is the eater of food [dwelling in all beings] and giver of wealth [the fruits of actions]. He who knows It as such receives wealth [those fruits]."[15] Śaṅkara remarks that it is God who connects all beings with the results of their respective actions.[16] Without the guidance of a conscious agent blind karma or its potency cannot lead to a future result with regard to the doer in the exact place and at the exact time.[17] It is the all-knowing Lord who dispenses the fruits of karma according to the merits and the demerits of the doers. So it is said that in ordaining the fruits of actions God considers the efforts made by the doers; otherwise the directions and the prohibitions of the scriptures become meaningless.[18] Śaṅkara observes:

> God acts solely as a general instrumental cause, dividing the resulting fruits of actions unequally in accordance with the inequality of merit and demerit acquired by the individual beings, even as rain does. It is seen in the world that rain becomes the common instrumental cause of long and short creepers, etc., or of rice and barley, etc., which grow in accordance with their own seeds, and yet unless there is rainfall they can have no differences in sap, flower, fruit, leaves, etc., nor can they have these in the absence of their own seeds; so also it stands to reason that God ordains good and bad for the individual beings in accordance with the efforts made by the beings themselves.[19]

Further, in creating the universe with diverse living beings, high and low, God takes into account their merits and demerits. Therefore no partiality and cruelty can be charged against Him for the inequalities among them.[20] Śaṅkara remarks: "Since the unequal creation is in accordance with the virtues and the vices of the jīvas that are about to be born, Īśvara is not to be blamed for this."[21]

5. *The law of karma is based on the recognition of man's free will.*

Thus, according to the law of karma, man is the architect of his own life. It lays stress on personal effort. Man's self-determination is the core of the law. He reaps as he sows. He gets what he deserves, what he qualifies himself for. Whatever karma he performs inevitably produces a corresponding result. Man's progress and retrogression,

[14]Sv.U. VI:11.
[15]Br.U. IV:4.24.
[16]*Ibid.* S.com.
[17]See BS III:2.38,39.
[18]See BS II:3.42.
[19]*Ibid.* S.com.
[20]See BS II:1.34.
[21]*Ibid.* S.com.

his honor and dishonor, his happiness and misery proceed from his right and wrong way of living. His present life is the result of his past actions and his future life will be the result of his present actions.

So says the *Chāndōgya Upaniṣad:*

> Now verily a person consists of will. According to the will a person has in this world, so does he become on departing hence. Let him, therefore, form his will.[22]

Śaṅkara remarks:

> As is a person's determination [adhyavasāya, saṁkalpa] while living here on this earth so does he become after death.[23]

Every individual has to raise himself to higher levels of life by his determined effort. As stated by Manu:

> Pondering within himself that his upward and downward courses [here and hereafter] follow from virtue and vice man should constantly engage his mind in the practice of virtue.[24].

Man's progress, secular or spiritual, starts with self-reliance. "Heaven helps those who help themselves" is a well-known saying. The highest of all possessions is self-help, according to Carlyle.[25] "Ask, and it shall be given you; seek, and ye shall find; knock, and it shall be opened unto you." Such is the exhortation of Jesus Christ.[26] Even self-surrender to the Divine Will is not possible without self-effort. It requires persistent practice of the resignation of the ego. "For every man shall bear his own burden," says St. Paul.[27]

6. *How karma bears fruit. The three kinds of karma and man's control over them.*

From day to day every individual (other than a seeker of liberation) is shaping his own future by accumulating within himself the subtle impressions of his thought, words, and deeds. These may be white, black, or mixed — conducive to happiness, unhappiness, or

[22]Ch.U. III:14.1.
[23]*Ibid.* S. com.
[24]MS XII:23.
[25]See Thomas Carlyle's *Sartor Resartus,* ed. by Archibald MacMechan, Boston, Athenaean Press, Ginn and Co., 1896, Bk.2, Ch.3, p.104.
[26]Matt. 7:7.
[27]Gal. 6:5.

the mixture of the two.[28] It may be noted in this context that the activities of a man of self-knowledge, or of a seeker of God, who is free from all attachment to the temporal, leave no binding impression on his mind. They are taintless being selfless. Says Śrī Kṛṣṇa:

> He who is devoted to yōga [selfless action] and is pure in mind, whose body is subdued, whose senses are under control, who recognizes his self as the Self of all beings, even though acting, is not tainted [by the good and the evil impressions of actions].
>
> He who performs actions dedicating them to God and giving up attachment, is not tainted by sin [the impressions of actions] as a lotus leaf is not moistened by water.[29]

The accumulated impressions of the various activities of a seeker of temporal values usually lie latent within him and accompany him beyond death. Only exceptionally good and evil deeds bear fruit in his present life. Of the remaining impressions some await fructification in his next life and the rest in his future life or lives, unless thwarted or eliminated by proper measures.[30] "One gets rid of sin by righteousness," says one of the Vedic scriptures.[31] The Manu-smṛti has specified various penances for the expiation of different sins.[32] The evil consequences of sinful actions can be checked, eliminated, or averted by prayer, penance, austerity, or the expiatory deeds of charity, service, or virtue. If a person prays to God for forgiveness for a sinful act he is sure to be forgiven provided he makes sincere effort not to repeat the same sin. God does not listen to the prayer of a hypocrite. Sincerity and humility are the essential prerequisites for God's grace.

At death a person leaves the gross body, but not the subtle body, which comprises the mind where the impressions of karma are stored. The self clothed with the subtle and the causal body departs. "This [the physical] body dies being left by the living self, but the living self dies not," says the *Chāndōgya Upaniṣad.*[33] As declared by Śrī Kṛṣṇa, "When the master [the self] obtains a body and when he leaves it he takes these [the mind and the senses] and departs, as the wind takes away the scents from their seats [the flowers]."[34] With the mind the self carries all its contents and with the senses all their special characteristics. It is reborn with them.

[28]See YS IV:7.
[29]BG V:7,10.
[30]See YS II:12; com.
[31]Tai. Ar. X:63.7 (dharmeṇa pāpamapanudati).
[32]MS XI.
[33]Ch.U. VI:11.3.
[34]BG XV:8.

In this way the continuity of individuality is maintained through successive births and deaths. An individual's present birth is actually a case of rebirth. A considerable portion of the residual impressions of his preceding life carried by the departing self, having fructified, has brought about his present human birth with inborn aptitudes. This portion is called *prārabdha* (fructifying or fruit-bearing) *karma.* The same also determines his term of life and the nature of the experiences, pleasant and painful, that he will go through during this lifetime.[35] The rest of the residual impressions remain within him in a dormant state until their fructification in his future life.

While experiencing prārabdha karma, that is to say, reaping the fruits of the past karma in his present life, a person performs new karma. The psychophysical constitution and the circumstances created by his fruit-bearing karma can condition his freedom of action but cannot annul it. So he has the capacity to choose his present course of action while reaping the fruits of past actions. For instance, when a person carries a load on his back, it restricts his movements no doubt, yet he retains his freedom to move. The point is this: the real agent is not the mind, nor any of the organs, nor the body, but the free self within that acts through them. As the instrument of the indwelling self the psychophysical system can restrict his freedom but cannot nullify it. A man's present life is the resultant of a twofold karma, the fruit-bearing karma and the new karma acquired in this life.

The term *karma,* in a wide sense, applies to the impressions created by it. From the foregoing account of one's karma, which includes the residual impressions of the past and the impressions of the current actions, it is evident that this can be arranged in three groups:

1) The accumulated (sañcita) karma, the stored up latent impressions of the past that will fructify in a future life or lives.
2) The fructifying (prārabdha) karma, the past impressions that are bearing fruit in the present life.
3) Prospective (āgāmi) karma, the impressions of the current activities that are accumulating and will fructify in due course. These are also called *sañcīyamāṇa karma* (the impressions that are being accumulated) or *kṛyamāṇa karma* (the impressions that are being created).

[35]See YS II:13.

We have stated above that man can make amends for his accumulated karma and has control over his prospective karma. But the fructifying karma, which is responsible for his present human body, the inborn aptitudes, the term of life, and the experiences he has to encounter, is, strictly speaking, beyond his control. A classical example of a bowman with a quiver of arrows is cited to illustrate man's control over the threefold karma. The bowman has no control over the arrow which he has already shot at his target. This is the analogy of the fructifying (prārabdha) karma. But another arrow which the bowman has fixed to the bow and is about to shoot he can throw away if he chooses to do so. This is the analogy of the prospective (āgāmi) karma. The bowman can discard the whole quiver of arrows he has on his back, if he so chooses. This illustrates man's control over accumulated (sañcita) karma.

7. *Is the fructifying (prārabdha) karma utterly beyond man's control?*

We must not say however that a man's prārabdha (fructifying) karma is totally out of his control, that nothing can be done about it. Although the structure of the fruit-bearing karma as a whole is unalterable, yet it admits of modifications in certain aspects. As a result of this karma every individual has a particular kind of physical body. No two bodies are quite alike. None can make his dark body fair or fair body dark. None can make his short body tall or tall body short. He who is born stark blind remains blind all his life. Yet man can ameliorate the conditions of life under which he is born.

For instance, it is up to him whether or not he will maintain his body in good health. Even a sickly body can be well developed by regular exercise and moderate living. Whoever understands that his present distress is due to his own past karma, instead of being fretful, will strive after its alleviation, being hopeful of the future. By proper remedial measures man can overcome many of his physical handicaps congenital though they may be. Moreover, by cultivating endurance, strength of mind, spiritual insight, and resignation to the will of the Lord man can rise above his physical disabilities, though incurable they may be, and turn life to the highest direction possible.

A person is not to be judged a saint or a sinner by the sufferings he undergoes but by his capacity to rise above them, by his attitude towards life. Therefore, he who is born blind is not necessarily a sinful man. In whatever situation a man may be he must make the best of it physically and mentally. This is what the law of karma points to. He is responsible for his present; he is responsible for his future.

Due to prārabdha (fructifying) karma each person is born with certain trends of body and mind. Some of these lead him to certain actions, good and evil, high and low; others lead him to certain experiences, pleasant and painful. A man has more control over the first variety than over the second. Each person is expected to curb wrong tendencies and develop right ones. This is the purpose of self-culture. Moral and spiritual training aim at this. So others can help us in this field by guidance and inspiration. Our inborn aptitudes generally lie within us as potencies. They do not develop without cultivation. A person may be born with artistic talent, or administrative ability, or political astuteness, or philosophic acumen, or the spiritual bent of mind, yet none of these will be manifest unless there are proper facilities for its growth, which can be provided by one's own endeavor and by others' help as well.

Of the second variety of inborn trends there are some that lead a person inevitably to circumstances involving such experiences as gain or loss of wealth, union with desirable or undesirable persons, bereavement of friends and family, loss of life. Over these man has little control. To cite an instance, a happily wedded couple had a child born blind. Neither parent had any control over it.

Then there are other trends which lie mostly in a potential state. Just as a seed germinates only when there are favorable conditions, similarly, these trends await favorable conditions for their actualization as experiences. These conditions can be created by the experiencer himself or by others, or by both. If *A* maliciously sets fire to *B*'s house, it cannot be said that *B* lost his house just because of his karma. *A*'s karma has been no less responsible in this case than *B*'s, because the one has had the active role and the other the passive. If a person inadvertently leaves the entrance door of his home open at night and a thief finds the opportunity to enter the house and steal some property, the owner is responsible no doubt for creating a situation favorable for the loss of property, yet the main responsibility is that of the thief for taking the aggressive part.

Similarly, a person himself and others can contribute to his well-being and to the mitigation of his sufferings by creating conditions favorable to the fructification of his good karma. Once a holy man of India advised a schoolteacher to prepare an indigenous medicine (a specific remedy for lung ailment) on a large scale and to sell it at a small profit so that it could reach the indigent people. Within a few years there was such a demand for the medicine that the gentleman decided to give up his job as a schoolteacher and start the wholesale manufacture of specific medicines. People had such confidence in the genuineness of his products that before long he made a fortune by an extensive sale of the medicines all over the country. Helping others is by no means inconsistent with the doctrine of karma, but follows naturally from it, as we shall see later.

8. *The experience of the fructifying (prārabdha) karma by a jīvan-mukta, a living free soul.*

Rare is the sage who succeeds in realizing Brahman before his term of life is over. Because of the momentum of prārabdha karma, which determines the span of life, his body continues to run its course, even though the ego-consciousness that drives it is withdrawn. It is somewhat like the potter's wheel that continues to revolve after the turning rod is removed. Consequently, an illumined person has to undergo such physical conditions as hunger and thirst, heat and cold, fatigue and sickness. In case he has any incurable bodily defect, such as blindness or deafness, he cannot get rid of that. So it is said that even an illumined soul has to bear the burden of prārabdha (fructifying) karma. Says Śaṅkara: "The work which has fashioned this body prior to the dawning of knowledge is not destroyed by that knowledge without yielding its fruits, like the arrow shot at an object."[36]

But truly speaking, an illumined person is above all physical conditions, because he does not identify himself with the body, being ever established in the knowledge of the Self. Other than prārabdha, the rest of his karma, that is to say, the accumulated (sañcita) and the prospective (āgāmi), are already eliminated, their root cause, avidyā, being eradicated by the knowledge of Brahman. Says the *Muṇḍaka Upaniṣad:*

> When He [the One who is omniscient and transcendent] who is high and low [who exists as the cause and also as the effect] is seen, then the knot of the heart is broken, all doubts are dispelled, and the deeds of him [the seer] are eliminated.[37]

In reference to the elimination of deeds Śaṅkara comments:

[36]VC 451.
[37]Mu.U. II:2.8.

But not the deeds that have brought about the present bodily existence inasmuch as they have started bearing fruit.[38]

In his *Viveka-cūḍāmaṇi* he says:

The prārabdha karma is certainly too strong for the man of realization; and is spent only by the actual experience of its fruit, while the actions previously accumulated and those yet to come are destroyed by the fire of perfect knowledge. But none of the three at all effects those who having realized their identity with Brahman are always living absorbed in that consciousness. They are verily the transcendent Brahman.[39]

Therefore, in the Upaniṣad it is said: "The seer [Knower of Truth] does not see death or disease, or sorrow. The seer sees all [Reality underlying all] and obtains all in every way."[40]

9. *The law of karma promotes individual and social well-being.*

Man strives to be prosperous and happy by fair and foul means time and again. After repeated success and failure, exaltation and humiliation in public career, after sweet and bitter experiences in social and domestic life, he becomes convinced of the inviolability of the moral law that righteous deeds invariably lead the doer to well-being and happiness, whereas unrighteous deeds invariably lead the doer to misery and suffering, here and hereafter. He who is thus convinced will do his best to abstain from unrighteousness and practice righteousness.

Whatever desire he may have for wealth, pleasure, beauty, position, power, knowledge, fame, and so forth, he will try to fulfill without deviating from the right path. By no means will he sacrifice virtue for the sake of material gain. A man of rectitude may or may not be in affluent circumstances, but he will always find himself in satisfactory condition and attain peace of mind and happiness. The practice of virtue invariably makes him pure-hearted and right-minded. As we have noted above, by good conduct one becomes good. "He who is pure-hearted is always filled with cheerfulness and hath no fear from any direction," says the *Mahābhārata*.[41]

He who is pure-hearted is also noble-minded, being free from all ill-feelings toward his fellow-beings, such as anger, hatred, jealousy, pride. Observance of moral principles, e.g., truthfulness, sincerity,

[38]*Ibid.* S. com.
[39]VC 453.
[40]Ch.U. VII:26.2.
[41]Mbh. (Śānti-parva) XII:259.14.

humility, kindliness, tolerance, is linked with due consideration for others and tends to make a person unselfish and charitable. While caring for his own good a virtuous man naturally devotes himself to the well-being of others. In doing good to the world he recognizes the gradations of good work: saving a person's life is higher than the fulfillment of his material needs. Higher than the saving of life is the giving of education. If one receives a sound education one can stand on one's own feet; one can solve one's own problems. Building of character thus becomes an essential part of a virtuous man's educational program. He knows that without moral backbone none can be self-reliant.

Higher than giving secular education is the imparting of spiritual knowledge, which alone can solve the problems of life permanently. A person can do good to the world to what extent he is good himself. This is the truth which many are apt to overlook in their over-zealousness to help the world. They want to do good to others without caring to be good themselves. "He who is not good himself can hardly do good to others," admonished Swami Brahmananda.

On another occasion he remarked: "Those who are good will do good by their very nature, and those who are wicked will do harm by their very nature." Then he related the following story:

> Once a holy man, seated on the bank of a river, was meditating. Suddenly he saw a scorpion floating on the water. He took pity on it and with the palm of his hand scooped it out of the water. But as he did so the scorpion stung him. The holy man suffered great pain. A few moments later the scorpion again fell into the water. The holy man again helped it out. Again the scorpion stung him. This happened a third time. Presently, a man who had been watching the whole thing asked: "Why do you help the scorpion when it stings you again and again?" The holy man replied: "It is the nature of the scorpion to sting, and it is my nature to help. The scorpion does not give up its nature, why should I give up mine?"[42]

10. *How the practice of virtue leads man beyond the relativity of good and evil to absolute good. Through obedience to the law one goes beyond law.*

Not only does virtue purify the heart; it also brightens the intellect. Consequently a virtuous person develops keen understan-

[42]Swami Prabhavananda, *The Eternal Companion* (Brahmananda — His Life and Teachings), 3rd edn., Hollywood, Vedanta Press, 1970, p.239.

ding and sound judgment. Before long he realizes the inherent limitations of virtuous deeds. He understands that whatever good one may secure in the world by righteous acts is not an unmixed blessing. One may gain prosperity, power, beauty, health, honor, and freedom from political and social disabilities, yet one cannot get rid of concomitant evil. Every situation has its own peculiar problems. In overcoming want by plenty one faces the problem of plenty. In ending war by peace the belligerent powers face the problem of peace. Just as lack of power creates problems so does power. Just as lack of beauty creates problems so does beauty. From actual experience one learns that good as well as evil creates bondage, the one like a gold chain, the other like an iron chain. But the gold chain is no less strong to bind than the iron chain, only its glitter hides its binding power.

As observed by Swami Vivekananda: "Evil is the iron chain, good is the gold chain; both are chains. Be free, and know once for all that there is no chain for you. Lay hold of the gold chain to loosen the hold of the iron one, then throw away both."[43]

He who strictly follows the right path clearly sees that good and evil are closely associated in the relative order, to which the world belongs. The one cannot be severed from the other. As a matter of fact they are inseparable like the obverse and the reverse of the same coin or like the two pages of a single leaf of a book. So he gives up the age-old wrong notion that good and evil are two cut-and-dried separate existences, that we can have the one to the exclusion of the other. He does not entertain the common visionary hope that by scientific research, technological devices, sound political ideologies, social organizations, international agreements, and other progressive measures, human conditions can be so ameliorated that in the long run evil will altogether disappear, and good and good alone will prevail in the world.

This does not mean, however, that in his view nothing can be done about the world. The position of the world is like that of a gymnasium for man's all-round development. It can be an ideal gymnasium but not an ideal home for perfected beings. This is the legitimate goal of all-world improvement. Or the position of the world is like that of a hospital. It can be a model hospital where every patient will be on the sure way to recovery, but not an ideal home for eternal life. Until a man attains perfection he will be born and reborn on the human plane. Birth and death are the necessary conditions of the earthly existence. Can these be eliminated?

[43]*Inspired Talks*, CW VII, pp.2-3.

In the relative universe good and evil are interrelated. The one does not exist without the other. There is nothing which is good and good alone. There is nothing which is evil and evil alone. There is no absolute good or absolute evil here. Strictly speaking, good and evil are not objective existences but the readings of the mind. Things appear as good and evil in the way we look at them. Neither is richness wholly good nor poverty wholly evil. Neither is beauty wholly good nor ugliness wholly evil. Just as richness and beauty can cause pride, even so poverty and ugliness can cause humility. Then again one and the same person can be counted rich from one standpoint and poor from another standpoint. One and the same person can be considered beautiful from one standpoint and ugly from another standpoint. The ugliest child is the paragon of beauty in the eyes of the affectionate mother.

Practice of virtue is not an end in itself. Morality is not an unmixed blessing. Kindness needs misery for its existence. Perpetuation of the one means the perpetuation of the other. Neither justice nor forgiveness can exist without wrongdoing. These are contingent ideals. For instance, as long as there is illness medical service is needed for its remedy. But the ideal is perfect health beyond illness and its remedy. Just as day exists in relation to night so virtue exists in relation to vice, but the ideal is neither day nor night but perpetual light. At first one has to overcome vice by virtue, then one can find the way beyond both.

What we generally consider as good and evil are but different manifestations of one ideal existence. The differences are in the degree of its manifestation. In what is known as good such as health, beauty, happiness, there is greater manifestation, while in what is regarded as evil such as disease, want, pain, there is less manifestation of the same reality. We have to rise from the lower to the higher manifestation and then go beyond both. Overcome evil by good and then give up both: this is the way, just as in order to remove the thorn stuck in your palm you take another thorn (or needle) and then discard both. No relative good howsoever high it may be is an ideal in itself. Scriptural knowledge counteracts our ignorance with regard to God. But He is beyond both knowledge and ignorance. God is the absolute Good beyond all dualities. He is the supreme Goal. In Him is life beyond birth and death.

Once a man said to Jesus Christ, "Good Master, what good thing shall I do, that I may have eternal life?" Jesus said unto him, "Why callest thou me good? *There is* none good but one, *that is,* God; but if thou wilt enter into life, keep the commandments."[44]

Only those who are established in righteousness, whose minds are purged of all wrong tendencies, become disenchanted of the relative good, in whatever form it may be, and seek the absolute Good beyond all dualities. Their minds turn to God in the true sense. They do not seek God for temporal values. They hold to God as the supreme Goal, as the sole refuge. They worship God with single-minded devotion and with firm resolve. We have explained how righteousness leads to spiritual awakening (see Ch.III, sec.19). Through the practice of virtue one becomes disillusioned of dualities and turns to the absolute Good.

It is evident from the foregoing discussion that the intention of the law of karma is to take man beyond law. Law is for the weak, for the bound. Through obedience to law the weak become strong, the bound become free.

[44]Matt. 19:16,17.

CHAPTER VI

MAN'S DAILY MIGRATION: WAKING, DREAM, AND DREAMLESS SLEEP STATES

1. *Man's daily migration to the three states successively testifies to the indwelling self beyond them.*

From day to day a human being normally experiences three different states — waking, dream, and dreamless sleep. This means that the embodied self, the experiencer within, daily dwells on three different planes of consciousness. Consequently, he encounters three types of experience, which contradict one another. The waking experience is counteracted by dream or dreamless sleep. Dream is counteracted by dreamless sleep or the waking state. Dreamless sleep is counteracted by the waking or the dream state.

In dreamless sleep a person is aware of unspecified ignorance. It is a state of experience. Therefore he can say on waking, "I was asleep, I did not know anything." This shows that there is consciousness underlying ignorance (ajñāna)[1] in deep sleep; the luminous self is aware of ignorance unspecified, with which he is then associated like fire enveloped by smoke. This is why he can recall "I did not know anything." In the waking state a person knows what he knows and what he does not know; that is to say, he is aware of his specific knowledge and his specific ignorance. But in dreamless sleep he is aware only of his indeterminate ignorance.

The one and the same experiencer has the threefold experience. While the experiences vary the experiencer remains constant. So a person says, "I wake, I dream, I sleep." Evidently, the same "I" or the experiencer is at the back of the varying experiences, external and internal. That which is invariable in the midst of the variable must be distinct from the variable. So none of these three states are inherent in the self, the experiencer. Even the waking state is not

[1]See fn. 10, p. 37; fn. 26, p. 181.

native to the experiencer; otherwise he could not get out of it. Besides, he daily needs dreamless sleep, short though it may be, for complete rest and restoration.

Just as a bird migrates from one region to another without belonging to any, even so does the real man, the experiencer within, move from one plane of consciousness to another without belonging to any of them. From the waking state he passes on to the dream state or dreamless sleep. From dream he passes on to dreamless sleep or returns to the waking state. From dreamless sleep he comes back to the dream state. or reverts to the waking state. Then again, from the waking state he passes on to the dream state or dreamless sleep. Such is a man's daily round of migration.

An investigation into the three states reveals the true nature of the self, their experiencer. Consciousness is the very essence of the experiencer, while the objects of experience are devoid of it. So the self is self-luminous. It is real to itself, ever aware of its own existence. It is pure, free and blissful. It is the single constant factor in human personality and is essentially united with Supreme Consciousness immanent in the universe. So the knower of the true nature of the self becomes sorrowless. Says the *Kaṭha Upaniṣad:*

> That by which one perceives the objects in both dream and waking states, by knowing that as the supreme and all-pervading Self, the calm man does not grieve.[2]

"A knower of the Self goes beyond grief," says the *Chāndōgya Upaniṣad.*[3]

2. *An account of the waking state.*

In the waking state the self, the experiencer within, associated with the organs and the mind, dwells on the physical body and even becomes identified with the same. As the body is, so he knows himself to be. His ego-consciousness is well defined, being based on the body-idea. He realizes himself as a distinct individual. He knows whether he is young or old, dark or fair, short or tall, male or female. He knows what family, community, nation, and country he belongs to. He knows who are his kinsmen, friends, and foes. He takes care of what he owns. He is aware of his secular interests and strives for them.

[2]Ka.U. II:1.4.
[3]Ch.U. VII:1.3.

It is through the medium of the physical body that the experiencer comes in contact with the physical universe. So in the waking state, as stated in the *Māṇḍūkya Upaniṣad,* an individual is conscious of the outside world (vahiṣprajña); he dwells on the gross physical objects (sthūlabhuk); he has nineteen avenues or means of attaining them (ekōnaviṁśatimukha).[4] These are the five sense organs, the five motor organs, the five vital forces, and the mind with its fourfold function, i.e., deliberation, determination, egoism, and recollection. All these are operative or ready for operation in the waking state.

While awake, a person is aware, on the one hand, of the external objects and, on the other, of the mental states. He knows what he likes and what he does not like. He is aware of his happiness and unhappiness, hope and despair, and love and hatred. But he can see only the surface of the mind, and not the entire mind. Most of his ideas, desires, aptitudes, and propensities lie hidden in the subconscious level. As we have noted (Ch. III, sec. 11), that part of the mind which is open to the waking ego is the conscious mind; that part which is below the range of ego-consciousness is the subconscious mind.

Every volitional action, physical or mental, leaves a corresponding impression upon the mind. This has a natural tendency to settle down in the subconscious level. Thus, all impressions of karma (deeds and experiences) are deposited there. Some of them are dormant, some are attenuated, some are overpowered. Usually the attenuated and the overpowered ones rise to the conscious mind being stimulated by some cause, external or internal. They influence our thoughts and actions considerably. It is the impression of a past deed or experience which, being manifest in the conscious mind, produces memory.

As noted by Śaṅkarācārya, the mind contains the impressions like a painted piece of canvas.[5] These are the sources of dream imagery as well. In the dream state the individual self attended with the organs, which belong to the subtle body, withdraws from the physical body and stays on the subconscious plane. What happens then? He loses all contact with the outside world and dwells on the imagery devised by the impressions of karma, worked upon by his desire and imagination prevalent at the time. In fact, the dream-imagery has a threefold cause — the jīva's avidyā (ignorance of the true nature of the self), kāma (desire), and karma (impressions of actions and experiences). Not

[4]Ma.U. 3.
[5]Ma.U. 4, S. com.

only the impressions of the present life, but also the residual impressions of the past life are stored in the subconscious mind. It is the impressions of karma deposited in the mind that appear as concrete objects in the dream state. The dream-objects are generally the reproductions of waking experiences, but there can also be new constructions; that is to say, dreams can be either presentative or representative.

An individual's volition and reason, more or less developed though they may be, are invariably associated with his waking ego, which is definite and pronounced. So they function only in the waking state, and not in the dream state or in dreamless sleep. In the dream state the experiencer recedes from the physical body to the subconscious level; consequently the individual loses body consciousness and becomes subject to subliminal impressions. Being dissociated from the body and driven by emotion and imagination, the ego of the experiencer of dream proves to be vague, fickle, and amorphous. There is no ego-idea in dreamless sleep, when the mind with all its features and functions becomes merged in indeterminate ignorance, the causal body. Man's physical, intellectual, aesthetic, moral, and spiritual culture depend on the exercise of reason and volition associated with the waking ego. Consequently, no human progress is possible but in the waking state. Emotion prevails both in the waking and the dream state, but there is no scope for the cultivation of emotion in the dream state in the absence of reason and volition. It goes without saying that nothing can be accomplished in the states of intoxication and coma, when the mind is stupefied more or less and reason and volition are benumbed. These are abnormal states and consequently degenerating, whereas dream and deep sleep states are normal.

3. *The dream state explained.*

As stated in the *Māṇḍūkya Upaniṣad,* in the dream state an individual is conscious of internal objects (antaḥprajñaḥ).[6] He does not actually go out of the body, although he may be travelling far and wide in his dream. He dwells on the subtle objects with the same nineteen avenues or means of attainment by which he operates on the gross objects in the waking state. These nineteen instruments —the five organs of perception, the five organs of action, the five vital forces, and the mind with its fourfold function — actually belong to

[6]Ma.U. 4.

the subtle body, although they act on the gross body in the waking state. But none of these means manifests the self, which is self-manifest, being of the nature of pure consciousness. As we have noted, consciousness is intrinsic in the cognizer and not in the cognized. It is the light of the self alone that manifests the objects of experience in the dream state when there is no external light to help as in the waking state.

It is primarily through the agency of the mind that the self experiences the dream objects. So says the *Praśna Upaniṣad:*

> In this dream state this deity [the self identified with the mind] experiences greatness. He sees again what has been seen, he hears again what has been heard. He experiences again and again what has been experienced in different places and directions. What has been seen or not seen [not seen in this life but in a previous one], what has been heard or not heard [not heard in this life but in a previous one], what has been experienced and not experienced [not experienced in this life but in a previous one], what is real and what is not real [like a mirage] he perceives all by becoming all [being conditioned by the mental impressions that turn into dream objects].[7]

Since dream objects are but transformations of the mental impressions, the self identified with the mind turns into dream objects, so to speak.

An individual becomes quite absorbed in dream-imagery. He does not at all miss the world of waking experience so real and dear to him. Nay, he nullifies it, so to speak, being totally oblivious of it. From the tangible physical universe he migrates to the dream world, which is all that exists for him at the time. It is said in the *Bṛhadāraṇyaka Upaniṣad:*

> When he moves about in dream these are his achievements: then he becomes an emperor as it were, or a noble brāhmaṇa as it were, or he attains states, high or low, as it were. Even as an emperor taking his retinue of subjects moves about in his territory as he pleases, so does the self thus taking the organs, move about as he pleases in his own body.[8]

While sleeping comfortably and safely on a luxurious bed in his royal mansion, a prince may dream that he is being chased by a tiger in the wilderness and running for his life. An affectionate mother

[7]Pr.U. IV:5.
[8]Br.U. II:1.18.

sleeping with the beloved child in her arms may know herself in the dream state to be a college girl playing tennis with other young girls. Indeed, the dream-experience is purely subjective. The ideas of time, space, and causality are imaginary. The objects are the creations of the dreamer's mind. They have no real basis.[9] They do not exist in the world of the waking state.

The *Bṛhadāraṇyaka Upaniṣad* gives a graphic account of the dream state:

> When he dreams he takes away a little of this all-embracing world [the impressions of the world of universal experience in the waking state], puts the body aside and creates [a dream body in its place], all by himself. Revealing his own lustre by his own light he dreams. In this state the man himself becomes the light.
>
> There are no chariots, nor animals to be yoked to them, nor roads there, but he creates the chariots, animals, and roads. There are no pleasures, joys, or delights there, but he creates the pleasures, joys, and delights. There are no pools, tanks, or rivers there, but he creates the pools, tanks, and rivers. For he is the agent.
>
> Regarding this there are the following verses:
> "The radiant indwelling self, who roams alone, puts the body aside in the dream state, and himself awake and taking the shining functions of the organs with him, watches those that are asleep. Again he comes to the waking state.
>
> "The radiant indwelling self, who roams alone, preserves the unclean nest [the body] with the help of the vital principle, and moves out of the nest. Himself immortal, he goes wherever he likes.[10]
>
> "In the dream world, the shining one, attaining higher and lower states, puts forth innumerable forms. He seems to be enjoying himself in the company of women, or laughing, or even seeing frightful things.
>
> "Everyone sees his sport but himself no one ever sees." They say, "Do not suddenly awaken him who is out. If he does not find the right organ [to enter the body] it becomes difficult to treat the body."[11] Others, however, say that the dream state of a man is the same as the waking state, because he sees in dreams only those things that he sees in the waking state. [Neither view is right.] In the dream state [in the absence of the organs and external light] the very self of the man becomes the light.[12]

[9]See BS III:2.3.

[10]"Though he dreams staying in the body, yet, having no connection with it like the ether in the body, he is said to be moving out." (Br.U. IV:3.12, S. com.)

[11]"The self may not get back to those gates of the organs through which it went out taking the shining functions of the latter; or it may misplace these functions. In that case defects, such as blindness and deafness may result, and the physician may find it difficult to treat them." (Br.U. IV:3.14, S. com.)

[12]Br.U. IV:3.9-14.

4. *The experience of dreamless sleep.*

In dreamless deep sleep the individual self recedes from the subtle body and being associated with the causal body, ajñāna, its basic adjunct, reposes on the Supreme Self. There it stays as the percipient of ajñāna. The ten organs with their respective functions merge in the mind, which again with all its features and functions merges in the causal body (also called the blissful sheath). (See Ch. II, sec. 16.) Consequently, in deep sleep none of the ten organs function, nor does the mind. Their functions depend on the radiance of consciousness transmitted from the individual self, which, having receded, they cannot operate any more. The fluctuations of the mind subside altogether; no thinking, no feeling, no volition, no imagination, no recollection, no cognition of any kind occur then. Consequently, the eyes do not see, the ears do not hear, the nose does not smell, the mouth does not speak, the hands do not grasp, the legs do not move.

In that state the self is subject to no stress or strain of any kind. It experiences unspecified ignorance and a state of bliss. Therefore, on waking from profound sleep a person can say, "I was sleeping happily. I did not know anything."[13] In waking and dream states a person's knowledge and ignorance both are specific: he knows what he knows and what he does not know. In dreamless sleep he is not aware of any specific knowledge or lack of knowledge. Yet this is not a state of complete unconsciousness or unawareness, but of awareness of noncognition, pure and simple, as is evident from the expression, "I did not know anything."

Dreamless sleep is thus described in some of the Upaniṣads:

> Uddālaka, the son of Aruna, said to his son, Śvetaketu: "Learn from me, my dear, the true nature of sleep. When a person is in deep sleep, 'Svapiti' as it is called, then my dear, he becomes united with Pure Being, he attains his own [Self]. That is why they say he is in deep sleep (svapiti); it is because he attains his own Self (svam). [Though resting on the Supreme Self, the individual self because of the veil of ajñāna does not realize oneness with the Supreme Self, Pure Being.]
>
> "Just as a bird tied by a string, after flying in various directions and finding no resting place elsewhere settles down where it is bound, even so my dear, the mind [the individual self with the limiting adjunct mind] after flying in many directions and finding no resting place elsewhere settles down in the Prāṇa alone, for the mind [the individual self with the limiting adjunct mind] is fastened to the Prāṇa [Pure Being, the Supreme Self]."[14]

[13]See Pd. XI:59 and VS sec. 8 (Jacob's edn.). [14]Ch.U. VI:8.1,2.

> Ajātaśatru said, "When this being whose essence is consciousness [that is to say, the individual self] is thus asleep, it absorbs at the time the functions of the organs through its own consciousness, and lies in the ākāśa that is in the heart [the Supreme Self]. When this being absorbs them then it is said to be in deep sleep [to be united with its own Self]. Then the nose is absorbed, the organ of speech is absorbed, the eye is absorbed, the ear is absorbed, and the mind is absorbed."[15]

> To him the sage Pippalāda said, "O Gārgya, just as all the rays of the setting sun become gathered in this luminous orb, and they emerge again from the rising sun, similarly, all these [the ten organs] become unified in the superior god, the mind. Therefore this person then [during sleep] does not hear, does not see, does not smell, does not taste, does not touch, does not speak, does not grasp, does not enjoy, does not eject, does not move. He is sleeping — so the people say."[16]

> That is the state of deep sleep wherein the sleeping person neither desires anything nor sees any dream. The third quarter [of the self] is Prājñā [lit. the one who is mostly ignorant], whose sphere is deep sleep, in whom all experiences are unified, who is verily a mass of cognition [because the cognition of unspecified ignorance is homogeneous], who is blissful and who is the doorway to knowledge [the experience of the dream and the waking state].[17]

In deep sleep even the ego-idea drops. While fast asleep a person does not know whether he is young or old, dark or fair, whether he is a man or a woman, whether he is a European, or an Asiatic, whether he is a Buddhist or a Christian, whether he is a teacher or a student. As stated in the Upaniṣad:

> In this state a father is no father, a mother no mother, the worlds no worlds, the gods no gods, the Vedas no Vedas. In this state a thief is no thief, the killer of a noble Brāhmaṇa no killer, a Caṇḍāla no Caṇḍāla, a Pulkasa no Pulkasa, a monk no monk, a hermit no hermit. [This form of his] is untouched by good work and untouched by evil work, for he is then beyond all the woes of his heart.[18]

An investigation into the three states reveals the fact that their cognizer is beyond ego-consciousness and beyond unconsciousness. The ever-shining self illuminates darkness. It is the central principle of consciousness in the psychophysical organism. It cannot be conceived as partly conscious and partly unconscious. It is altogether different from the psyche postulated by C. G. Jung, the renowned exponent of Analytical Psychology. The waking ego and the dream ego are but partial manifestations of the ever-shining self under

[15]Br.U. II:1.17.
[16]Pr.U. IV:2.
[17]Ma.U. 5.
[18]Br.U. IV:3.22.

various psychophysical conditions. Both these may be regarded as partly aware and partly unaware or as partly conscious and partly unconscious. But their basis — the luminous self, whose substance is consciousness — is ever-shining. It knows what it knows and what it does not know. It reveals man's knowledge and ignorance as well. It is the real man.

5. *The distinctness of the animating principle in the psychophysical organism.*

It becomes evident from the study of the dream and the dreamless sleep state that none of the ten organs, nor the mind, nor their conjoint action is responsible for the livingness of the body. In the dream state none of the organs function, but the mind continues to operate. In dreamless sleep the organs and the mind as well are inoperative. They become dormant. Still such involuntary vital processes as respiration, heart beats, digestion, and intestinal movements continue. It is because prāṇa, the life principle, which is distinct from the organs and the mind, keeps awake, while the others fall asleep. So says the *Praśna Upaniṣad:* "[When a person is asleep] it is the fires of prāṇa (the life principle) that remain awake in this city [the physical body]."[19] It is said in the *Bṛhadāraṇyaka Upaniṣad* that the luminous self, who is immortal and moves alone, preserves the unclean nest (the body) with the help of the vital principle (prāṇa).[20] Of the five phases of the life principle, three — mukhya prāṇa, apāna, and samāna (which are responsible for respiration, beating of the heart, digestion and assimilation) — carry on the involuntary vital processes through the autonomic nervous system.

6. *The self is untouched by the threefold experience.*

The gain or loss of wealth in dream does not make a man richer or poorer, nor does physical enjoyment or suffering in dream affect his body. It is because the dream experiences are illusory. Similarly, the indwelling self, the experiencer, is not the least affected by waking, dream, and deep sleep experiences, which are due to his identification with the not-self, that is to say, association with the body, the organs, and the mind, through ajñāna. As we have noted, the experiencer is ever distinct from all that is experienced. While the experiencer is self-

[19]Pr.U. IV:3. [20]Br.U. IV:3.12.

luminous, being of the nature of consciousness, the objects experienced, gross or subtle, are devoid of consciousness. It is the experiencer, the knower *per se,* that manifests the objects. The objects of experience undergo change, whereas the experiencer remains constant, being the witness of all changes. Changes cannot be recognized unless there is an unchanging observer to relate the succeeding with the preceding condition. Aloof and uncontaminated, the luminous self freely moves back and forth from one state of experience to another. This fact is graphically presented by the *Bṛhadāraṇyaka Upaniṣad:*

> The luminous self after enjoying himself and roaming and merely seeing[21] [the results of] good and evil deeds [in the dream state], stays in a state of profound sleep, and comes back in the reverse order to his former condition, the dream state. He is untouched by whatever he sees in that state, for this indwelling self is unattached.
>
> After enjoying himself and roaming in the dream state and merely seeing [the results of] good and evil deeds, he comes back in the reverse order to his former condition, the waking state. He is untouched by whatever he sees in that state, for the indwelling self is unattached.
>
> After enjoying himself and roaming in the waking state and merely seeing [the results of] good and evil deeds, he comes back in the reverse order to his former condition, the dream state [or that of profound sleep].
>
> Just as a great fish swims alternately to both the banks [of a river] eastern and western, even so does the luminous self move to both these states, the dream and the waking states.
>
> As a hawk or a falcon flying in the sky becomes tired, and stretching its wings, is bound for its nest, so does the self run for this state, where falling asleep he craves no [object of] desire and sees no dreams.[22]

Just as the dream experiences are unreal, so are the waking experiences. The self is affected by neither of them. The primary cause of both is the wrong knowledge, or the misconception, of the self. The dream experiences are known to be false on awaking to the empirical order, to which the waking state belongs. Similarly, the waking experiences of the empirical order are known to be illusory on being awakened to the Ultimate Reality, nondual Brahman, that the

[21]The dreamer is not really affected by the dream-imagery created by the impressions stored in the mind. It is to be noted that all dream perceptions and actions are involuntary and cannot be counted as karma. The impressions they leave on the mind can produce memories, but not karmic effects; they do not serve as retributive forces.

[22]Br.U. IV:3.15-19.

individual self essentially is. All the three states — waking, dream, and deep sleep — are cases of ajñāna, the ignorance of the true nature of the self. So they are all characterized as sleep,[23] because of the inapprehension of Truth in all of them.

The difference between the waking and the dream state on the one hand and the deep sleep state on the other is this: in deep sleep there is only nonapprehension of Truth; in the two others there is not only nonapprehension but also misapprehension of Truth. The dream state is related to the waking state as a dream within dream. By proper inquiry in the light of the Upaniṣads into the threefold experiences — waking, dream, and dreamless sleep, which are common to all human beings — the individual self is recognized as the central principle of consciousness ever shining in the psychophysical organism and unaffected by the varying objects of experience external and internal.

7. *The individual self is inseparable from the Supreme Self.*

A clear grasp of the true nature of the self beyond the states of waking, dream, and profound sleep leads to the realization of the all-pervading, all-knowing supreme Self. As declared by the *Praśna Upaniṣad:*

> Verily, it is this that sees, touches, hears, smells, tastes, thinks, cognizes, and works. This is the self of the nature of consciousness that pervades the body and the senses. It is this that becomes fully established in the supreme, immutable Self.
>
> Verily, he attains the supreme, immutable Self who knows that shadowless, bodiless, colorless, pure, undecaying self. He who knows this, O my good friend, becomes all-knowing, becomes all. As to this there is the following verse:
>
> He becomes all-knowing and enters into all who knows that immutable Self, O my good friend, wherein rest the intelligent self and also the prāṇas and the elements together with the deities [the intelligent forces controlling cosmic processes].[24]

The *Kaṭha Upaniṣad* expresses the same truth:

> That by which one perceives the objects of both sleep and waking states, having known that as the great and all-pervading Self, the wise man does not grieve [goes beyond all sorrows].[25]

[23]Ai.U. I:3.12.
[24]Pr.U. IV:9-11.
[25]Ka.U. II:1.4.

The self is realized in transcendental perception as the Supreme Self, nay, as nondual Consciousness undifferentiated, beyond the distinction of the subject and the object. This is the state of Self-realization. This is said to be the fourth (turīya) in relation to the other three states superimposed on the self through ajñāna. Truly speaking, this is not a state, but the very nature of the Self. It baffles description in positive terms. The *Māṇḍūkya Upaniṣad* distinguishes it from the three aforesaid states and indicates it by negative terms:

> The wise know that to be the fourth (turīya), which is not inwardly conscious [as in dream], nor outwardly conscious [as in the waking state], nor conscious both ways [as in a state intermediary between waking and dreaming], which is not a mass of dormant conscious processes [as in dreamless sleep], nor omniconscious, nor unconsciousness; which is ungraspable, imperceptible, indeterminable, uninferable, inconceivable, undefinable; which is pure and simple Self-awareness, which endures after the negation of the manifold; which is nondual, calm, and blissful. That is the Self. That is to be realized.[26]

8. *The One Supreme Being ensouls the individual and the cosmos in all aspects.*

The One Infinite Self, Pure Being-Consciousness-Bliss, underlies the manifold. In association with the microcosm this is the individual self. In association with the cosmos this is the cosmic self. The one and the same Self exists in three different ways in the microcosm and also in the macrocosm. In association with an individual's physical body the individual self is the experiencer of the waking state and is called *viśva.* In association with his subtle body the individual self is the experiencer of the dream state and is called *taijasa.* In association with his causal body (ajñāna) the individual self is the experiencer of dreamless sleep and is called *prājñā.*

Says Gauḍapāda in the opening verse of his *Māṇḍūkya-kārikā:*

> *Viśva* is the cognizer of the external objects and is all-pervading, while *Taijasa* is the cognizer of the internal objects; similarly, *Prājñā* has homogeneous experience [because in dreamless sleep all diversity, nay, even the distinction of the external and the internal is merged in unspecified ajñāna witnessed by the self]. One and the same entity [the self] is acknowledged in the three different states.

Similarly, the cosmic self exists in three different states. The

[26] Ma.U. 7.

cosmic self associated with the entire physical or gross universe is called *Virāt*. This is also called *Vaiśvānara*. The cosmic self associated with the entire subtle universe underlying the gross is called *Hiraṇyagarbha*. The cosmic self associated with the entire causal universe (undifferentiated māyā or avyākṛta) is called *Īśvara*. As we have noted above, the microcosm and the macrocosm are similar in structure. By practicing meditation on the essential oneness of the individual self with the cosmic self in all the three aspects of the world of appearance, one can realize the self as the sole reality behind all phenomena and ultimately as Nondual Consciousness free from all superimposition. At the back of every finite center of consciousness is the all-pervading consciousness, the Self of the universe. What is innermost in the individual must be innermost in the cosmos.

9. *The homogeneity of the dreamless sleep experience. The one immutable self behind the three states.*

The waking experience of every individual is different and so is the dream experience. But the experience of profound dreamless sleep is alike for all. In this there is no diversity nor distinction of inside and outside. All differences are merged in homogeneous causal ajñāna. In the deep sleep state, when even the ego-idea is lost, there is no difference between a saint and a sinner, between a king and a peasant, between a sage and an idiot, between a man and a woman, between a child and an adult. "In sleep what difference is there between Solomon and a fool?" is an old saying.

Sleep is the soothing balm for all agony, an unfailing restorer of tired limbs and mind. "He that sleeps feels not the toothache," they say. But unperturbed resposeful sleep is hardly the lot of those who are of perverted nature. It is said that sound sleep is the privilege of the virtuous. "He giveth His beloved sleep."[27] A man's ego-idea or "I-consciousness" is the yoke or the bond that drives him in the world. All his physical and mental incentives proceed from this. Hence it is so ordained that once in twenty-four hours a human being has to throw off the yoke to find complete rest.

In the waking state an individual experiences both happiness and sorrow in diverse forms. So does he in the dream state. But in deep sleep all that he experiences is unvaried calmness or happiness and unspecified ignorance. As stated in the *Kaivalya Upaniṣad:*

[27] Psalms 127:2.

> The same ātman as the individual self deluded by māyā gets identified with the physical body and performs various deeds; it is he who in the waking state gains pleasure from diverse objects of enjoyment, such as the opposite sex, food, drink.
> In the dream state this very self [the jīva] experiences pleasure and pain in the world of the living created by his own māyā. In the state of dreamless sleep when all things overpowered by tamas [ajñāna] disappear [become latent in ajñāna, the causal body] he attains simple happiness.[28]

The one and the same changeless self experiences the three states — waking, dream, and dreamless sleep — being associated with the gross, the subtle, and the causal body in due order of succession through its reflection on a particular modification of the mind (antaḥkaraṇa), which belongs to the subtle body. It is the mental modification characterized by "I-ness" that manifests the self as the ego, in other words, the self identified with the not-self. The stable basis of the varying ego-consciousness is the immutable self, the one that is invariable in the midst of the variables. It is distinct from the threefold body, which constitutes the fivefold sheath — the physical, the vital, the mental, the intelligent, and the blissful (see Ch. II, sec. 10-16). As such it is "the witness of the three states (avastha-traya-sākṣi)." It is also called *kūṭastha* (the rock-steady).

10. *How can a person recollect the dreamless sleep state in which the mind with the ego subsides?*

"I slept happily; I did not know anything" — this is how a person gives expression to his experience during deep sleep when he wakes up. It is to be noted that the experience of happiness and ignorance during deep sleep is universal. This is a case of recollection, which must be preceded by experience. But in the deep sleep state the organs and the mind disappear; even the ego subsides. How can there be experience in their absence? The fact is that they do not vanish in the deep sleep state, but remain latent in ajñāna, the causal body.

As we have noted, the cognitive mind (buddhi) with the organs of perception constitutes the intelligent sheath (vijñānamaya kōśa). This functions as the experiencer in the waking state, being characterized by egoism, a mode of the cognitive mind. This is the empirical self that operates on the mental and the vital sheath. The empirical self experiences the deep sleep state, being associated with ajñāna, the causal body, in which this (the intelligent sheath with the

[28] Kai.U. 12,13.

ego) remains latent temporarily. It is by means of the indrawn mode of ajñāna bearing the reflection of consciousness that the self perceives its innate bliss and also ajñāna.

Just as there can be modifications of the mind (antaḥkaraṇa), similarly there can be subtle modifications of ajñāna illuminated by consciousness.[29] Since ajñāna, the causal body, emits the blissfulness of the self in the deep sleep state it is also called "the blissful sheath." With the emergence of the intelligent sheath from the causal body in the waking state, the self becomes manifest distinctly as the ego in the waking state; it remembers its experience in the deep sleep state and says: "I slept happily; I did not know anything."

In his *Pañcadaśī* Vidyāraṇya explains how an individual remembers in the waking state his experience of happiness and ignorance during deep sleep when the organs and the mind, including the ego, disappear:

> "I slept happily, I did not know anything then" — thus a person recollects his happiness and ignorance in deep sleep state when he wakes up.
>
> Recollection results from experience. Therefore there must be experience in that state. Happiness becomes self-manifest being identical with consciousness [that the self is] and this manifests ignorance [ajñāna that veils the self].
>
> "Brahman is of the nature of Consciousness and Bliss," say the Vājasaneyins.[30] Therefore self-luminous Bliss is but Brahman and nothing else.
>
> What is called *ajñāna* (basic ignorance); in that the intelligent and the mental sheath become latent [see Ch. II, sec. 12-14]. Deep sleep is the state in which these [the empirical self with the mind and the organs of perception] remain hidden and this is the state of ajñāna (ignorance).
>
> Just as molten butter becomes solid again, so does the intelligent sheath [the empirical self associated with the mind and the five organs of perception], which becomes absorbed in ajñāna, the blissful sheath [in the deep sleep state], becomes manifest again [in the waking state]. In the state of absorption this self is called "the blissful" [being associated with the blissful sheath].
>
> That modification of the mind which [being indrawn] immediately before deep sleep reflects the bliss of the self, being absorbed in ajñāna together with the reflection turns out to be the blissful sheath.

[29]See VS VIII, S. com. *Subōdhinī*.

[30]Br.U. III:9.28. Vājasaneyins are the followers of the *Śukla* (White) *Yajur-Veda*, to which the *Bṛhadāraṇyaka Upaniṣad* belongs. Vājasaneya is the name of Yājñavalkya, the compiler of the *Śukla Yajur-Veda*. Vājasaneyin is derived from Vājasaneya.

> Then the indrawn self associated with the blissful sheath experiences the bliss of Brahman by means of the modifications of ajñāna bearing the reflection of consciousness [the modification of the mind bearing the reflection of the self being latent there].
>
> The modifications of ajñāna [operative in deep sleep state] are indistinct, whereas the modifications of the mind [operative in the waking state] are distinct.
>
> This is what those proficient in the established truths of Vedānta declare.[31]

Consequently, when the mental modifications become distinct in the waking state, the self by their means can recollect the deep sleep experience.

11. *The mysteriousness of the dream state. The Vedantic view of its cause.*

From ancient times dreams have proved to be a great mystery to the human mind. Thinkers, ancient and modern, have held different views of this inner experience common to all human beings. Various interpretations have been given of dream phenomena. Some attribute them to external causes, some to internal causes, some to both. It is an ancient belief that dreams are visitations from gods. However, most thinkers agree on the point that dream betokens the dreamer's inner nature. Each man makes his own dream. It is a common belief that dreams often foreshadow the future. Some hold that in the dream state the dreamer goes out of the body. It is quite likely that from the study of dreams man got the idea of the soul's survival of death, which means its final departure from the physical body that faces consequent destruction. He also discovered that the mind could be active even when the body was inert to all appearance. In the Vedantic view nothing goes out of the body in the dream state.

It is the subliminal impressions of past deeds and experiences in waking life that serve as materials for dream-imagery. But various factors can be its stimulating cause, such as the condition of the body, the immediate surroundings, and the mental state of the dreamer. For instance, it is a common experience that nightmares are often caused by indigestion. Atmospheric heat, cold, hard or soft beds, loose or tight clothing sometimes determine the nature of dreams. A person sleeping with a heating pad at his feet may dream that he is walking

[31]Pd. XI:59-66.

over a volcano. Hope, fear, desire, or a thought prevalent in the mind before sleep may also cause cognate dreams.

Hopeful of recovery, a young man crippled by an accident often dreamt that he had left his crutch and had been walking freely like a normal person. Another young man had a strong desire to make a fortune but found no way to do so. One night he dreamt that while walking in the woods he came by chance upon a hidden treasure to his great delight. Living happily in a summer resort and yet apprehensive of leaving the place, a person dreamt that the news of sudden illness in the family had called him back home; but when he woke up he was joyously surprised to find that he was still living in the same summer resort.

Besides such fleeting stimuli, one's deep-seated tendencies or merits and demerits acquired by past karma in this or in a previous life can arouse cognate impressions and create the dream-imagery. Ordinarily, one's secular disposition and desires give rise to dream images. In rare cases dreams betoken the dreamer's innate spiritual disposition. I shall quote from *The Gospel of Sri Ramakrishna* one such dream:

> He [Sri Ramakrishna] asked a devotee, "Do you ever have dreams?"
>
> Devotee: "Yes, sir. The other day I dreamt a strange dream. I saw the whole world enveloped in water. There was water on all sides. A few boats were visible, but suddenly huge waves appeared and sank them. I was about to board a ship with a few others, when we saw a Brahmin walking over that expanse of water. I asked him, 'How can you walk over the deep?' The Brahmin said with a smile: 'Oh, there is no difficulty about that. There is a bridge under the water.' I said to him, 'Where are you going?' 'To Bhawanipur, the city of the Divine Mother,' he replied. 'Wait a little,' I cried, 'I shall accompany you.' "
>
> Master [Sri Ramakrishna]: "Oh, I am thrilled to hear the story!"
>
> Devotee: "The Brahmin said: 'I am in a hurry. It will take you some time to get out of the boat. Good-bye. Remember this path and come after me.' "
>
> Master: "Oh, my hair is standing on end! Please be initiated by a guru as soon as possible."[32]

I have first hand knowledge of some dreams indicative of the dreamers' inborn spiritual tendencies. About sixty years ago a young brother-disciple of mine dreamt of receiving initiation from Swami Brahmananda, the spiritual son of Sri Ramakrishna about whom he

[32]GSR, pp.122-23.

had heard, and whose picture he had seen. But as he awoke from sleep he forgot the mantra (the mystic formula) that had been communicated to him in his dream. Later he had an opportunity to see Swami Brahmananda personally. He then begged for initiation, but was told to wait patiently. After several years when he was initiated by Swami Brahmananda he at once recalled that the mystic formula that was then imparted to him was the same one he had received in the dream.

A similar incident happened some years later. A young girl of about twenty had a dream of the same kind. But unlike the boy, she distinctly remembered the mantra that Swami Brahmananda gave her in the dream. Afterwards she came to see the Swami, who had been living in Calcutta — far from her native town. She found him seated side by side with another elderly disciple of Sri Ramakrishna, Swami Shivananda. As she related her dream to Swami Brahmananda, whom she had not met before, he said to her while pointing to the other Swami, "Are you sure that you saw me in a dream and not this Swami?" "Yes, Revered Maharaj. I saw *you* in a dream," replied the girl. Then Swami Brahmananda forbade her to tell him the mantra that she had received in her dream. Later when Swami Brahmananda initiated her she found to her great joy and assurance that he gave her the very same mantra she had received in the dream.

The following dream also testifies to the innate spiritual tendency of the dreamer. It was in January, 1921, in the city of Varanasi, that a young Swami of our Order recounted to Swami Turiyananda in the presence of others, including myself, a dream that had solved one of his long-standing spiritual problems. For some time he had been pondering whether the great spiritual leaders adored as Divine Incarnations formed a special order of ever-free souls, or whether they belonged to the class of the liberated souls of the highest type. Before he could reach a conclusion, he dreamt one night that he saw before him an infinite expanse of water with rolling waves.

Standing on the beach as he was watching the surging billows, there appeared before him a row of great spiritual personages generally adored as God incarnate in human forms, e.g., Rāma, Kṛṣṇa, the Buddha, Jesus Christ, Sri Caitanya, Sri Ramakrishna. He observed that they proceeded to the ocean and walked over the billows far, far away until they disappeared; then they reappeared and walked back to the beach with ease.

Next he saw ranged on the beach the great spiritual teachers worshipped as prophets, sages, saints, and living-free souls beginning with Śukadeva down to Swami Vivekananda. They too walked over the breakers without difficulty, but could not proceed very far and returned to the beach. This dream convinced him of the immense difference between the two orders of spiritual leaders. Those belonging to the former order were never bound and were ever free. The others had gained freedom from a state of bondage in the past and had attained permanently the status of free souls. They are reborn as such for the enlightenment and guidance of humanity from age to age, as necessity arises.

So we find that the main source of dream-imagery is the repository of the impressions in the dreamer's subconscious mind accumulated by his own deeds and experiences during the waking state in his present and past lives as well.

12. *Aristotle's view of the origin of dreams.*

Aristotle's view that the origin of dreams is within the dreamer himself is closer to truth than the dream theories of many other thinkers — philosophers, psychologists, and scientists, ancient and modern. As observed by Medard Boss:

> Aristotle no longer sought the origin of dreams outside man but inside his own nature. Dreams, he said, were the necessary manifestations of this nature. They derived from the experiences and personal attitudes of the dreamer, from his cares, his hopes, and also from his biological processes, especially from the coursing and warmth of blood. In his later writings he even tried to give a psycho-physiological explanation of prophetic dreams. However, the mere fact that he granted the possibility of prophetic dreams clearly proves that he too still based himself on the metaphysical foundations of the ancient Greeks.[33]

But it is a proven fact that some dreams foreshadow future events. It is not just an ancient belief. This is also evident from the foregoing discussion: a careful study of man's threefold experience — waking, dream, and dreamless sleep — points to the metaphysical foundation of human personality, which is verified by the suprasensuous experiences attained by the greatest seers and saints of the world in all ages. The three types of daily experience are so interrelated that we cannot understand any of them without recognizing one and the same unchanging experiencer underlying them all, and this is realized as

[33] Medard Boss, *The Analysis of Dream*, New York, Philosophical Library, 1958, pp.14-15.

the all-pervading Supreme Self in transcendental experience. What is innermost in man is innermost in the universe.

13. *Sigmund Freud's interpretation of the dream state and of the motivation of man is not tenable. The Vedantic view of the basic urge of man.*

We have noted above some instances of the dreamer's wish fulfillments in dreams. But this does not mean that all dreams are cases of the dreamer's wish fulfillment. Nor does it mean that the nature of the wish must be the same in all cases. According to Sigmund Freud, the pioneer of depth psychology, all dreams are wish fulfillments;[34] they are invariably motivated by infantile instinctual wish. In his opinion the primary source of a man's energy is the sexual urge, called *libido*. Such a view lowers man to the animal level. It leaves unexplained the development of moral virtues in man, morality for the sake of morality, the practice of unselfishness and self-denial as an ideal. And it is self-denial that leads to self-expansion. By restraining the lower self man attains the higher self. Moreover, Freud's view cannot account for the spiritual urge in man, which is based on the awareness of his spiritual self, the central principle of consciousness ever shining and immutable, while the sexual urge is rooted in his body-idea, the identification of himself with the body, from which proceed the sense-desires, the root cause of all vices. The two are of contrary nature. The one cannot be the outcome of the other.

To all appearance man is mortal, bound, and imperfect. Yet deep within his heart there is a longing for immortality, for complete freedom, for perfection. Sooner or later he becomes dissatisfied with anything finite. Man's urge for the Infinite, for the highest and best, is a universal fact. So the question arises: Why does the mortal man seek immortality, the bound man freedom, the imperfect man perfection? The point is: man is not what he appears to be. He is not the everchanging psychophysical organism, but its knower and ruler. He is the pure, free, immutable self, the principle of consciousness ever shining within, although for the time being, he is more or less identified with the adjuncts being reflected on them.

[34]Freud held this view at the beginning and continued to hold that this is the primary function of dreams. But the way soldiers who had undergone war trauma relived their traumatic experiences time and again in their dreams led him to see in dreams another function. Compulsive dreams are an effort of ego to *master* traumatic experiences. See *Beyond the Pleasure Principle*, New York, Liveright, 1950, pp.39-40.

There is kinship, nay, unity between the finite self and the Supreme Self. Essentially both are alike, being of the nature of pure consciousness. This is why the fundamental urge in man is the urge for the highest and best, the urge for perfection, the urge for the Infinite. It is the urge of the finite self to be reinstated in its pristine purity, freedom, and blissfulness. It underlies all physical, biological, and psychical urges. The divergencies are due to the differences in the psychophysical adjuncts with which it becomes associated, even as the same pure water assumes the attributes of the various channels through which it flows. The body, the organs, the vital principle, and the mind function because of the radiance of the immutable self, the unobserved observer. This radiance being all but withdrawn during deep sleep, the vital principle sustains the body through what gleam is left.

14. *The importance of the waking state. The way to manipulate the subconscious.*

The very presence of the luminous self serves as the moving power in the entire psychophysical organism. The greatest manifestation of power in man is in his waking state. It is the waking ego that takes the initiative in all his physical and mental achievements. The subliminal impressions with all their potencies are initially acquired by his volitional actions in the waking state. It is they that produce the dreams, as we have noted.

From man's conscious deeds — right and wrong, intentional and unintentional — are derived the instinctive drives and complexes in the subconscious region, which react on the conscious level. By manipulating the conscious plane with will and understanding one has to rectify and remold the subconscious plane. This is the method of self-culture that the Indian sages have recommended from time immemorial.

If man be at the mercy of the subconscious urges, if he has no control over the unconscious forces, over his hidden propensities, then there is no hope for him. On no account should man dread the subconscious, inveterate though it may be. He has to undo his own doing. In no human being is the subconscious all bad, howsoever degraded he may be. In some individuals there is the predominance of good elements in the subconscious, in some the predominance of evil elements, in some the balance of the two in the subconscious region of the mind.

15. *Carl Jung's conception of the psyche and consciousness leaves man subject to the Unconscious.*

Both Freud and Jung acknowledge an innate driving force in human beings and call it *libido.* But their conceptions of *libido* are very different. Freud identifies *libido* with sexual energy and sees its manifestation as the primary impelling force in every individual. According to Jung *libido* is the energy of the psyche, the totality of consciousness and the unconscious in man operating as a self-regulating system. It powers every involuntary and voluntary drive of an individual. It is at the back of all human deeds and development.

But, as we have explained above (see Ch. I, sec.4), the real self of man is other than the psyche. It is the central principle of consciousness that reveals man's waking, dream, and deep sleep states. It is the light that never goes out. As the waking ego it perceives the external objects and the mental states within its scope, and is also aware of the deeper levels of the mind. As the dream ego it experiences certain disclosures of the subconscious level. In dreamless sleep it is cognizant of the homogeneity of the causal state of the mind. Man's cultural development depends on volitional action, which is possible only in the waking state. There can be no volition without self-determination, which characterizes the waking state.

The fundamental urge in man, as we have stated, is the urge for perfection, the urge for the highest and best. It is the urge of the finite self for the Supreme Self. It is innate in the luminous self of every individual. This has varied expressions through multifarious psychophysical systems of human beings, just as pure light becomes manifest variously through diverse mediums.

Jung's conception of "The Personal Unconscious" has a certain resemblance to the Vedantic view of the subconscious region of the mind as the repository of the impressions of karma. But in his psychology the unconscious is preponderant. Along with "The Personal Unconscious" he postulates "The Collective Unconscious," which is deeper. Jung's conception of the psyche reduces man virtually to an automaton with an admixture of consciousness. He says:

> Psychic processes antedate, accompany, and outlive consciousness. Consciousness is an interval in a continuous psychic process; it is probably a climax requiring a special physiological effort, therefore it disappears again for a period each day. The psychic process underlying

> consciousness is, so far as we are concerned, automatic, and its coming and going are unknown to us. We only know that the nervous system, and particularly its centers, condition and express the psychic function, and that these inherited structures start functioning in every new individual exactly as they have always done. Only the climaxes of this activity appear in our consciousness, which is periodically extinguished.[35]

We have already pointed out that consciousness is the very being of man. It is the basis of his ego through which it becomes manifest on the physical and the mental plane. It persists even when the ego subsides, as it happens in deep sleep. It is the witness of unspecified ignorance or unconsciousness that marks the deep sleep state. The witness self shines as the luminous self within every individual in the waking, dream, and deep sleep states. It underlies the ego.

The existence of the luminous self is evident from the universal fact that each and every human being knows that he is. No material object, not even the vast, resplendent sun, ever knows that it exists; it is unaware of its own existence and of the existence of all else. The basic difference between a material and a spiritual entity is that the one is devoid of consciousness, while the other has consciousness as its very being. Within each individual dwells the immortal spirit, the ruler and cognizer of the psychophysical organism. It is this that daily experiences the waking, dream, and dreamless sleep states. It is self-aware and is aware of what is within its scope. It is contrary to physical light, which is unaware of itself and all else.

16. *Jung's hypotheses of the Collective Unconscious and the Archetypes seem to us superfluous.*

As far as we can see, Jung has postulated the Collective Unconscious, an assemblage of the Archetypes, as the basis of the Personal Unconscious in order to explain the similarities of the dream images and the legendary and the mythological concepts prevalent among widely divergent groups of human beings. To us it seems that the same can be explained by the relation between the particular and the general without assuming the Collective Unconscious. The general underlies the diversified particulars.

[35]C. G. Jung, "The Structure and Dynamics of the Psyche," in *The Collected Works of C.G. Jung,* Bollingen Series XX, Vol. 8, R.F.C. Hull, trans.; G. Adler, M. Fordham, H. Read, eds., New York, Princeton University Press, Pantheon Books, 1960, #227, p. 110. Reprinted by permission of Princeton University Press.

Consequently, the essentials of the general are common to all its specific forms. Every human body is a particularized universal human form. Similarly, every individual mind is the universal mind particularized. This is why similar traits are noticeable in the ideas, imaginations, and sentiments of different types of people despite their divergencies.

Further, according to the doctrine of reincarnation there is continuity of the mind of an individual from life to life. As we have noted, a person leaves the physical body at death; but the mind, which is other than the physical body and belongs to the subtle body, passes out with the departing self, the knower *per se*. The mind and the body being characteristically different, the hereditary transmission of the mind or the mental traits is not possible through the physical ingredients of the reproductive cells of the parents. The mind carries the remnants of the impressions of past lives. These are deposited in the subconscious mind and can account for strange dream images and legendary concepts, which cannot be explained by the impressions of the deeds and experiences of the present life.

17. *Modern psychotherapy in the light of Vedanta.*

Modern psychologists in general have tried to understand the dream state by the analysis of dreams and by referring it to one or another aspect of human personality. Just as the physical, physiological, and the psychological aspects of an individual are inter-related, so are the three normal states of human experience — waking, dream, and dreamless sleep. An isolated study of any of them cannot lead us to truth. The central fact in a human being is the luminous self, the experiencer of the three states. Behind all experiences, external and internal, there is but one experiencer. While the experiences vary, the experiencer remains constant.

We have explained how by a coordinated study of the threefold experience — waking, dream, and dreamless sleep — Vedanta has tried to determine the real nature of man and his relation to the three states and the different aspects of the psychophysical organism. Since human personality is a graded organization, Vedanta recommends a comprehensive and consistent view of it as a whole in order to evaluate its different constituent factors.

Although the knower within, the real man, is ever shining, pure, free, and immortal, and distinct from the psychophysical adjunct, yet, being veiled by ajñāna like fire shrouded by smoke, it gets identified with the not-self and loses control over it. The more an individual realizes his distinction from the body, the organs, and the mind, the greater is his mastery over them. The mind has a unique position in human personality. It is the chief instrument of knowledge and of action as well. None of the organs of perception or of action can function unless the mind conjoins with it.

On the one hand the mind is distinct from the body and the organs and on the other from the knowing self. The more a person can realize his distinction from the mind the better he can objectify it and manipulate it. This, according to Vedanta, is the only way to prevent mental distress and ailment. "Prevention is far better than cure" is a well-known proverb.

A person who fails to recognize his distinction from the mind naturally becomes identified with it. Being submerged in the mental waves he loses control over them and can hardly be free from internal turmoil and affliction. In such a case a curative method is the only recourse, and there cannot but be increasing demand for clinical observation and hospitalization for the remedy of mental malady.

Further, human anatomy is based on the study of the structure of the human body in its normal state and physiology on the study of the normal functioning of the body: similarly, psychology should be founded on the study of the human mind in its normal condition. Freud's Psychoanalysis, Jung's Analytical Psychology, and later schools of psychiatry are built primarily on the data of the pathological state of the human mind, and cannot therefore attain the status of standard psychology, the science of the human mind.

Though distinct, the body and the mind are closely associated. Consequently one can affect the other. Yet physical ailment rooted in the bodily condition is not necessarily attended with mental ailment, nor is mental ailment rooted in the mind necessarily attended with physical ailment. The point is, every disorder in a human constitution cannot be regarded as psychosomatic. What originates particularly from the bodily condition has to be treated on the physical level.

In the same way, what originates particularly from the mental condition has to be treated on the mental level. The cases in which the source of the trouble is in the mind cannot be dealt with by purely physical methods, such as drug therapy, electric shock, lobotomy. The cause has to be determined by a psychological process, which need not be the same as psychoanalysis, that is, probing into the lowest depth of the mind. The Vedantic psychotherapy aims to cure mental distress and functional disorders due to fear, anxiety, grief, frustration, internal conflict, a sense of guilt, suppressed desire, and so forth, by rectifying the patient's inner attitude towards the object concerned — things, beings, or events, as the case may be — and thereby transforming his reactions to them. Vedanta also stresses the necessity of moral observance for the calmness of the mind. (See Ch. III, sec. 15; Ch. IX, sec. 5.)

There is a tendency in modern times to stress the objective approach to mental life. But a purely objective study of the human mind cannot succeed. Unlike a physical object, the mind is imperceptible by the senses. The study of the mind and its functions through analysis of behavior is indirect and consequently cannot lead to definite and decisive knowledge, as we have noted (see Ch. III, sec. 18). Introspection is the only direct approach to the human mind. None but the individual himself can observe his mind. If there is any possibility of mistake in reading one's own mind it can be rectified by comparing notes with others. There are many factors which are common to most human minds. The study of behavior also can serve as a test, even though it may be misleading in certain cases. There is the possibility of error in sense-perception too. Still, sense-perception is generally accepted as a criterion of knowledge of physical objects and serves as the basis of physical science. Just as physical science is based primarily on the objective approach, psychology has to be based primarily on the subjective approach; it cannot be included in the category of physical sciences.

CHAPTER VII

DEATH AND AFTER

1. *A jīva's present existence is but a link in a continuous chain of life marked by a succession of birth and death. Liberation is attainable only in human life.*

Human life as limited by birth and death is not self-explanatory. It is intricate and anomalous. We cannot account for it without knowing what is before and what is after. Severed from its past and future, "One life, a little gleam of Time between two Eternities" in the words of Carlyle,[1] is an enigma. Too often it is cut short abruptly or prolonged unduly. It does not satisfy our sense of justice or consistency. It runs its course heedless of our cherished hopes and longings. Its favors and disfavors appear to be groundless oftener than not. No wonder men have held widely divergent views of this short span of life. Some look upon it as a comedy, some as a tragedy, some as a tragi-comedy. To some it is an empty dream, to some it is a severe battlefield, to some it is a wilderness, to some it is a sleep or a state of oblivion. Indeed, we cannot find the meaning and purpose of life until we know where we come from and where we go. It may be an exile's long, long, journey homeward-bound.

As we have indicated, in the Vedantic view a man's present existence is but a link in a continuous chain of life marked by a succession of births and deaths; it is a chain forged by his own karma and its consequence. Although man is intrinsically pure, free and immortal, yet by this very chain he is tied down to the death-bound world of dualities, totally oblivious of his true nature. Many a time he is born, many a time he dies — until he knows what he really is.

After having sweet and bitter experiences and good schooling through the ups and downs of a chequered journey of life in this and other worlds, he learns the lesson that his own hands hold the chain that binds him to the wheel of birth and rebirth. He learns that

[1]Thomas Carlyle, *On Heroes and Hero-worship and the Heroic in History,* Lecture V, London, Oxford University Press, 1963, p. 231.

through his own karma, good as well as evil, he remains in bondage and that through his own karma he can gain freedom, being disenchanted of the dual experience. With this conviction he turns from the search of the temporal to the search of the Eternal. He learns that while the temporal are many and limited, the Eternal is One and limitless; while the temporal are marked by interdependences, the Eternal is ever-free. This is how he finds the way from bondage to freedom, from death to immortality, from darkness to the Light of all lights.

Just as birth is followed by death, so is death followed by birth.[2] This is true in the cases of all bound souls. Rare personages who succeed in realizing Brahman, Saguṇa or Nirguṇa, during their lifetime, become released forever from the cycle of birth and rebirth. Liberation is attainable only in human life. This is its special privilege. But without a long course of preparation and hard spiritual discipline none can be qualified for it. This is why an individual has to be born and reborn as a human being until he is capable of realizing Brahman by withdrawing from the temporal. But human birth is not easy to attain. In an immeasurably long course of evolution, the individual soul gains the competence for being born as a human being. As declared by the *Śvetāśvatara Upaniṣad:*

> This [the individual soul] is not female, nor is this male, nor even neuter is this. Whatever body he assumes, with that he becomes identified.
>
> According to his deeds, the individual soul assumes successively various physical forms in various conditions. By the abundance of food and drink and by means of desire, touch, sight, and [consequent] delusion are the birth and growth of the [embodied] self.
>
> The individual soul, in accordance with the guṇas [sattva, rajas, and tamas] superimposed on himself, assumes various forms, coarse and fine. Being the cause of his union with them according to the nature of his actions and thoughts, he appears as another [different from what he is].
>
> By realizing the Divine Being — who is without beginning and without end, who pervades the entire universe, who creates the cosmos in the midst of the chaos, who is manifest in various forms — one becomes free from all fetters.
>
> They give up the mortal body once for all who realize the Divine Being, the cause of creation and dissolution, who is known to be without a

[2]Cf. Chuang Tzu, "Life follows upon death. Death is the beginning of life. Who knows when the end is reached." *Philosophy,* Ch. 5.

> body, who is the maker of the sixteen parts,[3] who is all-good and can be seen by the purified heart.[4]

As stated in the *Muṇḍaka Upaniṣad:* "He who cherishing objects desires them is born again here and there led by his desires. But of him who is established in the Self and has thus attained the fulfillment of desires, all desires vanish even here."[5]

2. *Of the threefold body only the physical tenement is left behind at death and nothing else.*

At death the embodied self leaves only the gross physical body, but departs with the subtle body and the causal body underlying it. With the subtle body all its components, i.e., the five prāṇas (the five phases of the vital principle), the five organs of perception, the five motor organs, and the mind (antaḥkaraṇa), go with him.[6] With the mind all its contents go. Nothing belonging to the physical body or the outer world can the departing soul take with him, but nothing of the mind can he leave behind. The impressions of his karma, comprising his merits and demerits, his right and wrong ideas, his good and evil tendencies and capacities, invariably go with him. These are the factors that determine his journey beyond. Just as a man's inner attitudes and thoughts determine his life's course before his death, so do they after his death. His immediate course depends on what thought prevails in his mind at the time of death. A man's habitual thought naturally becomes predominant at the time he leaves the body.

Says Śrī Kṛṣṇa: "Thinking of whatever object at the time of death a person leaves the body, that very object, O son of Kuntī, he attains, being constantly absorbed in its thought."[7]

In the waking state a man's organs, mind, and the five prāṇas, though belonging to the subtle body, operate on the gross body. In the dream state the organs and the mind are withdrawn to the subtle body, and in dreamless sleep to the causal body; but the five prāṇas continue to function in the gross body as in the waking state. The

[3]See Pr.U. VI:4, "He created prāṇa, from prāṇa faith, ākāśa, air, fire, water, earth, the organs, mind, food, from food vitality, austerity, hymns, sacrificial rites, the worlds, and in the worlds names."

[4]Sv.U. V:10-14.

[5]Mu.U. III:2.2.

[6]See Ch. II, sec. 7, "The constitution of the subtle body."

[7]BG VIII:6.

organs, the mind, and the five prāṇas of a dying man recede from the gross body and enter the subtle body, to which they belong. They all gather in the heart, where the subtle body in association with the radiant self is located. Then the subtle body along with the self leaves the gross body. Its departure means death. It is the gross body that becomes dead, and not the departing self. But people say that the man is dead. Or, it can be said that the self clothed with the subtle body withdraws the subtle organs, the mind (antaḥkaraṇa), and the five prāṇas, and then leaves the gross body. As we have noted above, the causal body underlies the subtle body.

3. *How a person dies.*

The process of death is thus described in the *Bṛhadāraṇyaka Upaniṣad:*

> When this [embodied] self apparently becomes weak and loses the power of discrimination [here the conditions of the body and other adjuncts are attributed to the self], the organs come to it. Completely withdrawing these particles of light [the organs and their functions] it comes to the heart [because the radiance of consciousness is withdrawn and becomes manifest only in the heart]. When the presiding deity of the eyes turns back from all sides [when the eyes fail to receive the light of the sun], the man cannot notice color.[8]

Further, it is said that every organ and the mind as well become united with the subtle body of the dying man:

> [The eye] becomes united with the subtle body; then people say, "He does not see." [The nose] becomes so united; then they say, "He does not smell." [The tongue] becomes united; then they say, "He does not taste." [The vocal organ] becomes united; then they say "He does not speak." [The ear] becomes united; then they say, "He does not hear." [The manas] becomes united; then they say, "He does not think." [The skin, the organ of touch] becomes united; then they say, "He does not touch." [The buddhi, cognitive mind] becomes united; then they say, "He does not know."[9]

After all the ten organs, the mind (antaḥkaraṇa), and the five prāṇas unite within the heart, the self leaves the body. How? The same Upaniṣad describes:

[8] Br.U. IV:4.1.
[9] *Ibid.* IV:4.2.

The top [nerve-end] of the heart brightens [the impressions of karma gathered in the mind are lit up by the luminous self as in the dream state. Those thoughts, experiences, and desires that prevail at the time determine the way the self departs].[10] Coming out through the brightened top, the self departs through the eye, or through the head or through any other aperture of the body. When it departs the prāṇa follows; when prāṇa departs all the organs follow. [The self is accompanied by prāṇa and all the organs including the mind. In fact, they leave together.][11]

A knower of Saguṇa Brahman leaves the body through the aperture in the crown of the head, which is called *Brahma-randhra.* He goes to Brahmalōka, from where there is no return to the mortal plane.[12] The souls departing by other channels are subject to rebirth. Śaṅkara observes:

Although the brightening of the top of the heart is the same for him who has the knowledge [of Saguṇa Brahman] and for him who does not have the knowledge and although the exit is lighted up thereby, yet the knower of Saguṇa Brahman departs invariably from the crown of the head, whereas others depart from other parts of the body. Why? It is due to the power of knowledge.[13]

The Upaniṣads quote the following verse on this point:

There are one hundred and one nāḍīs [nerves][14] of the heart, one of which pierces the crown of the head. Going forward by it, a man attains immortality. Other nerves going in different directions, only serve as channels for his departure from the body.[15]

4. *The attainment of immortality.*

Śrī Kṛṣṇa describes how a worshipper of Saguṇa Brahman leaves the body meditating on Him at the time of death and attains immortality:

He attains that ever shining Supreme Being who meditates at the time of death on the omniscient, ancient Internal Ruler, the One Sustainer of all, subtler than the subtle [being the finest of all existences],

[10]Cf. Ānanda-giri's gloss on S. com.
[11]Br.U. IV:4.2.
[12]See Br.U. VI:2.15; BS IV:4.22.
[13]BS IV:2.17, S. com.
[14]The Sanskrit term of the text is *nāḍī.* See footnote 14, p. 106.
[15]Ch.U. VIII:6.6; Ka.U. II:3.16.

> incomprehensible, resplendent as the sun, and beyond darkness, with a steady mind, filled with devotion and the power of concentration, wholly fixing the prāṇa between the eye-brows.[16]
>
> Closing all the doors of the senses, confining the mind within the heart, fixing the life-breath in the head, engaged in yōgic concentration, uttering the monosyllabic Ōm, which is Brahman, and meditating on Me, he who departs leaving the body, attains the Supreme Goal.
>
> I am easily attainable, O Pārtha, by that ever steadfast yōgī who constantly remembers Me from day to day with single-mindedness.
>
> Having attained Me, the great-souled ones have no more birth, which is the abode of misery and transitory, for they have reached the highest Goal.[17]

After dwelling in Brahmalōka, the highest realm in the cosmic order, for aeons, the knowers of Saguṇa Brahman realize Nirguṇa Brahman and attain final liberation at the cosmic dissolution, along with Hiraṇyagarbha, the Presiding Deity of Brahmalōka.[18] This is called "Gradual Liberation (krama-mukti)" as distinct from "Immediate Liberation (sadya-mukti)" achieved by those who realize Nirguṇa Brahman in this very life. In both cases the final Liberation is the same, whatever difference there may be in the way of reaching the Goal, which is complete absorption of the individual self in formless, featureless, attributeless Brahman, in which there is no distinction of any kind whatsoever.[19]

Even while living in the body a seeker of Nirguṇa Brahman can realize identity of the individual self with Brahman without the one being completely merged in the other. So says the *Kaṭha Upaniṣad:*

> When all desires that cling to one's heart drop, then a mortal becomes immortal and attains Brahman here [while living on the earth].
>
> When all the knots of the heart [ego-ideas rooted in ajñāna] are broken even while one is living, forthwith a mortal becomes immortal [by realizing the true nature of the self]. This much only is the instruction [of all the Upaniṣads].[20]

After leaving the body he traverses no path. So it is said:

> Those who are eager to go beyond paths [the journey of life here and hereafter] tread no path.[21]

[16]BG VIII:9,10.
[17]*Ibid.* VIII:12-15.
[18]See BS IV:3.10; also *Kūrma-Purāṇa* I:12.269 quoted in VP VII.
[19]See Pr.U. VI:5; Mu.U. III:2.8.
[20]Ka.U. II:3.14, 15.
[21]Quoted in S. com. on Mu.U. III:2.6.

> Just as the footmarks of birds cannot be traced in the sky or of fish in water, so is the departure of the illumined.[22]

The body of the jīvanmukta (the living-free) drops as soon as the remnant of the impressions of past karma, to which it owes its existence, runs out. Forthwith his individualized self, freed from the limiting adjuncts rooted in ajñāna, merges in Brahman. So says the *Kaṭha Upaniṣad:* "As pure water poured in pure water becomes verily the same, so also does the self of the sage who realizes [Nirguṇa] Brahman."[23]

His subtle body readily dissolves, whereas the physical body is cast off, like the slough of a snake, and disintegrates in due course. As stated in the *Bṛhadāraṇyaka Upaniṣad:*

> Of him who is without desires, who is free from desires, the objects of whose desires have been attained, and to whom all objects of desire are but the self — the organs [which belong to the subtle body] do not depart. Being but Brahman, he is merged in Brahman.
>
> Regarding this there is this verse: "When all the desires that dwell in his heart are eradicated, then the mortal man becomes immortal and *attains Brahman here* [in this very body]."
>
> Just as the slough of a snake lies dead and cast away on an anthill, so does the body lie. Then the self becomes disembodied and immortal, becomes the Supreme Self, Brahman, the Light.[24]

The attainment of the Ultimate Goal by the knower of Nirguṇa Brahman is graphically presented by the *Muṇḍaka Upaniṣad:*

> As rivers flowing down merge in the ocean, giving up their names and forms, even so do the illumined ones, being free from names and forms, attain the resplendent, all-transcendent Being. He who knows that Supreme Brahman verily becomes Brahman.[25]

The process of death is the same for the illumined and the unillumined, that is to say, for those who realize Nirguṇa Brahman and others who do not. At the time of death each soul — together with the organs, the mind, and the prāṇas — reposes in Pure Being, Brahman. While the soul of a knower of Nirguṇa Brahman merges in Brahman, being altogether free from the veil of ajñāna, the souls of

[22] Mbh. (Śānti-parva) 239.24, *ibid.*
[23] Ka.U. II:1.15.
[24] Br.U. IV:4.6,7.
[25] Mu.U. III:2.8.

others, including the knowers of Saguṇa Brahman, do not because of the intervening ajñāna.[26] Therefore, they emerge from that state and depart from the body. In Śaṅkara's view even a knower of Saguṇa Brahman is without the fullness of knowledge (avidvān), because he has not realized his identity with Brahman and gained the vision of the Ultimate Reality, Nondual Brahman. Consequently, his soul departs from the body although he is not reborn, whereas other departing souls are subject to rebirth.[27]

It is to be noted that in the case of a knower of Saguṇa Brahman the projecting power of ajñāna persists all along, its veiling power being eliminated at the time of realizing Brahman, but he knows multiplicity to be unreal. An ignorant man may see the mirage and be misled by it, while a wise man may see the mirage and know it to be false.

5. *On the eve of the soul's departure.*

That the souls of all become united with Brahman at death is thus indicated by the sage Uddālaka Aruṇi to his son Śvetaketu:

> Around a [dying] man afflicted with the infirmities of age, my dear son, his relatives gather and ask, "Do you know me?" "Do you know me?" He recognizes them as long as his organ of speech is not withdrawn into his mind, his mind into his prāṇa [vital air], and his prāṇa into heat [udāna] and the heat [udāna] into Supreme Being.
>
> But when his organ of speech is withdrawn into his mind, his mind into his prāṇa, his prāṇa into heat [udāna] and the heat [udāna] into the Supreme Being then he does not know them.[28]

Behind a man's speech is his thought. As he thinks so he speaks. Indeed, the mind is at the back of all the organs. Even when all the organs cease to function the mind can still function. This happens particularly in the dream state. Then again, when the mind ceases to

[26]Ajñāna or avidyā, usually translated as ignorance or nescience, does not mean the absence or the negation, but the reverse, of knowledge. It is anti-knowledge, which terminates with the knowledge of Reality. It has two distinct functions: (1) it veils Brahman the Supreme Being, and (2) it projects the manifold. It is because of this that the jīva fails to perceive the unity or the identity of the self with Brahman, and experiences multiple things and beings as real in themselves. His ajñāna or avidyā is the cause of both inapprehension and misapprehension. There can be inapprehension of the Real without its misapprehension, as in deep sleep, but hardly can there be misapprehension without inapprehension.

[27]See BS IV:2.7.

[28]Ch.U. VI:15.1,2. See also S. com.

function, still the life principle (prāṇa) continues to function as in dreamless sleep. When the breath of a dying man fails, that is to say, when the vital air (mukhya prāṇa, responsible for respiration) ceases to function, even then udāna maintains heat in the body. Therefore, we can know whether he is alive or not by feeling the warmth or heat in the body. So it is said prāṇa is withdrawn into heat (udāna). Udāna is the last to be associated with the self. The self in association with udāna is withdrawn into the Supreme Being.

It is said that udāna guards the upper part of the heart.[29] It leads the soul out of the body at death. Then the body loses all heat. So says the *Praśna Upaniṣad:*

> And the udāna moving upward through one of them [one of the one hundred and one nāḍīs (nerves) that is called suṣumnā] leads the departing soul to the world of the virtuous in consequence of his virtuous deeds, to the world of the sinful in consequence of his sinful deeds, and to the human world in consequence of both.
>
> Fire verily is udāna. Therefore, he whose fire has ceased goes to rebirth with his organs entered into the mind.
>
> Whatever is a [dying] man's thinking [according to the impressions of his karma prevalent at the time] with that he enters into prāṇa. Prāṇa joined with udāna and in association with the self leads to the world contemplated.[30]

As stated by the *Bṛhadāraṇyaka Upaniṣad:*

> Then [at the time of the departure] the self has a particular consciousness [mental modifications arising from the impressions of karma as in dream]. Attended with that consciousness he moves towards the goal related to it. He is equipped with acquired knowledge of all sorts, with work [righteous and unrighteous], and with the past experience [of the results of his endeavors].[31]

It is the impressions of knowledge, work, and past experience that are particularly meant here. Śaṅkara remarks in this context:

> The self journeying to the next world is attended with knowledge of all sorts, those that are enjoined or forbidden and those that are neither enjoined nor forbidden; with work enjoined or forbidden, and neither enjoined nor forbidden; and also with past experience (pūrva-prajñā), that is, the impressions of experiences regarding the results of past endeavors. These impressions take part in initiating fresh actions and

[29]Ch.U. III:13.5.
[30]Pr.U. III:7,9,10.
[31]Br.U. IV:4.2.

> also in bringing past actions to fruition; hence they too accompany. Without these impressions no action can be done, nor any results of past actions achieved, for the organs are not skillful in unpracticed work.
>
> But when the organs are prompted to work by the impressions of past experience, they can easily attain skill even without practice in this life. It is frequently observed that some are expert in certain kinds of work, such as painting, from their very birth, even without practice in this life, while others are unskillful even in some very easy tasks. Similarly, in the experience of sense-objects some are observed to be naturally skillful or dull. All this is due to the revival or nonrevival of past experience. Therefore, without past experience we cannot understand how anybody can proceed to do any work or to enjoy the fruits of past work.
>
> Hence these three — knowledge, work, and past experience — are the provisions on the way to the next world, corresponding to a migrant's cartload of equipment. Since these three are the means of attaining another body and experiencing the fruits of one's past karma, therefore one should cultivate only the salutary forms of them, so that one may have a desirable body and desirable experiences. This is the purport of the whole passage.[32]

While leaving the old body the departing soul assumes a very fine physical vesture caused by the impressions prevalent in the mind at the time. This has the potentiality of the next gross body intended for reaping the fruits of his karma. It is constituted of the subtle parts of the five gross elements. These are called *bhūta-sūkṣmas,* and are distinct from the sūkṣma-bhūtas, the five subtle elements.[33]

The Upaniṣad gives an illustration on this point:

> Just as a leech supported on a straw goes to the end of it, takes hold of another support [blade of straw] and contracts itself, so does the self throw this body aside, make it senseless [by withdrawing itself from it], take hold of another support [body], and contract itself [dwells within].[34]

Śaṅkara remarks:

> The impressions, called past experience [pūrva-prajñā], under the control of the person's knowledge and work, stretch out like a leech, from the body, retaining their seat in the heart, as in the dream state, and build another body in accordance with his past karma; they leave their seat, the old body, as the new body is made.[35]

[32] Br.U. IV:4.2, S. com.
[33] See BS III:1, S. com.
[34] Br.U. IV:4.3.
[35] *Ibid.* S. com.

It is worthy of note that until the individual self merges in Nondual Brahman it has all along the three bodies — the gross, the subtle, and the causal. Speaking generally, the departing souls take the following courses: (1) the way to Brahmalōka (Kingdom of God), (2) the way to svargalōka (heaven or paradise), (3) the way to the human plane, (4) the way to the subhuman region. Excepting the first all lead to birth and rebirth.

6. *The way to Brahmalōka.*

Those who worship Saguṇa Brahman with whole-souled devotion and succeed in realizing Him, go to Brahmalōka, which is the highest plane in the relative order. They clearly discriminate the self from the not-self as light from shade.[36] They perceive the reality of the one and the unreality of the other. To them the Supreme Lord becomes manifest as the One Self of all. Presumably they dwell in Satyalōka, the topmost realm of Brahmalōka. According to Advaita Vedānta the highest heavens of all genuine worshippers of the Personal God are included in Satyalōka. The two lower regions of Brahmalōka are Taparlōka and Janalōka. With their minds purged of all merit and demerit accruing from work and released from all attachment to the temporal rooted in ajñāna, these worshippers get free forever from the cycle of birth and rebirth. Having seen the Light of all lights they no longer live in darkness.

After leaving the gross body their souls invariably traverse a luminous path leading to Brahmalōka. It makes no difference whether they die in broad daylight or at pitch-dark tempestuous night, whether a funeral service is held for them or not. They invariably enter the luminous path signalized by fire, light, daytime, the bright lunar fortnight, the six months of the sun's northward journey (from the winter to the summer solstice, when the day gains daily over night). "Departing by this path the knowers of (Saguṇa) Brahman attain Brahman," says Śrī Kṛṣṇa.[37] This is the way usually called *deva-yāna,* lit. the path of the gods marked by light. The ardent seekers of God develop spiritual consciousness, get out of darkness and walk in light during their lifetime. No wonder after death they traverse the path of light and reach the realm where God is ever manifest beyond the panorama of dualities. This is the Kingdom of God (Brahmalōka) other than Paradise (Svargalōka).

Says the *Chāndōgya Upaniṣad:*

[36]See Ka.U. II:3.5. [37]BG VIII:24.

> When such persons who meditate on Brahman as the seer of sight, as the repository of all blessedness, as the dispenser of all blessings, as the Light that manifests all, depart, whether funeral rites are performed for them or not, they go to light, from light to day, from day to bright lunar fortnight, from bright fortnight to the six months of the sun's northward journey, from these to the year, from the year to the sun, from the sun to the moon, from the moon to lightning. There a person, who is not a human being, meets them and leads them to the Conditioned Brahman, the presiding deity of Brahmalōka. This is the path of gods, the path to Brahmalōka. Those who go by it do not return to the turmoil of human life; yea, they do not return.[38]

In the *Bṛhadāraṇyaka Upaniṣad* there is a similar account of the soul's journey to Brahmalōka.[39]

Only those who turn away from the noneternal and wholeheartedly seek the Eternal by appropriate methods go there. They reach the end of the transmigratory process and do not return to the human world.

As stated in the *Praśna Upaniṣad:*

> But those who seek the Self through austerity, chastity, faith, and knowledge proceed along the Northern course and attain the sun [the Self as the source of all life and light]. This is verily the sustainer of all lives. There is no death nor fear. This is the final goal. From this they do not come back. This is closed for the ignorant.[40]

The *Muṇḍaka Upaniṣad* specifically mentions those who are qualified for attaining to Brahmalōka:

> The forest-dwellers living on alms [the anchorites and others who retire from the world for religious meditation] and the self-controlled, wise householders who perform the duties pertaining to their respective stages of life and practice meditation [on Saguṇa Brahman], after being free from merit and demerit [consequent on work attended with secular desires] go by the path of the sun [the bright route] where is manifest the immortal, undecaying Puruṣa [the Omnipresent Being].[41]

Brahmalōka is the legitimate abode of the ardent worshippers of Saguṇa Brahman. Once there, they never return to the death-bound world. They get out of the cycle of birth and rebirth forever. Others may go there by virtue of their extraordinary achievements, such as

[38] Ch.U. IV:15.
[39] See Br.U. VI:2.15.
[40] Pr.U. I:10.
[41] Mu.U. I:2.11. See also Ch.U. V:10.1,2.

the knowledge of "the doctrine of the five fires (pañcāgni-vidyā),"[42] the performance of aśvamedha (horse-sacrifice), and the observance of unflinching continence; but they cannot stay there permanently. They have to come back to the plane of dualities sooner or later. Presumably they reach the lower regions of Brahmalōka, such as Taparlōka and Janalōka.

Nonreturn from Brahmalōka is assuredly for such as adore Saguṇa Brahman for the attainment of Liberation through the knowledge of Nirguṇa Brahman. It is they who merge in Nondual Brahman at the dissolution of Brahmalōka, which after all belongs to the order of becoming.[43] The ardent seekers of Nirguṇa Brahman who fail to reach the Goal during their lifetime usually go to Brahmalōka. According to the Upaniṣads, there is no return for the released souls that have attained Saguṇa Brahman and reached Brahmalōka.[44] In the case of the seekers of Nirguṇa Brahman who get rid of their ignorance (ajñāna), Liberation, which is uncaused and self-existent, naturally proceeds. There cannot be any question as to their nonreturn. It is a settled fact.[45]

7. *The way to Svargalōka (Paradise).*

Not satisfied with the enjoyment of prosperity and pleasure in this earthly life, which is of short duration and yet infested with obstacles, human minds hanker after perpetual happiness in the world beyond, where there is no impediment of any kind. From ancient times there have been men and women among various nations of the world who have dreamt of a heaven or paradise where there is no misery, no disease, no decrepitude, no death, no evil whatsoever and where the dwellers enjoy perpetual youth, beauty, and strength to the full satisfaction of their desires. The Vedic teachers do not deny the existence of such a heaven, or celestial region where the highest fulfillment of man's sense desires is possible. Nay, they even prescribe courses for its attainment. Human beings in general cannot relinquish relative good within reach and strive after the far off Supreme Good until they are fully convinced of the inherent inadequacy of the former by actual experience here and hereafter. Children cannot turn away from toys and dolls until they outgrow their child-mentality.

[42]Ch.U. V:5-10.
[43]BS IV:3.10.
[44]Br.U. VI:2.15; Ch.U. VIII:15.1; Ka.U. II:3.16.
[45]BS IV:4.22, S. com.

While recommending the ways to the celestial region or paradise (Svargalōka) the Vedic teachers at the same time point out its limitations. There is no access to eternal life through it. None can stay there forever. The seekers of celestial enjoyments have to come back to the human plane, where alone they can find the way to Liberation, freedom from all misery and the attainment of Supreme Bliss. It is foolishness to delay the attainment of Peace and Bliss everlasting while coveting transitory treasures and pleasures here and hereafter.

In the *Kaṭha Upaniṣad* the Brahmin boy Naciketā speaks to the King of Death about Svargalōka:

> In Svargalōka there is no fear whatsoever. You, O King of Death, are not there. No apprehension of old age is there. Going beyond both hunger and thirst, and beyond the reach of sorrow, all rejoice there.[46]

Yet Naciketā rejects the most covetable pleasures and possessions here and hereafter liberally offered by the King of Death. Says the boy:

> Ephemeral are they, O King of Death. Yet they sap the vigor of all the organs of the mortal man. Moreover, the longest life is short indeed. Let these chariots, dances, and music ever be yours.
>
> Man cannot be gratified by possessions. . . . What decaying mortal on the earth here below having come close to the undecaying immortals and knowing the truth (that his highest purpose can be attained through them) will exult in long life, while convinced of the futility of music, dalliance, and enjoyments? Tell me, O King of Death, of the Great Beyond regarding which man has misgiving. No other boon than this that penetrates the inscrutable does Naciketā ask for.[47]

Apart from the seeker's faith in the existence of the soul after separation from the body, it is the observance of daily duties, the practice of righteousness including charity, and the performance of humanitarian deeds that pave the way to heaven. This threefold duty is indicated by the terms *Iṣṭa* and *Pūrta.* Iṣṭa includes daily oblation to fire called *agnihōtra,* austerity, truthfulness, kindness to all creatures, hospitality, and the offerings to all deities. Pūrta includes such philanthropic deeds as the excavation of water-tanks, wells, canals, etc., and the establishment of temples, almshouses, and resthouses. According to Manu, Iṣṭa and Pūrta steadily performed with earnestness and devotion by means of wealth earned by honest

[46] Ka.U. 1:1.12. [47] *Ibid.* 1:1, 26-29.

means leads to enduring bliss (Svargalōka). The same is preparatory to Liberation if performed with no desire for the temporal.[48]

The *Chāndōgya Upaniṣad* adds to Iṣṭa and Pūrta a third type of righteous deeds called *Datta* (gift) as a means of going to heaven (Svargalōka). By this threefold work the householders can acquire adequate merit for reaching heaven by the same dark path which is marked by smoke, nighttime, etc.[49] Datta includes the rescuing of refugees, noninjury of creatures, the giving of gifts other than those at the altar.

That man can also go to Svargalōka by the right performance of his duties according to his social order and stage of life (svadharma) is thus indicated by Śrī Kṛṣṇa:

> Fortunate indeed are the Kṣatriyas, O Pārtha, who are called to fight in such a battle that comes unsought as an open gate to heaven.
>
> Dying on the battlefield as a hero thou gainest heaven; conquering, thou enjoyest the earth. Therefore arise, O Son of Kuntī, resolved to fight.[50]

The way to Svargalōka is through darkness typifying the seekers' ignorance of Truth. After death they traverse a dark path signalized by smoke, nighttime, the dark fortnight, the six months of the sun's southward journey (from the summer to the winter solstice when the night gains daily). "Taking this path, the seeker, attaining the lunar light [heaven where the semi-darkness of ignorance prevails] returns," says Śrī Kṛṣṇa.[51] One cannot get out of the cycle of birth and rebirth by staying in heaven, no matter how long.

Says the *Muṇḍaka Upaniṣad:*

> Deluded persons regarding Iṣṭa and Pūrta as most important do not know anything higher [the way to Liberation]. Having enjoyed on the heights of heaven the fruits of their good deeds by which they go there, they enter again this world or an inferior one.[52]

The way to Brahmalōka and the way to Svargalōka are thus contrasted by Śrī Kṛṣṇa: "Verily, these two — the path of light and the path of darkness — are regarded the perennial routes of the world

[48]MS IV:226, Kullūka's com.

[49]Ch.U. V:10.3.

[50]BG II:32,37. The duty of the Kṣatriyas is to protect the virtuous and subdue the wicked.

[51]BG VIII:25.

[52]Mu.U. I:2.10.

[which is without beginning and end]. Following the one a man does not come back and following the other he is reborn."[53]

8. *Descent from Svargalōka and rebirth.*

When the merits of righteous deeds that take the seekers to Svargalōka are exhausted, they cannot stay there any more. The impressions of their residual deeds that were dormant so long or were overpowered by the meritorious deeds, being now ready to bear fruits, lead them to the human plane or to a lower order of life according to the nature of the residual deeds. So says Śrī Kṛṣṇa: "Having enjoyed that vast heavenly sphere (Svargalōka) until their merits are exhausted, they enter the mortal world. Thus, the seekers of the objects of sense-desire who follow the way of the Vedic rites are destined to come and go."[54] They are bound to the round of birth and rebirth.

In Svargalōka none has to work to fulfill his desire. Where there is no karma no new acquisition is possible. It is like a vacation resort where people go and live happily without work and spend what they earned elsewhere by the sweat of their brow. As soon as their earnings are spent they have to come back to the place of work. The denizens of Svargalōka are like the happy-go-lucky scions of wealthy families who do not take life seriously and spend their time in innocent diversions. Human life is the only sphere of karma. Consequently, when their resources are exhausted the departed souls, after their stay in Svargalōka, descend with the residual karma along the same path by which they ascend or by a different path.

The *Brahma-sūtras* affirms the soul's return to the mundane life: "On the exhaustion of the meritorious deeds [that lead to Svargalōka] the soul returns with residual karma by the same route by which it went or by a different route, as declared by the Śruti and the Smṛti."[55]

The soul's descent to the world is thus depicted by the *Chāndōgya Upaniṣad:*

> Having dwelt there [in the lunar world, Svargalōka] till their merits are exhausted they return again [because this is not their first descent] the same way they came. They come to ākāśa, from ākāśa to air. Having become air they become smoke. Having become smoke they become light cloud.

[53]BG VIII:26. [54]BG IX:21. [55]BS III:1.8.

> After having become light cloud they become rain-bearing cloud. Having become rain-bearing cloud they fall as rain. They are born in the world as rice and barley, herbs and trees, as sesame plants and beans. From these the release is more difficult [than in earlier stages]; for whoever [with the power of procreation] eats the food and sows the seed, the soul becomes like unto him [assumes the similar physical body].[56]

Only the soul's temporary contact with ākāśa, air, smoke, cloud, rain, etc., is meant here. The soul does not turn into any of these inanimate objects, or assume their forms. Nor is the soul born as rice, barley, herb, tree, or any other plant. It merely becomes associated with them as with vehicles. All these various objects, inanimate and animate, serve only as the mediums of transmission or as the successive stages in the soul's journey to the kind of birth to which it is directed by the residual karma. To pass through these stages is less difficult than to pass through a woman's womb.[57] It is the law of karma that determines the soul's movement towards its destination, and not natural force, or chance, or destiny.

We quote below the pertinent remarks of Śaṅkara:

> As the attainment of the states of air, smoke, etc., by the souls coming down with residual karma consists in their mere contact with these [inanimate objects], so also the attainment of the states of paddy, etc., consists merely in their contact with those that are such because of birth.[58]
>
> So the souls with residual karma have mere contact with paddy, etc., in which other souls are dwelling. For this reason, one has to reject the primary meaning of the word *born* and also the state of plant life as the seat of experience [for the descending souls]. Yet we do not deny the plant life being a state for experiencing the fruits of work. Let this be a seat of experience for those souls which, owing to their lack of merit, have attained the state of plant life. But the souls descending from the moon [Svargalōka] with their residual karma do not experience the fruits of their karma [of paddy, etc.] by being identified with plant life. This is what we hold.[59]
>
> Hence the mere association with paddy, etc., of the souls descending from the moon [Svargalōka] with their residual karma is indirectly spoken of as becoming those plants.[60]

The soul gains its new body from a womb.[61] After being

[56]Ch.U. V:10.5,6.
[57]See BS III:1.23.
[58]BS III:1.24, S. com.
[59]*Ibid.*
[60]BS III:1.25, S. com.
[61]BS III:1.27.

connected with a progenitor the soul with the residual karma enters a womb and gains a body suited to the experience of its karma. The birth is high or low according to the nature of the residual karma.

As long as a person is attached to the temporal his stock of impressions accrued from work cannot be exhausted, nor can it be wholly good or wholly evil; so there must be the predominance of good, or the predominance of evil, or the evenness of the two. While experiencing the results of fructifying karma man performs new karma and accumulates new impressions. Besides, he has other impressions in store, which he has carried over from the past life and which must be of mixed character. These impressions may be partly dormant and partly overpowered. The impressions other than the fructifying can be rectified or eliminated by different methods, including expiatory deeds as we have noted before. (See Ch. V, sec. 6.)

Whoever works with secular desires must acquire impressions good or evil according to the nature of the work. But even good work cannot be altogether free from evil elements. Charity without discrimination can do more harm than good. So even in doing good work a person cannot avoid evil impressions altogether. Then again, even a virtuous person cannot do good consistently. He may also do wrong unintentionally for lack of understanding. Similarly, a wrongdoer cannot do wrong and wrong alone. Even his misdeeds may have some good elements in them. For instance, a keen sense of obligation to his family may drive a person to an act of theft.

We have seen how good as well as evil results of work cause bondage for the worker who seeks them (see Ch. V, sec. 6). In order to be free he has to relinquish the desire for both. In the words of Śrī Kṛṣṇa: "The threefold fruit of action — disagreeable, agreeable, and mixed — awaits the nonrelinquishers [of fruit] after death, but not the relinquishers."[62] So we find that a man who goes to heaven as a result of his meritorious deeds may perchance have some evil impressions predominant in him on the exhaustion of his merits. Consequently, such a person, on coming down from heaven (Svargalōka) will have a low birth in the human plane or may even descend to the subhuman level. But this rarely happens. Usually those who return from heaven are reborn on high levels of life. Yet there is a remote possibility of low birth even for them. Says the *Chāndōgya Upaniṣad:*

[62]BG XVIII:12.

> Those whose conduct here [on earth] has been good [and consequently their residual karma] will quickly attain some good birth — birth as a brāhmaṇa, birth as a kṣatriya, or birth as a vaiśya. But those whose conduct here has been evil [and consequently their residual karma] will quickly attain some evil birth as a dog, birth as a pig, or birth as a caṇḍāla [an outcast].[63]

Here the main purpose of the Upaniṣad is to encourage the doers of good deeds and admonish the evildoers.

Those who return from heaven have, as a rule, good saṁskāras (impressions of karma) prevalent in them. Consequently, they are born as noteworthy human beings in a favorable situation. As declared by one of the Smṛtis:

> Men belonging to different castes and stages of life who are steadfast in their respective duties experience the fruits of their actions in the next world, and then by virtue of their residual karma they are born in notable places, castes, and families, endowed with beauty, longevity, knowledge, good conduct, wealth, happiness, and intelligence.[64]

9. *But no woe ever betides a spiritual aspirant even though he may fail to reach the Goal in his lifetime.*

As we have noted above, the spiritual aspirants who succeed in realizing Brahman, Saguṇa or Nirguṇa, are not reborn. All others are subject to rebirth. A spiritual aspirant who fails to reach the Goal before death is invariably born under very favorable circumstances. This is evident from the following dialogue between Arjuna and Śrī Kṛṣṇa:

> He who, though possessed of faith, is not steadfast in practice, whose mind wanders away from the Ideal — failing to reach the goal of Yōga, what way does he go, O Kṛṣṇa?
>
> Does he not, O mighty-armed one [Kṛṣṇa], fallen from both [the temporal and the eternal] and without support, perish like a cloud rent asunder, being deluded on the way to Brahman?
>
> This doubt of mine, O Kṛṣṇa, Thou shouldst completely dispel; for there is none but Thee who can dispel this doubt.
>
> Verily, neither here nor hereafter, O Pārtha [Arjuna], is there destruction for him; for he who strives after the Supreme Good never comes to grief, O dear friend.

63Ch.U. V:10.7.

64Quoted by Śaṅkara, BS III:1.8, com.

> Having attained the worlds of the righteous and lived there for many, many years, he who has fallen from Yōga [because of the subliminal desires for experiencing the fruits of his meritorious deeds] is reborn in the house of the purehearted and prosperous.
>
> Or, he is reborn only in the family of the yōgīs possessed of wisdom. Such a birth is rare indeed in this world.
>
> There he regains the understanding acquired in the previous birth and strives for perfection harder than before, O descendant of Kuru [Arjuna].
>
> By that very previous practice he is irresistibly carried away. Even an inquirer after Yōga [spiritual knowledge] goes beyond the Vedas [attains greater results than the results of the Vedic rites intended for temporal good].
>
> Verily, a yōgī [spiritual aspirant] who strives assiduously, being purified of all sins and gaining perfection through many births, then reaches the supreme Goal.[65]

10. *The departing soul assumes a body according to the nature of its karma (thoughts and deeds). Reincarnation in human form is inevitable in due course.*

Among the seekers of temporal good there are some in whom merits (the impressions of righteous deeds) far exceed their demerits (the impressions of unrighteous deeds). They go to Svargalōka in case they crave it. Otherwise, they are soon reborn as virtuous human beings in conditions favorable to spiritual awakening. Then there are many in whom merits and demerits are more or less balanced. They, too, after leaving the body do not go very far, but are reborn as human beings in a year or so. None but the extremely depraved persons who grossly abuse the privileges of human life — who prove to be brutes in human garb — go down to subhuman level after death. After leaving the human body they appear in their true forms. Some of them may be born as animals; some may degrade to plant life.[66] Others may enter the nether region.

But even in the subhuman level the impressions of their good karma whatsoever it be, remain overpowered for the time being. As soon as the impressions of vile thoughts and deeds that lead them there are exhausted, they are reborn on the human plane by virtue of their good saṁskāras. It is to be noted that according to Vedanta

[65]BG VI:37-45.

[66]It is to be noted that according to modern biologists, there is no clear-cut line of demarcation between plant life and animal life.

there is no perpetual retrogression, nor eternal perdition. Going down to hell or the nether region is like entering into a penitentiary. As soon as the evildoer's character is mended through suffering and grief he returns to the human plane in due course. Just as there is no new acquisition in Svargalōka, so it is in the nether region. The one is the place of vacation for enjoyment, the other is the place of suffering like a penitentiary. Neither is the sphere of karma.

The departing soul does not pass on to another body as is often assumed. In no case does it enter into a ready made habitation; rather it develops a new body in due course with the materials gained from heredity and environment. As we have noted above, at the time of passing out of the body the soul assumes a minute physical vesture that contains the potentiality of the next gross body. Just as a seed develops into a corresponding plant or tree by securing the necessary elements, so does this minute physical vesture develop into the corresponding body. The kind of physical body the departing soul assumes depends on the nature of the thoughts and the deeds (the impressions of karma) that prevail within him at the time of death. Says the *Kaṭha Upaniṣad:*

> Some souls enter into wombs for acquiring bodies, others enter into stationary life [such as plants] in accordance with their deeds and in accordance with their thoughts.[67]

But sooner or later every soul must come back to the human plane, where alone there is scope for the fulfillment of its highest destiny. There is no access to eternal life but through the human birth. Not only that. The human body is indispensable to life's development.

The doctrine that after leaving the human body the soul may successively assume animal and plant forms has been held by eminent Greek philosophers, such as Pythagoras, Empedocles, Plato. But unlike the Greek theory of metempsychosis, the Hindu view of transmigration emphasizes reincarnation in human form.

The force behind the whole process of evolution is the urge of the soul to be reinstated in its pristine purity and blissfulness, by regulating nature external and internal. The process is continuous throughout the living world.

[67]Ka.U. II:2.7.

CHAPTER VIII

HOW IS A MAN REBORN?

(Heredity and Environment Are Not Adequate to Account for a Man's Birth and Growth)

1. *The worldwide acceptance of the doctrine of reincarnation is due to its reasonableness.*

The doctrine of reincarnation is avowed particularly by Hinduism and Buddhism. It affirms the rebirth of a man in a new human body until he gets free from all attachment to the temporal. There are, however, subtle differences between the Hindu and the Buddhist views of reincarnation. I shall dwell on the subject from the Hindu viewpoint, that is to say, from the viewpoint of Vedanta.

The belief in the transmigration of the soul has not been confined only to Hinduism and Buddhism. Clear evidences of this belief are to be found in Greek thought; in the Zoroastrian scriptures; in the teachings of the Essenes, of the Pharisees; in the teachings of the early Fathers of the Christian Church, such as Justin Martyr, St. Clement of Alexandria, Origen; and also in the sayings of the Sufi mystics and poets. Primitive and tribal races in different regions of the world also hold to this belief. From the very beginning the human race has been confronted with the mysteries of birth as well as of death. Where does man come from? Where does he go? These are the natural inquiries of the human mind.

Concomitant with the belief in man's future existence there has been belief in his past existence as well. The words of Jesus Christ corroborate the doctrine of rebirth. Referring to John the Baptist he says: "And if ye will receive *it,* this is Elias, which was for to come. He that hath ears to hear, let him hear."[1] Existence after death presupposes existence before birth. What is beyond death must be

[1]Matt. 11:14,15.

beyond birth. Man's origination as well as destruction does not depend on the physical body.

The Scottish philosopher and historian, David Hume (1711-1776), observes: "The soul, therefore, if immortal, existed before our birth; and if the former existence no way concerned us, neither will the latter. . . . The Metempsychosis is therefore the only system of this kind that philosophy can hearken to."[2]

So says Swami Vivekananda: "If you are going to exist in eternity hereafter, it must be that you have existed through eternity in the past; it cannot be otherwise."[3] Eternal existence with a beginning is absurd. What begins in time must end in time.

The doctrine of reincarnation is a complement to the doctrine of karma. Man is reborn for the fulfillment of his karma. As he sows, so he reaps. The law of karma is the chain that ties man to the wheel of birth and rebirth. It is through karma that man is bound. And it is through karma that he can get free. Karma proves to be the cause of his bondage as long as a man clings to the temporal; but when he turns to the Eternal, karma opens the way to freedom. The twofold doctrine is based on a comprehensive and consistent view of human personality comprising its present, past, and future. It accounts for the settled facts of life. Being a rational interpretation of the drama of life and its mysteries, the doctrine has commended itself to the great thinkers of the world from ancient times to the modern age. Indeed, the doctrine of reincarnation, a sequence of the law of karma, has its supporters among the world's theologians, philosophers, mystics, scientists, poets, and psychologists. Writing on *Reincarnation and Karma, a Spiritual Philosophy Applied to the World Today,* L. Stanley Jast, Chief Librarian, Manchester, England, observes:

> The basic testimony to the truth of reincarnation is of a purely intellectual order. It rests on the ability of the conception to give significance and meaning to what would otherwise be without either, and this is the only kind of evidence of *any* truth, whether in the world of phenomena or the world of thought, which has ultimate value. It can be deduced from rigorous logic from the most elementary assumption of a moral order in the universe, and without *that* assumption there is not even a universe: there is merely a monstrous futility of a colossal nightmare.[4]

[2]David Hume, "On the Immortality of the Soul," in *Essays,* London, George Routledge and Sons, [1900?], pp.424-27.

[3]CW II, p.218.

[4]*Reincarnation, An East-West Anthology,* compiled and edited by Joseph Head and S. L. Cranston, New York, Julian Press, 1961, p.161.

2. *The recollection of one's past life and its verification.*

The fact that we do not remember the previous lives we lived does not disprove the doctrine of reincarnation. It is often argued: If we lived before as human beings, why do we not remember our past incarnations? Since we do not remember them the theory of reincarnation is not acceptable. But the point is, our existence or nonexistence does not depend on our memory. We do not have full recollection of our childhood days. Does this mean that we did not exist as children? We are likely to forget early periods of this very life. No wonder we do not remember our former life or lives. And it is a great blessing that we do not. Otherwise our present existence would have been complicated to the extreme. There would have been many a pretender, to say the least.

Even though human beings in general are oblivious of their previous lives, yet there have been exceptional cases of individuals in ancient and modern times who had memories of their past incarnation or incarnations. In many instances their recollections of past lives were verified.[5] According to Patañjali, by a special method

[5]It may not be out of place to record from personal knowledge an authentic case of intuitive memory of past life. In 1935 when I was in New Delhi I heard from an intimate friend, a teacher of Sanskrit in a high school, that a Brahmin girl of nine, Śanti Devi by name, who had been living with her parents in the old city, had had memories of her former life since she had been a child. The secretary of the local Y.M.C.A. personally requested me to investigate into the matter and ascertain the truth. But because of my preoccupation as the leader of the Ramakrishna Mission Ashrama in New Delhi I could not take up the investigation. Shortly after that I had to leave the city to make arrangements for my journey to the United States.

I gathered from different reliable sources that since the age of five the girl would remark from time to time with regard to certain food and dress, "I have eaten this before," "I have put on this before." The mother paid little attention to the child's prattle. But as she grew up she spoke more definitely of her experiences in her previous life. She often asserted that she had lived in Mathura (a city about 150 miles to the southeast of Delhi), that her husband was a cloth merchant, that she remembered his name but would not give it out (because an orthodox Hindu woman does not as a rule utter the husband's name). A grand uncle elicited from her the name and address of the husband, who was not a Brahmin, and who even came to Delhi when the case was related to him. He was accompanied by his son, who was one year older than Śanti Devi. As she saw the son she was deeply moved.

It was known upon inquiry that the mother of this boy died in a hospital in Mathura in 1925, shortly after giving birth to the son. Śanti Devi was born in Delhi in 1926. To verify the case a party of about ten noteworthy citizens, including the editor of a local daily paper, a commissioner of Delhi Municipality, and a college professor, went by train to Mathura accompanied by Śanti Devi, who had never been there before in this life. They discovered that Śanti Devi was well acquainted with the place and knew many details of the house where she claimed to have lived in her past life. She also visited with her former parents and had no difficulty in finding the house where they lived even then.

of meditation a person can awaken the memories of his past life. As stated in his Yōga-aphorism, "As a result of the perception of subliminal impressions one gains the knowledge of former lives."[6] The Sanskrit term for such recollection is *jāti-smara.* The Buddha is said to have remembered all his past lives.[7] Śrī Kṛṣṇa speaks of His past incarnations: "O Arjuna, many are the lives I have passed through and thou too. But I know them all, whilst thou knowest not, O Scorcher of foes."[8]

3. *A clear knowledge of man's present existence is the key to the knowledge of his past and his future existence.*

It is by knowing what man is and how he lives that we can determine where he comes from and where he goes. Without understanding his real nature we cannot understand what his birth or death really means. It has been well said that man is the central fact in all investigation.

A careful study of a human being and the allied facts points to the truth that man is not just a physical, or a biophysical, or a psychophysical being. The real man is the knowing self, the central principal of consciousness, which is the unchanging witness of the changing conditions of the body, the organs, the mind, and the external world. The indwelling self is the only constant factor in human personality that integrates all the physical and the psychical factors into a coherent whole, and coordinates the diverse functions of the mind, the organs, and the body. It maintains the identity of man despite all changes, external and internal. Man is essentially immortal spirit ever shining and it is this that is mainly responsible for the livingness of the psychophysical organism. "He is the life of life," says the Upaniṣad with regard to the real man.[9]

It is because of the real self — of the nature of pure consciousness — that every individual knows spontaneously that he is. He is aware of his own existence and the existence of all else that comes his way. It is this self-awareness that distinguishes all sentient creatures from material things. It is self-evident. It requires no proof. Being of contrary nature the changeless luminous self cannot originate from the body, the organs, or the mind, or from their functions. It is fundamental. It exists in the psychophysical organism from the very beginning. It is the sole regulatory principle of the changeful

[6]YS III:18.
[7]See *Samannaphala Sutta.*
[8]BG IV:5.
[9]Ken.U. I:2.

heterogenous factors in an individual. Its presence is the antecedent condition of the purposive behavior of a living being. Wherever there is livingness there is sentiency. Devoid of consciousness, explicit or implicit, any physical organization must be either a mechanical device or a material structure. Herein is the basic difference between the living and the nonliving.

Being immutable the self is beyond birth, growth, decay, and death. It is not born with the birth of the body, nor does it die when the body drops. As declared by Śrī Kṛṣṇa:

> This [the self] is never born, nor does it die. It is not that not having been it again comes into being. (Or, it is not that having been it again ceases to be.) This is unborn, eternal, changeless, though ancient ever new. It is not killed when the body is killed.[10]

4. *Neither the self nor the mind is inheritable.*

Now the question arises: Where does the self of a human offspring come from? The unborn self cannot originate either from the male or the female parent. Not the parent's body, nor the mind, nor any of the ten organs, none of which has consciousness inherent in it, can generate the luminous self, which is of contrary nature. It is absurd to hold that the self of the child can emerge from the father's or the mother's self, which is indivisible and immutable. Modern biology recognizes the mind but not the self. But without the recognition of the self, an unvarying spiritual principle in the psychophysical organism, the integration of the ever shifting physical and psychical factors and their processes, and also the direction of the whole towards a definite end, remains unexplained. As observed by Edmund Sinnott: "What pulls together the separate parts and processes of a plant or animal and knits them into an organism, and what draws this organism toward a developmental goal prefigured in its living stuff — these are problems where the confident progress of biology has made but little headway."[11]

It is equally impossible for the child to inherit the mind from either parent. An individual's mind is distinct from the self and the body as well, although closely associated with both. These three constituents cannot be identified with one another. Mental states and

[10]BG II:20.

[11]Edmund W. Sinnott, *The Bridge of Life: From Matter to Spirit*, New York, Simon and Schuster, 1966, p. 128.

functions are other than those of the body and the organs (see Ch. III, sec. 4). None of the organs can function unless the mind joins with it. But the mind can function even when the organs and the body are inoperative. It is through the mind conjoined with the senses that the self perceives physical objects. An individual functions as an organized system because of the coordination of these three primal constituents — the self, the mind, and the body. There can be no living organism without their correlation. From the organism's inception, the three exist as distinct principles. None of the three derives from the two others. Living processes are invariably psychophysical. A plan for self-development is immanent in the very embryo. With the plan there must be a planner. "It is *as if* an immanent principle inspired each cell with knowledge for the carrying out of a design," says Sir Charles Sherrington, the eminent physiologist.[12]

Unlike the physical body the mind is impartible. It is too subtle to be broken into parts. Amputation of the body does not cause the amputation of the mind. The receptacle of the mind remains the same while the contents change. It is the identity of the mind that maintains one's individuality beyond death and rebirth. Hence the child's mind cannot be a fragment of the parental mind. Nor can it arise from either parent's body or the self, being different by nature from both. What the offspring actually receives from the parents are the rudiments of its physical body. These can serve more or less as the medium for the transmission of the parents' physical characteristics to the offspring. Can the child's mind, and the self as well, develop from this physical source? If not, where do they come from?

5. *The meaning of heredity. The individual variations must have a real cause. These cannot be a matter of chance.*

The doctrine of reincarnation recognizes the general biological law that "like begets like." Humans are born of human parents, elephants of elephant parents, ants of ant parents. The same is true of plant life. A fig tree originates from another fig tree, an apple tree from another apple tree. A living thing comes from another living thing of the same species and never from lifeless matter. This property of self-reproduction common to all living things is known as heredity. It differentiates a living thing from nonliving matter. It is because of a

[12]Charles Sherrington, *Man on His Nature,* Gifford Lectures, 1937-38, New York, Macmillan and Co., 1941, p. 106.

vital difference between the two that the one cannot derive from the other. I quote below modern biologists' definitions of heredity:

> *Heredity, in the last analysis, is self-reproduction,* the common property of all life and the property that distinguishes living from nonliving matter.[13]
>
> Each new generation of organisms closely resembles its parents; the mating of two cats always produces cats and the mating of two Siamese cats always produces Siamese cats and not a different variety. Certain distinctive characteristics appear frequently in successive generations of a given family tree. Man has been aware for many centuries that "like begets like" and that new types of animals and plants may result when unlike forms are crossed. This tendency of individuals to resemble their progenitors is called *heredity.*[14]

This resemblance does not exclude individual variations. Heredity, in a wide sense, is inclusive of both similarity and divergence. Every creature, despite the resemblance it bears to its progenitors and to other creatures of the same descent, retains its individuality. Indeed, every living being is a distinct individual. What is the cause of this distinctiveness? The basic difference between one individual and another lies in their mental constitutions, which are not acquired from the parents. Even twin brothers widely differ in their inner nature despite the closest physical resemblance. Every individual brings into this life his own mind and develops in his own way. The root cause of variation is in the inner nature of the living being and not in environmental conditions. Modern genetics has not been able to find a satisfactory solution of the problem of variations.

Vedanta does not contradict modern biologists' delineation of the process of human reproduction so far as the body of the offspring is concerned, but does not consider it an adequate explanation of the origin of the offspring as a whole. Had an individual been primarily a body instinct with life, then the transmission of the parents' physical particles through the reproductive cells might account for his origination. But far more important than the body are his mind and the self, neither of which can be attributed to his parents, as already explained. Even for his body the parents cannot be held wholly responsible. Its roots are to be traced to his past life. A human being cannot result from chance conjunction of material units, that is to

[13]Edmund W. Sinnott, L.C. Dunn, Theodosius Dobzhansky, *Principles of Genetics,* 5th edn., New York, McGraw-Hill, 1958, p. 2.

[14]Claude A. Villee, *Biology,* 4th edn., Philadelphia, W. B. Saunders, 1962, p. 452.

say, the physical ingredients of the reproductive cells of the parents, the sperm and the ovum.

6. *Human reproduction according to modern biology.*

According to modern biology the human body like other multicellular living things, plants or animals, consists of innumerable minute cells, which are responsible for its structure and function. Each cell is a miniature organism and is regarded as the fundamental unit of life. "New cells come into being by the division of previously existing cells." As noted by Dr. Villee, "The cell theory includes the concept that the cell is the fundamental unit of both function and structure — the fundamental unit that shows all the characteristics of living things."[15] Other than the ordinary body cells are the germ cells, which have the property of reproduction. The reproductive cell in the male body is called the *sperm,* and the reproductive cell in the female body is called the ovum or *egg.* The common name for both is the *gamete.* Each gamete is a single cell. The sperm is smaller but more active than the egg. The sperm is not observable by the unaided eye.[16]

While the acquired traits of parents belong to the body cells, their inherited characteristics belong to the gametes — the egg and the sperm. So the inherited characteristics are transmitted to the offspring but not the acquired traits, according to present-day biologists. This refutes the former Lamarckian view that the acquired as well as the hereditary characteristics of parents are inherited by the offspring. The German zoologist, August Weismann, contended for the first time that "acquired" characteristics are never inherited. His view has prevailed since then, being supported by many evidences.

Inside the reproductive cell there are rod-shaped bodies called the *chromosomes.* In each cell of the human species there are twenty-three pairs of chromosomes.[17] Within the chromosomes lie the material units called the *genes.* Each one of the genes controls the inheritance of one or more characteristics. They are generally known as heredity units. As noted by William Beck:

> No one could examine a naked gene, for its properties were assayable only by genetic analysis of the progeny. It itself remained an inferred

[15]Villee, *Biology,* p. 35.

[16]The human egg is about 1/25 of an inch in diameter. It can be seen without a microscope, but is at about the limit of unaided human vision.

[17]Before 1956 the number counted was twenty-four pairs.

entity and a thoroughly remarkable one, for its small size and durability suggested that its material construction must be startlingly complex in detail.[18]

That the theory of genetic inheritance is founded on assumption is acknowledged by later biologists:

> It should be clearly understood that we are sure of the existence of genes not because we have seen them or analyzed them chemically (genetics has so far not succeeded in doing either of these things), but because Mendel's laws can be satisfactorily understood only on the assumption that genes exist. For the purpose of studying the inheritance of traits, it is sufficient to define the gene as a unit transmitted from parents to offspring, which is responsible for the development of certain characters in individuals living in certain environments. The gene so defined is a hypothetical unit, and the body of knowledge concerned with these genes has come to be known as formal genetics. The theory of formal genetics could have been developed even if chromosomes had been unknown and the microscope did not exist.[19]

> The gene with which Mendel and his followers worked was an imaginary unit, a "something" that caused pea seeds to be green or the eyes of *Drosophila* to be red. Now, with a more certain understanding of the gene's role, geneticists know better where to look for discontinuous traits whereby single genes can be investigated. Such investigations have already demonstrated that these "modern" genes can be analyzed by the same methods that Mendel used for his garden peas.[20]

Indeed, the only common link between the child and its parents is its genetic constitution. At copulation numerous sperm are ejaculated. One of them perchance meets one ovum and brings about a new germ-cell called the zygote, the fertilized egg, which develops into an individual in due course. It is said that "only one of the millions of sperm deposited at each ejaculation fertilizes a single egg."[21] Thus, according to current biology, the starting point of an individual's life is the zygote produced by the fusion of the nuclei of the male and the female reproductive cells. The fertilized egg contains twenty-three chromosomes from the male parent and twenty-three from the female parent. The hereditary units, the genes, of both the

[18]William S. Beck, *Modern Science and the Nature of Life,* New York, Harcourt, Brace, 1957, p. 214.

[19]Sinnott et al., *Principles of Genetics,* pp. 54-55.

[20]Villee, *Biology,* p. 584.

[21]*Ibid.* p. 424.

parents lie within them. The chromosomes and the genes function as a single unit. To quote contemporary biologists:

> From the very beginning, at fertilization, the body possesses a highly developed structure, or organization. As the development proceeds this organization undergoes an orderly series of changes, leading by stages to the formation of a fetus and then of an adult body.
> The only material objects that one inherits biologically from one's parents are the genes carried in the egg and sperm cells from which the body originates.[22]
> Indeed, the nuclei of egg and sperm, these tiny packets of reproductive substance, into which so much is packed and out of which so much emerges, are the most remarkable bits of living matter in existence.[23]

In explaining the origin and development of an individual, the biologists have had recourse to both assumption and chance. Says Dobzhansky:

> A child receives one-half of the genes of his father and one-half of the maternal ones; which particular maternal and paternal genes are transmitted to a given child is a matter of chance. Which mutations occur, and when and where, is also a matter of chance.[24]

7. *Modern biology gives no satisfactory explanation of the birth of a genius or a moron.*

According to Julian Huxley it is a matter of chance. Says he:

> Egg and sperms carry the destiny of generations. The egg realizes one chance combination out of an infinity of possibilities; and it is confronted with millions of pairs of sperms, each one actually different in the combination of cards which it holds. Then comes the final moment in the drama — the marriage of egg and sperm to produce the beginning of a large individual. . . . Here, too, it seems to be entirely a matter of chance which particular union of all the millions of possible unions shall be consummated. One might have produced a genius, another a moron . . . and so on. . . . With a realization of all that this implies, we can banish from human thought a host of fears and superstitions. No basis now remains for any doctrine of metempsychosis.[25]

[22]Sinnott et al., *Principles of Genetics,* p. 7.

[23]*Ibid.* p. 17.

[24]Theodosius Dobzhansky, *The Biology of Ultimate Concern,* New York, New American Library, 1967, p. 126.

[25]Julian Huxley, *What Dare I Think?,* New York, Harper & Brothers, 1931, pp. 82-83.

To hold that the birth of a genius or a moron is the result of a chance union of sperm and egg, as Julian Huxley does, is not a satisfactory explanation of a known fact. It is tantamount to saying, "I do not know the real cause." To attribute a universally observable fact to chance in this cosmic order regulated by the law of cause and effect, is indicative of one's inability to probe into deeper realms of existence. To have recourse to chance as an explanation is worse than submission to fatalism. Just as the biologists cannot explain certain observable facts of life without the assumption of something, e.g., the gene, which is beyond the range of observation, similarly, there are established facts in the sensible universe composed of the living and the nonliving, which cannot be explained without the recognition of subtle realities, such as mind and spirit, that are beyond the ken of the senses but are graspable by reason and open to suprasensuous vision.

According to the doctrine of karma, nowhere in the universe is there room for chance, neither in the domain of the animate nor in the domain of the inanimate. Nothing happens without a cause. As is the cause so is the effect. The effect corresponds to the cause. The law of karma on which the doctrine of reincarnation is based is the cosmic law of cause and effect functioning on the human plane as a moral law. As we sow, so we reap. Neither heredity nor environment, not even their interaction, can explain the birth and growth of an individual. Further, geniuses are born of mediocre parents, morons of normal parents, sane children of insane parents, wicked children of saintly parents. Only the law of karma can account for these anomalies.

The point is, the child comes to the parents and is not begotten by them. The prime factor in the origination and development of an individual is the individual himself: all else is subsidiary to him. This is particularly evident in the case of young prodigies. The world has witnessed not a few of them in both East and West in all ages. We shall mention only two instances during the historical period.

Śaṅkarācārya, the greatest exponent of Advaita Vedanta, lived only thirty-two years (868-718 A.D.). At the age of seven he mastered the Vedic literature, which is a library in itself. His erudite preceptor was astonished by the pupil's genius. The profound scholarship and wisdom of young Śaṅkara won the admiration of one and all. His fame extended far and wide. The King of Kerala came to pay his respects. At the age of nine Śaṅkara embraced monasticism. And he attained nirvikalpa samādhi, the apex of spiritual realization, before he was twelve. Most of his literary works, the masterpieces of Advaita

Vedanta, were composed by the time he was sixteen. A versatile genius — a seer, a philosopher, a saint, an indefatigable religious reformer, a poet, a prose-writer, and a debater par excellence, a spiritual teacher of the highest order — young Śaṅkara made the Vedic religion invincible. His great achievements within a short span of thirty-two years are among the marvels of the world.

The Scottish philosopher, Sir William Hamilton, who lived from 1788 to 1856 A.D., proved in his youth to be a marvelous prodigy of modern times. It is said that he started to learn Hebrew at the age of three. At the age of seven he was pronounced by one of the Fellows of Trinity College, Dublin, to have shown a greater knowledge of language than many candidates for a fellowship. At thirteen he could speak thirteen languages. Among these, besides the classical and modern European languages, were Persian, Arabic, Sanskrit, Hindustani, and Malayan. At fourteen he wrote a complimentary letter to the Persian Ambassador, who happened to visit Dublin, and the latter said that no one in Britain could have written such a document in the Persian language. At six he could look up from toys and answer a difficult mathematical problem; and when he was eighteen the Astronomer Royal of Ireland, Dr. Brinkley, said of him, "This young man I do not say *will be* the first mathematician of his age, I say he *is* the first mathematician of his age."[26]

Evidently, the extraordinary powers of prodigies are not due to heredity, or environment, or the interaction of the two. These must have been cultivated by the individuals themselves in their former lives.

The doctrine of reincarnation maintains the identity of an individual throughout a succession of births and deaths. One and the same individual appears in different physical garbs, but all along retains the same mind, which is separable from the body. His progress is dependent primarily on the development of the mind and secondarily on the development of the body. Modern biologists distinguish the mind from the body but consider it an annex. Consequently in their view the mind is inseparable from the body; there is no clear-cut distinction between the two; the same hereditary units, the genes, that bring forth the body also bring forth the mind — both arise from the same physical particles transmitted by the parents. But the difference in the nature of the mind and the body is so marked that both cannot have the same kind of material components.

[26]Originally narrated in *North British Review*, September, 1866; quoted in Johnson, *The Imprisoned Splendour*, p. 379.

8. *Hereditary transmission of mental characteristics is not possible. Neither heredity nor environment, but the child's own nature, is responsible for its development.*

A distinctive characteristic of the mind is that it can transmit consciousness, which is intrinsic in the self. The radiance of consciousness reaches the body through the mind and not *vice versa.* When the mind is diverted from the physical body the body loses sensation; none of the ten bodily organs, either of perception or of action, can function, but the mind continues to operate. In the dream state the body is almost inert, yet the mind functions intensely. Bodily functions and mental functions are altogether different. A person can intensely think, feel, will, imagine, recollect, when his body and his organs are inoperative. Unlike the bodily processes, mental functions give clear evidence of underlying consciousness. The mind cannot be disintegrated in the same way as gross matter. No chemical analysis of the mind is possible. The mind can wander anywhere, but not the body.

The body and the mind being characteristically different, bodily traits belong to the body and the mental traits to the mind. So the hereditary transmission of mental traits through particles of the body of either parent is not possible. "The inheritance of mental ability or intelligence is one of the most important, yet one of the most difficult, problems of human genetics," remarks Claude Villee.[27]

However, according to modern biology the mental as well as the physical traits of the parents are inherited by the offspring. How?

> The living substance of the sperm and egg nuclei transmits all the characters which the new individual inherits from his parents. The qualities themselves — color, size, shape, and so forth — are not present in the germ cells, but something representing them and capable of producing them in the new individual is present. In man, the color of hair, eyes and skin, the size and shape of the body and its parts, certain structural defects, resistance to various diseases, certain mental traits, capacities and defects are all inherited and therefore must be represented in the gametes. The latter, then contain factors which interact with each other and with the environment to produce the adult characteristics.

Biology acknowledges two determining factors in the development of an individual — heredity and environment. Of these two heredity is basic. The functioning of environment is dependent on

[27] Villee, *Biology,* pp. 503-4.

heredity, that is, the individual's physical and mental constitution acquired from the parents. So says Conklin:

> Unquestionably the factors or causes of development are to be found not merely in the germ but also in the environment, not only in intrinsic but also in extrinsic forces; but it is equally certain that the directing and guiding factors of development are in the main intrinsic, and are present in the organization of the germ cells, while the environmental factors exercise chiefly a stimulation, inhibiting or modifying influence on development.[28]

As observed by Claude Villee:

> At one time a bitter argument raged as to whether heredity or environment was more important in determining human traits. It is now abundantly clear that both physical and mental traits are the result of the interplay of both genetic and environmental factors.[29]

According to the doctrine of reincarnation an individual acquires from the parents whatever physical traits are merited by him in consequence of his karma. But he does not owe his mental characteristics to the parents in the same way. He brings his own mind with him. As we have noted, hereditary transmission of mental traits is not possible. Mental characteristics of the parents cannot pass on to the offspring through physical particles. Whatever similarity there may be between the mental characteristics of an individual and those of his parents must be due to the fact that like attracts like in accordance with the law of karma.

An individual's inborn nature, physical as well as mental, is mainly responsible for his development. The environmental conditions can only stimulate or retard his growth. There is no question but that man is deeply influenced by the surroundings in which he lives. Generally, his development is the resultant of the interaction of his inner nature and outer conditions. But his inner nature is the prevailing force. By no means can man be counted as a creature of circumstances. Very often he chooses his environment according to his inner tendencies and capabilities. He can modify the environmental conditions, use them to his best advantage, and can even rise above them. He can even develop the power to create his own environment.

[28]Edwin Grant Conklin, *Heredity and Environment in the Development of Men,* Princeton, N.J., Princeton University Press, 1919, pp. 59-60.
[29]Villee, *Biology,* p.506.

A man of self-knowledge is unperturbed by the changing conditions of life. Says Śrī Kṛṣṇa: "He whose mind is unworried in the midst of sufferings, who is free from desire in the midst of pleasures, who is devoid of attachment, fear, and anger — such a person of steady wisdom is said to be a sage."[30]

9. *The fertilized egg develops into a full-fledged human being because the same is latent in it. Where does he come from? Not from the parents. It is the psychophysical constitution that evolves and not the real self.*

According to modern genetics the very first stage of an individual's existence is the fertilized egg or zygote, the single cell formed by the fusion of the nuclei of sperm and ovum. This is what develops into an adult in due course. "At fertilization a sperm and an egg come together and unite, the nucleus of one fusing completely with that of the other. The single cell resulting from this union begins to divide, forming a group of cells, which develop into an embryo and finally into an adult organism." As conceived by the geneticists the single cell that develops into a full-fledged human individual is a minute but potent biophysical unit. They remark, "Indeed, the nuclei of egg and sperm, these tiny packets of reproductive substance into which so much is packed and out of which so much emerges, are the most remarkable bits of living matter in existence."[31]

But the fertilized egg that grows to be an adult person cannot be regarded merely as a material unit endowed with livingness. What develops into a human individual must have the same latent in it. According to Vedanta, development means unfoldment of inherent potency. What lies latent in the cause becomes manifest as the effect.

A fig seed is a fig tree in the potential state. A fig seed develops into a fig tree and a poppy seed into a poppy plant; it is because the fig tree exists in the fig seed and the poppy plant in the poppy seed as potencies. Only by studying the fig tree can we know the real nature of the fig seed. No chemical analysis of the seed will reveal its true nature to us. No microscopic observation can probe into its potency. Similarly, by studying the poppy plant we can know the poppy seed in the true sense and in no other way.

Therefore, in order to know the true nature of the fertilized egg we have to know its developed state as man. Truly speaking, it is a

[30]BG II:56.
[31]Sinnott et al., *Principles of Genetics,* p. 17.

miniature man. All the main factors of human personality — the body, the organs, the vital principle, the mind, and the self — must be there in potential states.

Involution precedes evolution. The evolvement of the seed into a tree is due to the fact that the tree is involved in the seed. Evolution is truly speaking the unfoldment of what is infolded. Without the recognition of involution, evolution is inexplicable. The differences in the seeds account for the differences in trees of the same species. As is the cause so is the effect. Something cannot come out of nothing. The cause of the variation of each individual is in its very nature. Neither environmental conditions, nor heredity, far less chance, can account for the new departure of every individual in the course of its development. Each individual develops according to its own pattern. The secret of its development is its innate creativeness. The fertilized egg develops into a human individual because the same is involved there. Modern evolutionists ignore involution; consequently they have had recourse to "chance variations" or "sporadic changes" in accounting for the individual evolutionary process.

To quote Swami Vivekananda:

> No rational man can possibly quarrel with these evolutionists. But we have to learn one thing more. We have to go one step further, and what is that? That every evolution is preceded by an involution. The seed is the father of the tree, but another tree was itself the father of the seed. The seed is the fine form out of which the big tree comes and another big tree was the form which is involved in that seed. The whole of this universe was present in the cosmic fine universe. The little cell, which becomes afterward the man, was simply the involved man, and becomes evolved as a man. If this is clear, we have no quarrel with the evolutionists, for we see that if they admit this step, instead of their destroying religion, they will be the greatest supporters of it.[32]

The central principle in human personality is the luminous self, the knower within, whose radiance sustains the psychophysical constitution and becomes manifest through it. There is neither evolution nor involution, neither expansion nor contraction, neither growth nor decay, in the ever-shining changeless self. All these variations characterize the psychophysical constitution alone. Consequent on its varied modifications there is diverse manifestation of the luminous self. Just as the same sunlight appears different through different transmitters — as dim or bright, as yellow or red, as

[32]CW II, pp. 207-8.

blue or green, similarly according to the development of the psychophysical system, the radiance of consciousness belonging to the self (ātmacaitanya-jyōti) becomes manifest variously — as more or less intelligence, as more or less strength, as more or less joy, and so forth.[33]

In the fertilized egg an individual's psychophysical constitution is in the nascent state. His mind as well as his body, minute though they may be, have just begun to develop with the concomitant manifestation of the self, howsoever faint it may be. Livingness is ever attended with consciousness. Any expression of consciousness or sentiency in a living thing must be due to the manifestation of the self through the mind. As we have noted, it is through the mind that the radiance of consciousness reaches the physical level.

Where do the mind and the self of the individual come from? Neither of the two can be inherited from the parents. The self is indivisible. Mind is impartible being composed of subtle elements beyond the operation of gross matter. Neither can derive from the physical elements transmitted by the parents, as we have explained. From this it follows that the real source of the human offspring is not the fertilized egg, that is to say, he does not originate from the male parent or from the female parent or from both. He must come from elsewhere.

10. *The birth of an individual.*

Truly speaking, the birth of an individual is the rebirth of one of the many individuals who died somewhere sometime previously. Death is not the end of an individual nor is birth the beginning of him. There is no place for accidentalism in human life, if it is to be considered meaningful. In order to find how a man is reborn we must find how he dies. At death, the self, the real man, leaves the physical body, but retains the subtle and the causal body. The mind with all its contents belongs to the subtle body. According to those impressions of karma (including volitional actions, experiences, and thoughts) that become prevalent in the mind of a dying man, a very fine physical vesture for the subtle and the causal body is formed at the time of his departure from the gross body. This fine garb carries the potencies of the next gross body he assumes. He may go to a higher or a lower region impelled by the impressions of karma. But when these are exhausted the residual karma will lead him eventually to this human

[33]See BS I:3.30; BG XV:12; S. com.

plane, where alone he has a chance for liberation. It is to be noted that unredeemed or unliberated souls are subject to rebirth and not the liberated.

When a bound soul is ready for rebirth on the human plane the impressions of his karma lead him to the parents from whom he can secure the materials for his gross body. The fine physical vesture that he wears has the potency to acquire the necessary material elements. Being associated with food he enters the body of the male parent suitable for his purpose. There he gets into the requisite sperm, which turns into a potent seed for his development as an individual. This is the seed that being united with the requisite ovum in the female parent turns into the zygote and becomes ready for germination. These are the two specialized male and female reproductive cells that are responsible for the birth of the offspring.

A tree may bear any number of fruits, yet they differ from one another in spite of their similarity due to common origin. Similarly, despite their resemblance every sperm differs from every other sperm in a male body. In the same way every ovum differs from every other ovum in a female body. Led by its karma the transmigrating soul gets into the requisite sperm and the ovum out of countless reproductive cells. The fusion of the sperm and the ovum required for its physical body is by no means a matter of chance. Nor is this brought about by blind natural force. Behind it is the universal law of cause and effect in the form of the law of karma. Neither the sperm nor the ovum can be counted as an individual in the sense in which the fertilized egg is. Just as the livingness of each fruit on a tree is dependent on the livingness of the tree, so is the livingness of the sperm dependent on the livingness of the male body, and the livingness of the ovum dependent on the livingness of the female body.

According to the Upaniṣads, it is the male parent that sows the seed of the offspring in the soil of the female parent. It is said in the *Chāndōgya Upaniṣad:*

> Woman indeed is the fire, O Gautama. Into this fire the Gods [presiding deities of the organs] offer the libation of semen. Out of this offering arises the foetus.[34]

As stated in the *Bṛhadāraṇyaka Upaniṣad:*

> Reaching the earth [while coming down from the celestial sphere] they [the souls of those who perform sacrificial rites and righteous deeds in

[34]Ch.U. V:8.2.

order to go to higher regions for sense-fulfillment][35] become food [being associated with rice, barley, etc.]. Then they are again offered in the fire of man, thence in the fire of woman, whence they are born (and perform rites) with a view to going to other worlds. Thus do they rotate [until they gain the saving knowledge, which frees them from the cycle of repeated birth and rebirth].[36]

Here the father is said to be the procreator. In this respect the Vedantic view is akin to that of the modern "spermists." The "ovists" hold a contrary view with regard to fertilization. As observed by Dr. Sturtevant:

> With the development of clearer ideas about fertilization two schools emerged: the "ovists" who thought the preformed parts were contained in the unfertilized egg and were merely activated by the sperm, and the "spermists" who thought of the sperm as a complete animalcule that was merely nourished by the egg.[37]

In the words of the *Aitareya Upaniṣad:*

> What exists in the male body as semen — the transmigrating soul is at first conceived as that. This is the extract of vigour from all the limbs of the body and this the man holds within himself as the self. When he deposits this in his wife he procreates it. That is its first birth.
>
> It becomes one with the wife as her own limb is. Therefore it does not hurt her. She nourishes this self of his that has entered into her. The father is regarded as reborn as the son.
>
> Being the nourisher she has to be nourished. The wife bears the embryo. Right after its birth the father protects the child [by natal rites] at first. Protecting the child from its birth onward he thus protects himself for the continuation of the worlds. For thus alone are these worlds perpetuated. This [the coming out from the wife's womb] is one's second birth.
>
> He [the son] who is like the second self of his [of the father] is made his substitute for the performance of righteous deeds. Then the other self of his [that is, the father] having accomplished his duties and having reached his age, departs. So departing hence he is reborn. That is his third birth.[38]

Śaṅkara comments on this:

> Is it not a fact that for the transmigrating soul the first birth is in the form of semen from the father? And his second birth has been stated to

[35]They are reborn on the human plane when the merits of their deeds are exhausted.

[36]Br.U. VI:2.16.

[37]A.H. Sturtevant, *A History of Genetics,* New York, Harper & Row, 1965, p. 121.

[38]Ai.U. II:1.1-4.

> be as a son from the mother [wife]. The turn now being for stating the third birth of that very soul [which is born as the son] why is the birth of the dead father mentioned as the third? . . . That son, too, just like his father, entrusts his responsibility to his son [in his own turn] and then departing from here takes birth immediately after. . . . What is stated with regard to the father is implied here with regard to the son.[39]

11. *The doctrine of reincarnation makes life meaningful.*

The doctrine of reincarnation explains man's present existence with reference to its past and future. If birth be the beginning of life then death must be its end. Rationally we cannot accept future life without acknowledging our existence in the past. The assumption of future life is based on the recognition of the present life as its preexistence.

Every child is born with a particular psychophysical constitution. What makes the difference? Heredity cannot logically explain the difference in the inborn aptitudes of the individuals. The doctrine of reincarnation provides the only satisfactory explanation of the inequalities of life. An individual's weal and woe, weaknesses and excellences, knowledge and ignorance, rise and fall, depend primarily on his own past thoughts and deeds. No external agency, parentage or Divine dispensation, chance or fate, is responsible for them. The doctrine rejects both heredity and predestination as the source of human life. It makes man self-reliant. It distinguishes the real man, the changeless self, from the everchanging psychophysical adjunct and points out the cause of his bondage and the way to freedom.

A clear knowledge of the interrelation of the body, the mind, and the self in human personality is the key to self-mastery. These three factors are distinct from one another, although closely associated. One does not originate from nor can one be identified with, either of the two others.

According to biology, heredity and environment are the two principal factors in the origin and development of an individual; and of these two heredity is basic. The biologist views the fertilized egg, the zygote, as a material unit composed of the physical particles derived from both the parents. To maintain the origin and development of man from this very source is to advocate the fundamental reality of matter. It is tantamount to saying that man's spiritual self, as well as the mind, originates from gross matter. Such a

[39] *Ibid.*, S. com.

position is untenable. Physical processes can produce physical light but not the light of consciousness marked by self-awareness, which distinguishes spirit from matter. Man's spiritual self is not actually born nor does it die, but transmigrates for the time being under the law of karma.

PART THREE

MAN'S TWOFOLD JOURNEY OF LIFE:

The Secular and the Spiritual Pursuit

CHAPTERS IX-XII

CHAPTER IX

MAN IN QUEST OF THE ETERNAL

1. *The human mind has not remained wholly occupied with the temporal, but has faced the fundamental problems regarding the world and man from the beginning of his development.*

From the earliest days humanity in general throughout the world has been preoccupied with diverse temporal interests — possessions, pleasures, position, power, friendship, beauty, knowledge, fame, and so forth; whereas the reflective minds in all ages and all places have generally turned to the ultimate reality beyond. Not a few men and women among races unknown to one another, have grappled with fundamental problems with regard to the world and man. To solve them some have made it their lifelong task.

The queries regarding the world as a whole have usually taken these forms: What is the true nature of this universe of heterogeneous things and beings varying continuously? What is its origin? How does it originate? How is it sustained? Ever marked by interdependence and transition, a shifting scene of dualities, e.g., origination and destruction, union and separation, order and disorder, light and darkness, this conglomeration of the animate and the inanimate can be neither self-existent nor self-supporting. Yet it functions as an orderly whole, as a veritable cosmos governed by laws universal and particular. There must be some Supreme Intelligence that brings this into being, and maintains it.

Both the macrocosm and the microcosm have proved to be enigmas. No less mysterious than the sensible universe is man the experiencer. Though quite fragile, yet a repository of inestimable potentialities is he. Consequently, inquisitive minds have tackled such problems with regard to him as these: What is man? Where does he come from? Where does he go? What is his final end? What is the meaning of this humdrum life—the same old drama of birth, growth, decay, and death — invariably marked by dual experience of agreeable and disagreeable, of good and evil in every sphere of life;

while at the same time the human heart craves for life beyond death, for light beyond darkness, for joy beyond sorrow. Can this innermost longing of the human heart for unalloyed joy, for unmixed blessing, ever be satisfied?

The speculative philosophers in East and West have tried to solve these fundamental problems by logical reasoning on the settled facts of life and the world as known to them. Their aim has been to explain the past with reference to the whole, to harmonize the many with the ultimate One as far as possible. To find unity in variety is the goal of knowledge.

While different branches of physical science seek unity in their respective spheres, philosophy seeks the unity of unities. The method followed by physical science is primarily the observation of the sensible facts, experimentation on them, and drawing of inferences. Philosophy investigates the truth of various theories as well as known facts, external and internal, in order to ascertain the final truth. The facts we experience are not self-explanatory. The philosopher has to determine their cause by the reasoning process. He has to find the explanation of the sensible in the suprasensible, of the known in the unknown, in order to determine the Cause of causes. Thus philosophical inquiry ends in the mediate knowledge of the ultimate One attained by inferences.

Since the main interest of the speculative philosophers in dealing with the above problems is intellectual satisfaction, they have remained contented with the mediate knowledge of the ultimate Reality. Even the knowledge of a concrete object gained by inference is indirect and indefinite. No wonder that the knowledge of the suprasensuous truths reached by dialectic reasoning is invariably mediate and hence lacking in certitude. Consequently, the conclusions of the speculative philosophers are as a rule indecisive. This is why they have held divergent views with regard to the ultimate Reality.

2. *How the spiritual aspirants' quest for the ultimate Reality differs from that of the speculative philosophers.*

On the other hand there have been spiritual philosophers whose main interest in dealing with these problems has not been just the mediate knowledge of the Supreme Reality for the satisfaction of their intellect. Regarding Its attainment as the highest goal of life they have sought the actual experience of It. They have not remained satisfied with the findings of speculative reason. Having derived preliminary knowledge of the Supreme Being from the authentic scriptures verified by the experiences of the seers and also from the words of the competent teachers, they have tried to be convinced of the nature of Reality and the method of attaining It by the rational interpretation of authoritative words. Not only that. They have followed disciplinary courses preparatory to the practice of meditation. This has served as the key to the realization of the Truth.

They have found that man's inmost self, the finite center of consciousness, is inseparable from Infinite Consciousness, the all-pervading Self of the universe. What is innermost in an individual is innermost in the whole universe. Self-effulgent Supreme Consciousness is the ultimate Reality. This is the finest of all existences. This permeates each and every thing, howsoever vast or minute it may be, and is not penetrated by anything. This is manifest as the experiencer only in living creatures because of the presence of the mind in them. The mind has the capacity to transmit consciousness, more or less, according to its development. There is no manifestation of consciousness in a material object because of the absence of the mind in it.

In a human being the Self of the universe is specially manifest as the indwelling self possessed of self-awareness and the awareness of all else within its scope. Through the requisite purification of the psychophysical constitution by ethical and spiritual disciplines, a seeker of Truth succeeds in recognizing the true nature of the self and in realizing its unity or even identity with the Supreme Self. As declared by the *Kaṭha Upaniṣad:*

> The Self, smaller than the small, greater than the great, abides in the hearts of all living creatures. The man who is free from all desires [for the temporal] realizes That (the glory of the Self) through the purification of the organs and the mind and thus goes beyond sorrow.[1]

It is said in the *Chāndōgya Upaniṣad:* "The knower of the Self overcomes grief."[2]

In the Upaniṣads there are many instances of spiritual aspirants making inquiries about the fundamental reality. The *Śvetāśvatara Upaniṣad* opens with the following inquiry about the Cause of the universe by the seekers of Brahman, the Supreme Being:

[1]Ka.U. I:2.20. [2]Ch.U. VII:1.3.

> The Vedic students [the seekers of Brahman] ask: "Is Brahman the Cause [of the universe]? Whence are we born? By what are we sustained? What is our destination? O ye, the knowers of Brahman, [tell us] under whose ordinance we undergo different conditions in happiness and in other than happiness. Time, inherent nature, destiny, chance elements, primordial cause (prakṛti), individual self — none of these can be considered the origin of the universe; nor their combination, because they combine for the individual self [for his experience and liberation]. The self also is not a free agent, being subject to happiness and misery."
>
> They [the seekers of Brahman], following the method of meditation, experienced the self-effulgent Supreme Being associated with His power hidden by its own constituents, the guṇas [sattva, rajas and tamas].[3] It is He, who, though One without a second, rules over all the causes beginning with time and ending with the individual self.[4]

In the same Upaniṣad one of the knowers of Brahman declares:

> I have realized this Supreme Being, resplendent as the sun, beyond all darkness. It is by knowing Him only that one overcomes death. There is no other way out [of the cycle of births and rebirths].[5]

In dealing with metaphysical questions the aim of the spiritual philosophers has been to reach a final solution of all human problems. How can a man get out of the maze of life once for all? The final solution of human problems is not possible without reference to the ultimate Goal. So these questions arise: How can man's deepest longing for immortality, for eternal life, be fully satisfied? How can he attain complete self-fulfillment? Where is the culmination of his knowledge? Where is the cessation of all his hankerings, of all his bondages and sufferings? The eternal life must be all-perfect, free from all grievances.

With the perpetuation of life the perpetuation of misery in any form whatsoever is unthinkable. Man seeks eternal life with perpetual peace and blessedness. Where else but in God, the Supreme Being, can he find this? He is the Eternal One underlying all that are noneternal. There cannot be two eternals. The Eternal is infinite. The Infinite alone is eternal. "It is the Infinite that is immortal; it is the finite that is mortal,"[6] said the sage Sanatkumāra to Nārada, who approached him for the knowledge of ātman (the all-pervading Self) in order to go beyond all sorrows. Despite his vast learning Nārada

[3]See footnote 13, p. 261.
[4]Sv.U. I:1-3.
[5]*Ibid.* III:8.
[6]Ch.U. VII:24.1.

had not succeeded in going beyond grief because of his lack of the knowledge of ātman.

The Infinite is all-perfect, being all-bliss. So Sanatkumāra said to Nārada: "It is the Infinite that is bliss. There is no bliss in the finite. Only the Infinite is bliss. One must desire to know the Infinite."[7]

Whatever joy the finite beings experience is derived from that One source. So says the sage Yājñavalkya to Janaka: "On a particle of this very bliss [that Brahman is] other beings live."[8] The knower of Brahman attains this fully.

3. *The urge for the Eternal, for the Infinite, is bound up with man's real nature.*

Now the questions may arise: Why does mortal man seek immortality, imperfect man perfection? Why does finite man aspire after the Infinite? Why does not man rest contented with his inherent limitations? Can his inordinate ambition ever be fulfilled? But the truth is that man is not really mortal, finite, or imperfect. He only appears to be so, being identified with the psychophysical garb he wears for the time being. As the knower of the body, the organs and the mind, he is distinct from them all. The knower should not be identified with the objects known. As the perceiver of the changing conditions that objects undergo he is beyond them all. The real man is the indwelling spirit, the central principle of consciousness, that shines with constant effulgence and rules over the psychophysical organism. It is the all-pervading Spirit, Supreme Consciousness, that shines within every individual as the finite self.

At the back of every wave in the ocean there is the same boundless mass of water; similarly, at the back of every finite center of consciousness there is Infinite Consciousness. Just as an apparent form differentiates the wave from the ocean without separating it, similarly the finite self is differentiated from the all-pervading Self by the veil of ajñāna that creates seeming separation. Ajñāna underlies the psychophysical constitution of an individual as his causal body (see Ch. II, sec. 11). It has a peculiar property that imposes forms on the formless, apparently limits the limitless, and makes something appear different from what it really is. Because of the presence of ajñāna in every individual, One Infinite Self is apparently divided into countless selves. (See Ch. I, sec. 7.)

[7]Ch.U. VII:23.1 [8]Br.U. IV:3.32.

The finite self cognizes ajñāna, hiding his true nature as self-luminous consciousness. It is evident from such a common experience as "I do not know myself." The knower does not know himself, does not recognize his own self as pure spirit shining with constant effulgence. Just as the cloud hiding the sun is manifested by the sun, similarly ajñāna that hides the luminous self is at the same time manifested by it. The presence of ajñāna is testified by the self, its cognizer.

Ajñāna is the cause not only of the inapprehension but also of the misapprehension of the self. Veiled by ajñāna the self becomes more or less identified with the psychophysical garb and appears as the ego. The self identified with the not-self is the ego (the individual who asserts himself as "I"). While experiencing the conditions of the body, the organs, and the mind, the individual self ascribes their properties and functions to himself. Thus the self appears as the knower and as the doer and as possessed of the characteristics of the body, the organs, and the mind. He virtually turns into a psychophysical being. Thus he appears to himself and to his fellow-beings as other than what he really is. All the while the indwelling spirit behind ajñāna shines with constant effulgence unaffected by the pairs of opposites experienced by the apparent man, such as birth and death, growth and decay, strength and weakness, virtue and vice, knowledge and ignorance, pleasure and pain.

This is why the apparent man, although immured in the psychophysical garb and engrossed with the transitory, feels the urge for the Eternal, for the Infinite, vaguely though it may be. It is the apparent man that seeks immortality as this urge develops. Bondage and liberation both concern the apparent man. He has to realize his true self, ever shining, pure, free, immortal. The urge for the Eternal, for the Infinite, is innate in him. Knowingly or unknowingly he is tending towards That all the while. Behind his search for wealth, for power, for happiness, for beauty, or for fame, is the search for the Infinite. He cannot remain satisfied with anything finite, anything limited. Even though all the treasures of the world be accumulated and laid at the feet of a seeker of wealth, yet he will seek more. Through greater and greater, man is seeking the greatest, through higher and higher he is seeking the highest, through better and better he is seeking the best. There can be many great and greater, but the greatest can be but One. The English word *God* signifies That. The Vedantic term for the same is *Brahman,* greater than whom there is none.

4. *The fulfillment of this urge for the Eternal, for the Infinite, is the true purpose of religion.*

The difference between a worldly man and a spiritual person is this — the former seeks God unknowingly and even wrongly, while the latter seeks God knowingly and by right methods. The true purpose of religion is twofold: to awaken the human mind to the supreme Goal of life, and to lead the way to its attainment. Religion is the only human pursuit that is concerned particularly with the Eternal, whereas all other pursuits of life are concerned particularly with the temporal. Even philosophy, arts, literature — considered as noble vocations of life — usually subserve man's secular interests. Religion holds before man the prospect of immortality, of perfection, of supreme beatitude, on attaining which all hankerings end, all struggles cease forever, all bondages drop.

The great saints and seers and spiritual leaders belonging to the different religions of the world declare in one voice that they have reached the Goal. Their exemplary lives and sublime teachings carry conviction. For centuries they have won the spontaneous allegiance of human hearts. Compared to that the respect and admiration commanded by the most eminent persons in all other fields is negligible. In this modern age Sri Ramakrishna demonstrated that God can be realized by different methods, and that every religion worth the name is a pathway to God. He also declared from his own experience that the realization of God is the Supreme Goal of life, and that a seeker can reach the Goal by following a spiritual course suited to his inner disposition and situation in life.

Now the point is, how can a man turn his mind Godward? How can he accept God as the supreme goal of life and strive for its attainment? This Godward urge requires cultivation. Man is born with strong sense-desires. His senses have a natural tendency to turn outward. As he experiences the sensible world he tries to derive pleasure from each and everything, and to avoid pain as far as possible. How to live in this world and live happily becomes his primary concern. With this end in view he cultivates various branches of knowledge, develops agriculture and arts and industries, founds social orders and political systems, establishes military powers, and so forth. Even religious associations are formed to subserve man's secular interests. Not a few seek religion for temporal good. Some pray to God for wealth, health, happiness, success, and so on; some for the redress of dire calamities. Some study scriptures for erudition.

None of them can be counted as seekers of God in the true sense. A genuine seeker of God seeks God for God's sake. He accepts God as the Supreme Goal. Whatever he seeks he seeks for the attainment of this Goal. He does not seek God for anything else. Those who supplicate God for worldly benefit only, forgetting spiritual values, are like beggars who approach the Emperor of emperors for trifles. They are like those foolish persons who, having come to the perennial spring of ambrosia, try to quench their thirst with ditch water.

When a person accepts God, the Supreme Spirit, as the highest Goal and strives for Its attainment, then begins his spiritual life. Until then a worshipper of God is in an undeveloped stage of religious life. To seek God for temporal interest is a low form of religion, though not irreligion. The central purpose of religion is to lead man to God, beyond whom there is none. He is the Adorable One. Religious life in the true sense begins with the search for God as the supreme Goal. "The highest ideal of every man is called God," says Swami Vivekananda.[9] A spiritual aspirant lives true to this purpose of religion. He is in an advanced stage of religious life.

5. *How does man develop this Godward urge? Not through frustration, but through ethical discipline leading to right understanding.*

It is not so easy to get over the inborn secular desires and turn away from the search for the temporal to the search for the Eternal. It requires the development of insight through ethical discipline, to realize the inherent shortcomings of all temporal values and the importance of spiritual values of all grades. One cannot gain this conviction without a certain measure of inner purification. Without this, no one can turn to God in the true sense.

Fear of the battle of life or failure in it, bitter experience of unforeseen calamities, sufferings caused by bereavement, penury, humiliation, or chronic disease, despondency consequent on vain efforts to attain a long cherished goal — any one or more of these can generate disgust with life or dislike of society, but cannot release the mind from inveterate sense-attachment and direct it Godward. Mental depression may develop misanthropy but not dispassion characterized by the search for the Eternal. Renunciation without the yearning for God is superficial. It is misleading and unsafe, nay, dangerous. This has been stated graphically by Śaṅkarācārya:

[9]CW III, p.89.

> There are seekers of Liberation who have but superficial renunciation and yet attempt to cross the ocean of relative existence. The shark of inner craving catches them by the throat and violently snatching them away, drowns them midway.[10]

How does ethical discipline lead to spiritual awakening? The ethical life of a person begins with due consideration of his fellow-beings interests. Just as happiness is agreeable and unhappiness disagreeable in his own case, so it is in the case of all others. With this understanding he tries to promote others' happiness and to prevent or remove others' unhappiness as far as he can. This practice is conducive to both individual and collective well-being. In order to carry this on he has to cultivate virtues and overcome vices. Any fellow-feeling towards one's fellow-beings is a virtue; it is moral. Similarly, any ill-feeling towards one's fellow-beings is a vice; it is immoral. Thus kindness, sincerity, charity, justice, truthfulness, admiration, humility, chastity — which represent the possessor's fellow-feeling towards his fellow-beings — are counted as virtues. They contribute to his inner calmness and cheerfulness. As a result, he can maintain self-composure, and thus see things clearly and judge them rightly.

Right understanding is essential to right living. External resources are of little help to a man who does not know how to use them for his best interests. "It is man that makes money; money does not make man," said Swami Vivekananda. A man with right understanding will never starve in this world. Human beings suffer more from the abuse of powers and possessions than from the lack of them. The only way to prevent this is by the development of right understanding through the practice of virtues.

On the other hand, all ill-feelings, such as anger, jealousy, hatred, pride, falsehood, fear, cruelty, insincerity, lust, greed, are condemned as vices. A man is the first victim of his own vices. They beset him with cares and worries and upset the mind. Naturally his vision becomes distorted and his judgment vitiated. He becomes liable to all kinds of mistakes. He does not know where his best interests lie. With all his intellectual powers he behaves like a clever animal. It is the concensus of the Vedantic teachers that virtues brighten human understanding, whereas vices darken it. From virtue proceeds happiness, from vice misery. Vices undermine human life, whereas virtues stabilize it at all levels — physical, intellectual, aesthetic, moral, spiritual.

[10]VC 79.

Because of his insight a virtuous man can see life as a whole. He can evaluate the different levels of life and grasp the inherent limitations of all secular pursuits. He finds that the search for the temporal in any form whatsoever cannot lead man out of bondage. It ends in a vain search for security in the insecure; yet the spiritual leaders declare that there *is* a way out of bondage to complete freedom, and that they have found the way. Even then the upright man cannot make up his mind to follow their way. More than the bitterness of adversity he has to realize the futility of prosperity by actual experience, in order to turn away from the temporal to the Eternal.

6. *Unless disillusioned of the dualities one cannot follow the spiritual path firmly.*

Practice of virtue is essential to man's well-being in all spheres of life without exception. It is indispensable to his secular development as well as to the spiritual. A seeker of temporal values in any form whatsoever who does not deviate from the path of virtue, derives the greatest benefit out of every situation in which he finds himself. From his own experience of the blessings of life which he can secure — such as affluence, power, position, beauty, knowledge, happiness, honor — he develops an insight by which he becomes convinced of the inherent inadequacy of all worldly achievements, howsoever great, glorious, and high they may be.

He finds that the whole world of experience consists of pairs of opposites, e.g., light and darkness, construction and destruction, order and disorder, prosperity and adversity, life and death, youth and old age, in which the contraries are inseparable: the one does not exist without the other. There is no good without the concomitant evil; yet the human mind desperately seeks the one to the exclusion of the other. This is the delusion of the dualities that keeps man tied down to the vain search for security in the insecure. It is but a wild goose chase for the unmixed blessings of life.

He who persistently follows the path of virtue does not take long to discern these facts. Being disillusioned of all the charms of the relative order he turns to the Eternal One, who is beyond all dualities, all relativity. He tries to approach Him with unfaltering steps, knowing Him to be the Supreme Goal of life. As his thoughts dwell on the Supreme Being he becomes convinced of the truth that none but He is all-free, all-pure, all-perfect; in Him alone is true life, true light, true freedom, true joy. On attaining Him there remains nothing more to attain; on knowing Him there remains nothing more to know. Where else should he seek refuge but in Him? Thus, the seeker of temporal values turns into a bonafide worshipper of God. Says Śrī Kṛṣṇa in the *Bhagavad-gītā:* "Those men of virtuous deeds whose vices have been eliminated become free from the delusion of the dualities and worship Me with firm resolve."[11]

7. *Though disillusioned of the dualities the seeker has to develop longing for God by the practice of Karma-yōga.*

Yet he has to go a long way to reach the Goal. Although he understands the necessity of seeking God, yet the natural longing for God does not easily grow within him. Without this quality he cannot tread the spiritual path with unfaltering steps. In order to cultivate this longing he has to practice Karma-yōga, that is to say, the performance of duties, domestic and social, with equanimity, with dispassion. There are different methods of Karma-yōga. We shall dwell on them later, as we proceed. (See Ch. XI, sec. 1, 2.)

Even though the spiritual aspirant may feel an urge to leave society and retire to solitude in order to devote himself exclusively to spiritual pursuit, yet he is not considered ready for this without further inner purification by the practice of Karma-yōga. He is advised to live in the world, but to live free from worldliness with a spiritual outlook on life. Since he holds to God as the Supreme Goal, he does not look upon anything mundane, howsoever great and glorious it may be, as an end in itself. Whatever he has he holds for the sake of the Lord. Whatever deed he performs he looks upon as a means to the supreme end. Naturally he is not indifferent to anything but takes proper care of everything. He who is attentive to the goal cannot be negligent of the means. Rather, he handles it with special care without being attached to it. This is what living in the world with dispassion (the practice of detachment) means. Without the spiritual goal in view no one can be a Karma-yōgī. This is the first spiritual course prescribed for a spiritual aspirant, the seeker of the Eternal.

8. *Through Karma-yōga he gains competence for the practice of Bhakti-yōga or Jñāna-yōga, either of which leads directly to the Goal.*

[11]BG VII:28.

Through the practice of Karma-yōga with the appropriate inner attitude, the spiritual aspirant gains competence for the practice of Bhakti-yōga (the way of devotion) or Jñāna-yōga (the way of knowledge) according to his aptitude. Either of these two ways leads directly to God-realization. Bhakti-yōga is the approach to Saguṇa Brahman, God possessed of all blessed qualities, usually called the Personal God, who, though without form, assumes form to favor His devotees. This is the way of devotion marked by the worshipper's feeling of relationship with the Divinity which is expressed by the terse formula "I am Thine, Thou art mine." All theistic religions are varied forms of Bhakti-yōga, the approach to the Personal God, Saguṇa Brahman.

Jñāna-yōga is the approach to Nirguṇa Brahman, Impersonal Absolute Being (Pure Being-Consciousness-Bliss), beyond the distinction of substance and attribute. This is the way of knowledge characterized by the follower's awareness of the essential identity of the individual self with the Supreme Self as Pure Consciousness. It is indicated by the terse formula "Thou art That." In mystical terminology *God* refers to Saguṇa Brahman and *Godhead* to Nirguṇa Brahman. Jñāna-yōga, which is the direct approach to Nirguṇa Brahman, is a very steep course. It suits only highly qualified spiritual aspirants, who can rise above the body-idea. To realize Nirguṇa Brahman after realizing Saguṇa Brahman by Bhakti-yōga is a less arduous course. Some seekers of Nirguṇa Brahman prefer this.

9. *How the practice of Bhakti-yōga leads to the Goal — the realization of Saguṇa Brahman.*

While practicing Karma-yōga as preparatory to Bhakti-yōga, the seeker of Saguṇa Brahman is expected to carry on the formal worship of God by physical, verbal, and mental methods for the cultivation of ardent devotion. Through these disciplinary measures the seeker's mind is purged of the subtle impressions of sense-desires accumulated in the subconscious by his past thoughts, experiences, and deeds in this or in a former life. As a result, genuine interest in devotional practices and natural longing for God develops. Then the practice of Karma-yōga is no longer compulsory; the seeker can devote himself wholly to devotional practices. This is the starting-point of Bhakti-yōga proper.

As the seeker's mind gets settled on God his sense of relationship with Him deepens. He feels the proximity of God. He approaches

God through one or another form of relationship with Him, such as between the Ruler and the ruled, between the Master and the servant, between the Father and the child, between the Mother and the child, between the Friend and the friend, between the Child and the parent, between the Supreme Beloved and the loving soul. It is to be noted that each succeeding form of relationship is closer than the preceding one. Gradually he turns more and more from the practice of physical and verbal modes of worship, to the practice of such mental modes of worship as constant remembrance of God, resignation to His will, and meditation on Him.

With the intensification of his devotion the worshipper develops an insight into the true nature of God as all-pervading Supreme Spirit, and into his own nature as pure, immortal spirit. He realizes that God is not just the Ruler, or the Master, or the Father, or the Friend. He is all-in-all. He is the Ruler, Father, Mother, Friend, Companion — all in One. Nay, He is the Soul of all souls. He, the all-pervading Self of the universe, dwells within each one of us as the inmost self. After searching for God far and near, in the starry heaven, in the sublimity of snow-capped mountain peaks, in the stillness of a dense forest, in the vast expanse of the rolling waves, in sacred books and temples, in ostentatious rites and ceremonies, in pomp and power, the seeker recognizes the truth that He who appeared to be the farthest is the nearest of all. He who seemed to be outside is the inmost of all. He realizes then that the shortest way to reach Him is by an inner approach. This turning of the seeker's mind towards the self within is illustrated by the Vedantic teachers with the example of the musk deer.

In the Himalayan heights, close to the snowline, there dwells a type of deer called the musk deer. As the male deer grows it develops musk inside the navel. The deer inhales the sweet fragrance emitted by the musk without knowing its source. Fascinated by the fragrance the deer tries to find the source. It wanders far and wide, over hills and valleys. At last it gets tired and lies down on the ground. All of a sudden it discovers that the source of fragrance it had been searching for was right within its navel. Similar is the case with the spiritual aspirant. Being under the right guidance, he discovers that the Eternal One, the all-perfect One he has been seeking here and there, is manifest within him as the indwelling Self.

Says Śrī Kṛṣṇa: "O Guḍākeśa [an epithet of Arjuna, lit. Conqueror of sleep], I am the Self dwelling in the hearts of all beings.

I am the beginning, the middle, and also the end of all beings."[12]

Says Jesus Christ: "The Kingdom of God cometh not with observation: neither shall they say, Lo here! or, lo there! for, behold, the Kingdom of God is within you."[13]

Now the devotee is at the threshold of God-realization. As observed by Sri Ramakrishna:

> As long as the devotee says, "God is there [pointing upward]," God is far away from him. But when he says "God is here [pointing inward]," God is very close to him. He will see God very soon.

At this stage the devotee meditates on God within the heart as his inmost self. At the back of the finite self he visualizes the all-pervading Self. He adopts a concrete form as the symbol of the Divinity for worshipping Him. And this he looks upon as the embodiment of the Infinite Consciousness existing at the back of each finite center of consciousness.

Because of his loving devotion to God, his clear grasp of the nature of God, and his intense longing for His vision, he succeeds in meditating on Him intensely within the heart. Through deep meditation a mental mode is formed corresponding to the nature of God. This eradicates the veil of ajñāna that shrouds the finite self and conceals the Supreme Self, just as a small patch of cloud appearing before the eyes hides the enormous resplendent sun. Then God becomes revealed to the devotee.

Says the *Bhāgavatam* with regard to God-vision: "Whom the yōgīs see with the mind completely absorbed in Him through deep meditation."[14] Those who surrender themselves to God also receive His grace. When the devotee sees God he finds himself in Him. He realizes his essential unity with the Divinity. One cannot objectify the inmost Self.

10. *Qualifications of the follower of Jñāna-yōga, the seeker of Nirguṇa Brahman.*

As a result of the purification of the mind through the practice of Karma-yōga and other disciplinary measures, a seeker of Nirguṇa Brahman acquires the four prerequisites of a follower of Jñāna-yōga. These are:

[12]BG X:20. [13]Luke 17:20,21. [14]SB XII:13.1.

1) Discrimination of the Real from all that is unreal.
2) Freedom from all desires for the enjoyment of the fruits of meritorious deeds here and hereafter.
3) A group of six virtues, namely, (1) control of the mind, (2) control of the organs, (3) fortitude, (4) withdrawal of the mind from external objects, (5) faith, (6) settledness of the mind on the self.
4) Longing for Liberation.

Then he must follow the triple approach to Nirguṇa Brahman consisting of:

1) Hearing of the Vedic dictum on the identity of the individual self and the Supreme Self from the texts and from a qualified teacher.
2) Reflection on the truth of the dictum for gaining conviction.
3) Meditation on the Self.

The sage Yājñavalkya thus speaks to his wife of the triple method:

> The Self, my dear Maitreyī, should be realized — should be heard of, reflected on, and meditated upon. By the realization of the Self, my dear, through hearing, reflection, and meditation, all this is known.[15]

As we have already noted, the approach to Nirguṇa Brahman is much harder to follow than the approach to Saguṇa Brahman. It particularly fits those who have gotten rid of the body-idea. This is evident from the words of Śrī Kṛṣṇa:

> The difficulty of those whose minds are set on the Unmanifest (Nirguṇa Brahman) is greater. For the way of the Unmanifest is hard to follow by those who are identified with the body.[16]

11. *Meditation is the proximate and sole means to the realization of Brahman, Saguṇa or Nirguṇa.*

It is evident from the foregoing discussion that meditation is the direct means to the realization of Brahman, Nirguṇa as well as Saguṇa. As such it is the final spiritual course for reaching the Goal. All other disciplinary measures are intended to prepare the mind for the practice of meditation. It is also to be noted that excepting this,

[15]Br.U. II:4.5. [16]BG XII:5.

there is no other method of realizing the Supreme Being and of being united with Him. Therefore, meditation is the only means to the attainment of the ultimate One. The direct experience of the Supreme Being is not possible by any other way. The two other ways to the knowledge of the suprasensible — verbal testimony and ratiocination — can give us only the indirect, and not the direct, knowledge of the Supreme Being. From the scriptural texts and from the words of the seers we can know much about God, yet we remain ignorant of Him, because they do not reveal God to us. Similarly, by logical reasoning we can have only mediate knowledge of the ultimate Reality; and this is indefinite and indecisive, as we have already noted.

When God is realized He becomes manifest as Supreme Spirit, as undifferentiated Consciousness beyond all diversities. This state of experience is called *samādhi,* the culmination of meditation. During meditation the threefold distinction — of the finite self as the meditator, of the Supreme Self as the object of meditation, and of the mental operation as meditation — persists. In samādhi this tripartite distinction vanishes. Pure Consciousness as an integral whole shines.

In the experience of Saguṇa Brahman the distinction between the finite self and the Supreme Self is not altogether obliterated. The finite self finds itself as belonging to the Supreme Self as the wave belongs to the ocean. This is called *savikalpa samādhi.* In the experience of Nirguṇa Brahman, the finite self becomes absorbed in the Supreme Self and the identity of the two as Pure Consciousness is realized. This is called *nirvikalpa samādhi.* Once the seeker realizes the Supreme Being in savikalpa or in nirvikalpa samādhi he does not lose sight of Him anymore. Even as an embodied being he lives in Him, moves in Him and has his being in Him. Such a person is said to be "living-free." Here ends man's quest for the Eternal.

But it is to be noted that most seekers of God succeed in realizing Him when the life's term is over. After leaving the body on the attainment of samādhi, the worshipper of Saguṇa Brahman retains his individuality and lives in perpetual loving relationship with Him in Brahmalōka, while the seeker of Nirguṇa Brahman merges in absolute Being.

12. *The place of Rāja-yōga in the quest of the Eternal.*

The reader may wonder why there is no mention of Rāja-yōga in the above context. "Is it not efficacious for the attainment of the Eternal?" he may ask. The point is, Vedanta considers three standard yōgas — Karma, Jñāna, Bhakti — adequate for reaching the Goal Supreme. They are suited to different types and grades of spiritual aspirants. Says Śrī Kṛṣṇa in the *Bhāgavatam:*

> The three yōgas of love, knowledge, and work have been told by Me to men for their Highest Good. Except through these there is no way to attain Freedom.[17]

Obviously, Śrī Kṛṣṇa does not consider Rāja-yōga as a separate yōga. But this does not mean that he ignores it. As a matter of fact, Vedanta accepts the practical features of Rāja-yōga (of which Patañjali is the first great exponent), adapts them to its own metaphysical background, and includes them in the three standard yōgas mentioned above. It does not accept Patañjali's philosophical basis, which is dualistic, being founded on the Sāṁkhya system of Kapila. References to the practical courses of yōga are found in some ancient Vedantic literature including the *Śvetāśvatara Upaniṣad.*[18]

The following are the eight limbs or accessories of yōga as prescribed by Patañjali:[19]

1) *Yama* (abstention from evil-doing) — this includes five moral observances: nonviolence, truthfulness (abstention from falsehood), nonstealing, continence (abstention from incontinence), non-covetousness. These rules of conduct are meant to be universally observed.

2) *Niyama* — while *yama* signifies prohibitions, *niyama* signifies prescriptions, such as (1) cleanliness of the body and the mind, (2) contentment, (3) austerities (self-discipline), (4) study of scriptures (including repeated utterance of a sacred text, formula, or word, which is a concentrated form of prayer), (5) dedication of the fruits of action to God (practice of Karma-yōga). The last two of this group come under devotional practices, which occupy a subordinate place in Patañjali's yōga. It is to be noted that moral observance forms the common basis of all yōgic disciplines. There is no way to the Eternal but through this.

3) *Āsana* (posture) — sitting in a steady position, easy and poised, with the backbone, neck, and head in one vertical line. This eliminates bodily resistance and promotes steadiness of breath and concentration of the mind.

[17]SB XI:20.6.
[18]Sv.U. II:8-14.
[19]YS II:29.

4) *Prāṇāyama* — regulation of breath. Even without conscious effort for the control of breath, this can be achieved through the cultivation of devotion to God and by fixing the mind on Him. Āsana and prāṇāyama are preliminaries to the practice of meditation.

5) *Pratyāhāra* — withdrawal of the organs and the mind from sense-objects and the directing of thoughts to the object of meditation.

6) *Dhāraṇā* (concentration) — attempt to steady the mind on the object of meditation, even though it may be for a very short period.

7) *Dhyāna* (meditation) — prolonged concentration of the mind on the object of meditation as a result of steady and persistent practice.

(It is to be noted that pratyāhāra, dhāraṇā, and dhyāna are the three stages of the concentration of the mind on the object of meditation.)

8) *Samādhi* — absorption of the mind in the object of meditation. Patañjali thus distinguishes between meditation and samādhi:

> Meditation is the uninterrupted concentration of thought on its object. This itself turns into samādhi when the object alone shines and the thought of meditation [and of the meditator] is lost as it were.[20]

As we have noted above, Vedanta also holds that the triple distinction that prevails in meditation does not persist in samādhi. Patañjali also agrees with Vedanta on the point that the direct experience of suprasensuous truths is attainable only in samādhi. So he says:

> In that state knowledge is said to be "truth-bearing."
>
> This knowledge is of a different order than the knowledge gained from inference and the scriptures. For it is definite in nature [being superconscious experience].[21]

By developing buddhi, the power of discrimination between the self and the not-self, the yōgī can discern the luminous self as distinct from the mind and meditate on this as such. A clear and steady perception of the self as other than the mind, to which buddhi belongs, is called *viveka-khyāti* (lit. the discriminating knowledge). It counteracts avidyā (wrong knowledge), the primal cause of the identification of the self with the not-self. Patañjali observes:

[20]YS III:2,3. [21]YS I:48,49.

> The cause of this [the identification of the self with the not-self] is avidyā.
>
> When avidyā has been eradicated, the identification ceases. Then bondage drops as the self becomes aloof [that is, reinstated in its innate freedom].
>
> The way to eradicate avidyā and sever bondage is the constant apprehension of the self as other than the mind [including the discriminating knowledge].
>
> At the seventh stage of this [discriminating] knowledge the yōgī reaches the highest level.[22]

This is *samprajñāta samādhi. Samprajñāta* literally means "fully conscious." This samādhi is so called, because it is attended with the discriminating knowledge that belongs to the mind.

Being established in this state the yōgī develops the power to attain *asamprajñāta samādhi,* in which the self is fully realized. Then the luminous self, completely withdrawn from the mind and its mode of the discriminating knowledge, shines all by itself without any subject-object relation. This aloofness is liberation. After this samādhi the yōgī dwells in the body as a free soul. At death the subtle body of the yōgī, of which the mind is the chief support, merges in basic prakṛti (undifferentiated nature), while the physical body drops and in due course resolves into its constituent elements. Thus, the yōgī attains final liberation, which is complete aloofness or isolation of the luminous self (puruṣa) from prakṛti.[23]

According to Yōgic dualism both puruṣa and prakṛti are ultimately real. Puruṣa is self-luminous, changeless, and immortal; whereas prakṛti is insentient and subject to transformations. There is only one prakṛti, while there are numerous puruṣas, and each is omnipresent and self-luminous.

It is evident from the foregoing discussion that meditation plays the most important part in the practice of Rāja-yōga. It is meditation on the true nature of the self that leads to self-realization and consequent liberation.

Vedanta recognizes this method, although its conceptions of the self and of liberation widely differ from those of Patañjali. Rāja-yōga is even counted as *the* yōga because of its great emphasis on the practice of meditation, which is also essential to Bhakti-yōga and Jñāna-yōga. Further, it is called *Dhyāna-yōga,* the way of meditation. Under this heading it has been included in the sixth

[22] YS II:24-27. [23] See YS I:51; IV:34.

chapter of the *Bhagavad-gītā*. Śrī Kṛṣṇa thus commends the practice of Dhyāna-yōga:

> That state in which the mind being restrained by the practice of concentration becomes tranquil, in which the yōgī seeing the Self through the purified mind rests satisfied with the Self; in which he feels utmost delight that is beyond the senses but perceivable by insight, being established in which he does not deviate from his real state; and having gained which, he considers no other gain greater than that, and being settled in which, he is not perturbed even by heavy sorrow; that is the state which one should know. It is designated "yōga" in which there is termination of all contact with pain. This yōga should be practiced with determination without dejection of spirit.[24]

Then the Yōgī, having realized the unity, or the identity, of the self with Brahman, experiences the supreme bliss of Brahman. So says Śrī Kṛṣṇa:

> To this yōgī who is taintless and free from desires, who is of a tranquil mind and identified with Brahman, comes supreme bliss.
>
> The yōgī, freed from blemish, thus fixing the mind constantly [on the Self] attains easily the supreme bliss of union with Brahman.[25]

From the above account one can see the vast difference between Patañjali's view of Liberation and the Vedantic view of Liberation.

[24]BG VI:20-23. [25]*Ibid.* 27,28.

CHAPTER X

THE PATH OF PROSPERITY AND THE PATH OF SUPREME GOOD; THEIR NECESSITY

1. *No inherent conflict between the two paths. The one can be conducive to the other.*

In the course of life's journey an individual who develops a sense of spiritual values comes to a crossing where two main roads lead in opposite directions. The one is the path of prosperity and the other the path of perfection. He finds that if he seeks prosperity he cannot attain perfection; if he seeks perfection he cannot gain prosperity. The one is marked by avarice and the other by renunciation. Indeed, the two ways appear as contrary as the goals. The search for possessions and pleasures here and hereafter keeps the seeker in bondage, ties him down to the temporal order of endless variety and ceaseless change, of insecurity and interdependence; whereas the search for the Highest Good leads the aspirant beyond the relative order, beyond the dualities of good and evil, to the Supreme Being, the Eternal One, who alone is good in the absolute sense. In the one case man is haunted by death, in the other he finds the key to immortality. In the one he gropes in darkness despite his pretension to knowledge; in the other he is led by the Light of all lights.

No wonder the world's religious leaders pronounce the two ways to be contrary: "One is the road that leads to wealth, another the road that leads to Nirvāṇa," says the Buddha.[1] "Ye cannot serve God and Mammon," says Jesus Christ.[2] "He who has little will receive," teaches Lao Tzu.[3] "Supreme Good is one thing and pleasure is another," declares the Upaniṣadic teacher.[4] The way of prosperity is not confined to the pursuit of riches; it embraces all secular pursuits — the quest for power, position, academic knowledge, fame, beauty,

[1] *Dhammapada* V:75.
[2] Matt. 6:24.
[3] *Tao Te Ching* XXII.
[4] Ka.U. I:2.1.

aesthetic pleasure, and so forth. While all other pursuits of life are concerned primarily with the temporal, religion is concerned primarily with the eternal. It holds before man the prospect of immortality, freedom from all bondages and miseries, nay, the attainment of absolute peace and blessedness. The prerequisite for this is declared to be the renunciation of pelf and power.

Indeed, from the earliest times the Vedic teachers have held renunciation to be the sole means to Supreme Good. "Not by work, nor by progeny, nor by wealth, but by renunciation some attained immortality," said the venerable Parameṣṭhin to Āśvalāyana, a teacher of the *Ṛg-Veda,* who approached him for the knowledge of Brahman, the Supreme Being.[5]

While speaking of Brahman as the Self within all, free from hunger and thirst, grief and delusion, decay and death, the sage Yājñavalkya points out the means of realizing the same: "Knowing about this very Self, the Brāhmaṇas renounce the desire for sons, for wealth and for the worlds, and lead a mendicant life."[6]

When Yājñavalkya was going to renounce the world, leaving behind all property, Maitreyī, his wife, inquired:

> "Sir, if indeed this whole earth full of wealth be mine, shall I be immortal through that or not?"
>
> "No," replied he, "your life will be just like that of people who have plenty of things, but there is no hope of immortality through wealth."
>
> Then Maitreyī said, "What shall I do with that which will not make me immortal? Tell me, sir, of that alone which you know to be the only means to immortality."
>
> Then the sage explained to her the nature of the Self and the methods of its realization. "The Self, my dear Maitreyī, should be realized — should be heard of, reflected on, and meditated upon. When the Self, my dear, is realized by being heard of, reflected on, and meditated upon, all this is known."
>
> After giving the instruction Yājñavalkya left home.[7]

Once a rich man, who was dutiful and virtuous, asked Jesus Christ, "Good Master, what shall I do that I may inherit eternal life?" Jesus said to him, "One thing thou lackest: go thy way, sell whatsoever thou hast, and give to the poor and thou shalt have treasure in heaven: and come, take up the cross, and follow me." But

[5]Kai.U. I:2.
[6]Br.U. III:5.1.
[7]*Ibid.* IV: 5.3,4,6,15.

the man did not want to part with his great possessions and went away aggrieved. Then Jesus remarked to his disciples, "Children, how hard it is for them that trust in riches to enter into the Kingdom of God! It is easier for a camel to go through the eye of a needle, than for a rich man to enter into the Kingdom of God."[8] It is worthy of note that these are the warnings that are intended for those who are ready to follow the path of perfection. The seekers of Supreme Good are expected to rise above all temptation of pelf and power.

Even though the great spiritual leaders declare in one voice that renunciation provides the only access to the Kingdom of God, yet how many can give up their earthly treasures for its sake? How many can turn away from the temporal values to the search for Supreme Good? Like the rich man of the Biblical story most human beings choose to hold their possessions, no matter how trivial they be, rather than hazard them for the sake of eternal life. Even those who have neither property nor position would passionately struggle for them rather than seek the Kingdom of God. Neither coercion nor inducement can turn a person from the way of prosperity to the way of Supreme Good. The sense-desires are too firmly rooted in man for him to submit to either of these means.

The way of Supreme Good cannot be pursued under compulsion. It is a way of inner development, the realization of man's innate perfection. It has to be chosen out of free will and followed with earnestness and devotion. Indeed, rare are the individuals who can fulfill the conditions for immortality laid down by the great teachers of the world. Consequently, the followers of the path of Supreme Good are few and far between, while the path of prosperity is always overcrowded. "Among thousands of men, one, here and there, strives for perfection," says Śrī Kṛṣṇa, "and of those who strive and succeed, one, perchance, knows Me in truth."[9]

Is the spiritual life then intended only for the scanty few who can forego all that is perishable for the sake of the Imperishable? Cannot the seekers of prosperity prepare for the Kingdom of God? Or, must they give up all endeavor, all desire, all hope for entering it as long as they care for the secular values? Is the overwhelming majority of human beings to be treated as lost souls? For the seekers of prosperity too there must be a way of proceeding towards the Ultimate Goal. For them also there must be an opening to spiritual life. Religion has to find it.

[8]Mark 10:17,21,24,25.
[9]BG VII:3.

2. *The Vedic religion takes into account both the ways. It views man as a whole and presents a complete scheme of life.*

Fully conscious of the mighty hold that the world of experience has on human minds, the Vedic seers formulated a scheme of religious life to include the seekers of temporal well-being as well as the seekers of spiritual values. So the Vedic religion has two distinct courses: (1) the way of activity (pravṛtti-mārga), and (2) the way of renunciation (nivṛtti-mārga), characterized respectively by desire and desirelessness. The former is intended to lead to plenty and pleasure here and hereafter, whereas the latter is intended to lead to Supreme Good. Manu, a well-known codifier of the Vedic rules of life, remarks: "Activity (pravṛtti) and renunciation (nivṛtti) are the two forms of the Vedic discipline for the attainment of prosperity and happiness and for the attainment of Supreme Good."[10] The way of activity and the way of renunciation are respectively the way of prosperity and the way of Supreme Good.

The guiding principle of the way of activity is the practice of virtue. In the search for wealth, or in the search for pleasure, the seeker should by no means deviate from the moral course. Renunciation does not necessarily mean giving up all activities and possessions. Primarily, it is a dispassionate attitude to the temporal consequent on spiritual awakening, that is to say, the turning of the mind to the eternal. The main condition for the way of renunciation is freedom from desires for all that is transitory and longing for the eternal. One can have both internal and external renunciation, or only internal. External renunciation without the internal has no value. A person may have the spirit of renunciation even though living in the family. He can be in the world without being worldly-minded. Such cases are, of course, not very common.

Through the discipline of the way of activity (pravṛtti-marga) a man can gain affluence and happiness not only in this world but also in the worlds beyond. He can strive for merit adequate to reach the very climax of temporal glory and enjoyment after death. This means an immeasurably long term of life in the highest realm of sense-fulfillment, such as a celestial paradise. But he cannot reside there forever. Having experienced the joys and splendors of the heaven-world (svargaloka) for a long, long period, until the merit that leads him there is exhausted, he comes back to this earth. Or, he may go farther down to a lower region in consequence of the severe demerit

[10]MS XII:88.

fructifying at the time.[11] When this demerit is worked out, he returns to the human world with remaining merit and demerit.

Thus, according to the predominance of merit and demerit accruing from work, the follower of the way of activity (pravṛtti-mārga) continues to pass from the lower to the higher world and from the higher to the lower, repeatedly undergoing four conditions of life — birth, growth, decay, and death — with happiness and misery alternating.[12] This migratory existence with continuous rotation of the wheel of life impelled by karma is called in Hindu religious terminology *saṁsāra* (lit., a continuous course).

It is to be noted that according to the Hindu view there is no absolute beginning or end of the creative order consisting of the jīva, jagat, and Īśvara. The creative process continues eternally in the succession of projection, preservation, and dissolution of the universe. Creation (sṛṣṭi) means projection of the manifold from the causal into the manifest state. Its continuation in the manifest state is its preservation (sthiti). Its reversion into the causal state is its dissolution (pralaya). The whole process is under the guidance of the Supreme Lord (Īśvara).

There is no escape from saṁsāra by the way of activity (pravṛtti-mārga) throughout the cycles of projection, preservation, and dissolution of the universe.[13] Its adherent keeps rolling on in the creative process. So the way of activity is called *pravṛtti-marga* (lit., the path of turning on). On the contrary, the follower of the way of renunciation gets out of the creative order, characterized by duality and dependence, by withdrawing the innermost self and realizing its unity with the Supreme Self, the fundamental Reality free from limitations, luminous, and blissful. So this is called *nivṛtti-marga* (lit., the path of turning away). As declared by the Upaniṣad, "Thus does the man who has desires transmigrate. But the man who has no desire (to whom all objects of desire are but the Self) never transmigrates."[14]

[11]As stated in the *Muṇḍaka Upaniṣad* (I:2.10): "Deluded persons regarding sacrificial rites and humanitarian deeds to be the highest do not know any higher good [the means of Liberation]. Having enjoyed [the fruits of their good deeds] on the heights of heaven attainable by meritorious work, they enter again this world or go to an inferior one."

[12]See SD III:53, Vijñānabhikṣu: "The suffering arising from decay, death, etc., is common to all beings going upward and downward — beginning from Brahmā down to the plant."

[13]See BG VIII:19, "The same multitude of beings, coming forth again and again, merge, in spite of themselves, O Pārtha, at the approach of night (dissolution) and remanifest themselves at the approach of day (projection)."

[14]Br.U. IV:4.6.

Pravṛtti and *nivṛtti* are very significant terms. They are also interpreted as "turning on the ego" and "turning away from the ego." Pravṛtti, then, implies ego-centeredness and nivṛtti surrendering the ego, that is, God-centeredness. In the words of Swami Vivekananda:

> Pravṛtti means revolving towards, nivṛtti means revolving away. The "revolving towards" is what we call the world, the "I and mine"; it includes all those things which are always encircling that "me" by wealth and money and power and name and fame, and which are of a grasping nature, always tending to accumulate everything in one centre, that centre being "myself." That is pravṛtti, the natural tendency of every human being; taking everything from everywhere and heaping it around one centre, that centre being man's own sweet self. When this tendency begins to break, when it is nivṛtti or "going away from," then begin morality and religion. Both pravṛtti and nivṛtti are of the nature of work; the former is evil work[15] and the latter is good work. The nivṛtti is the fundamental basis of all morality and all religion, and the very perfection of it is entire self-abnegation, readiness to sacrifice mind and body and everything for another being.[16]

The work section (karma-kāṇḍa) of the Vedas deals primarily with the way of activity, and the knowledge section (jñāna-kāṇḍa) with the way of renunciation. The way of activity is also intended to lead to the same Ultimate Goal, although its immediate purpose is the attainment of prosperity. As preparatory to the way of renunciation, it is an indirect approach to Supreme Good. So it is the remote cause of Liberation. As an indirect means to the highest end, while it promotes secular well-being, the way of activity paves the way to Supreme Good. On the relative importance of these two ways, Śaṅkara, the staunch supporter of the way of renunciation (nivṛtti-mārga), observes:

> Having created the world, the Lord, willing to preserve it, at first created the Prajāpatis[17] — Marici and the rest — and enjoined on them the way of activity (pravṛtti dharma) as stated in the Vedas. He then created Sanaka, Sanandana and the rest[18] and instructed them in the way of renunciation (nivṛtti dharma) characterized by knowledge and desirelessness.

[15]Any ego-centered work, honest and pious though it may be, is a cause of bondage, and therefore evil.

[16]CW I, pp. 83-84.

[17]Literally, "the lords of created beings," the progenitors. The ten founders of the way of activity, according to Manu, are Marici, Atri, Angiras, Pulastya, Pulaha, Kratu, Pracetas, Vaśiṣṭha, Bhṛgu and Nārada (MS I:35).

[18]The four founders of the way of renunciation are Sanaka, Sanandana, Sanatkumāra and Sanātana.

The religion of the Vedas is a twofold way: the way of activity and the way of renunciation. This twofold religion, in which one of the ways is the direct means to prosperity and the other to Supreme Good, is the basis of world order and security, and was followed by the members of the different castes[19] (the brāhmaṇa, the kṣatriya, and the rest) and of the different āśramas,[20] desirous of their welfare. . . . The aim of the twofold religion expounded by the Gītā is the attainment of Supreme Good.[21]

For world order and security both the ways are essential. Both of them are as old as mankind. They exist side by side. Without the way of activity the way of renunciation cannot function. And the former, unless directed to the latter, cannot hold its own. It goes out of bounds and disrupts life, individual and social. It is a truism that man's sense-appetites are insatiable. They grow and multiply indefinitely, unless well regulated. The two ways of religion (dharma) are, as it were, the centrifugal and the centripetal forces that make the human world rightly run its course. The Sanskrit word *dharma,* which is usually translated as "religion" is very significant. Etymologically, it means "that which upholds" in the words of the *Mahābhārata.*[22] It denotes particularly "the Law or the Principle that upholds the world order."[23] It has also restricted meanings, viz., virtue, duty, and the characteristics of a person or a thing. Dharma, according to Kaṇāda, is that which leads to the attainment of prosperity (abhyudaya) and Supreme Good (niḥśreyas) as well.[24] This means that the way of prosperity and the way of Supreme Good both are in accord with the Law or the Principle which maintains the world order.

3. *The four main human objectives. The imperative need of virtue in the pursuit of wealth and happiness.*

In formulating the scheme of life the teachers of the Vedic religion have kept in view four main human objectives (puruṣārtha): virtue

[19]The four social orders (Varṇas) — brāhmaṇa, kṣatriya, vaiśya, and śūdra (see Ch. XII, sec. 1). The word *brāhmaṇa,* wrongly spelt as "brahmin," should be distinguished from *Brahman,* the Supreme Being, and from *Brahmā,* the Cosmic Soul. The latter part of each Veda is also called *Brāhmaṇa,* such as *Aitareya Brāhmaṇa, Taittirīya Brāhmaṇa,* and so forth.

[20]The four orders or stages of life (see Ch. XII, sec.3).

[21]S. com. on BG, intro.

[22]Mhb. XII:109.14.

[23]In early Vedic literature the term *ṛta* is used in this sense.

[24]The *Vaiśeṣika Sūtra* I:1.2.

(dharma), wealth (artha), pleasure (kāma), and Liberation (mōkṣa). Wealth and pleasure belong to pravṛtti-mārga (the way of activity), Liberation to nivṛtti-mārga (the way of renunciation); virtue is common to both. Of these four, Liberation or Supreme Good is the ultimate value; the rest are instrumental, being preparatory to the knowledge of Truth, which alone makes man free.[25] Virtue is the *sine qua non* for the Supreme Good, as no spiritual unfoldment is possible without it. Not only that; it is indispensable to material welfare also. Any progress in life, material as well as spiritual, must be based on man's moral worth. So virtue, and not wealth, is considered to be the primary object of life.

Such a view may not readily appeal to the man of the world. To him economic values rather than the moral values are of primal necessity. He thinks that money can solve the problems of life more effectively than morality. And for gaining wealth also, he finds cleverness and technical devices more effective than honesty. In his view, moral scruples considerably hamper worldly success. He believes he has a greater chance for securing prosperity and happiness by sacrificing moral principles than by adhering to them. The dictum "Honesty is the best policy" may be good, according to him, for winning the Kingdom of Heaven but not the citadel of Fortune. The ancient seers, however, saw things differently. Why? We shall see.

Virtue (dharma) means inner excellence and worthiness for the performance of an individual's duties towards himself and others. So it includes intellectual abilities as well. Manu enumerates wisdom and knowledge under virtue (dharma), which according to him, consists of ten qualities, viz., contentment, forgiveness, uprightness, nonstealing, cleanliness, self-control, wisdom, knowledge, truth, and equanimity.[26] According to the Vedic standard the early part of life has to be devoted exclusively to the cultivation of virtue. It emphasizes moral development more than intellectual; whereas the modern system of education stresses intellectual growth, ignoring the moral. In the *Taittirīya Upaniṣad* we find that a preceptor gives the following instruction to his pupil on the eve of his returning home after graduation:

> Speak the truth. Do your duties. Swerve not from your study. After satisfying the teacher with gifts due to him,[27] you shall marry and have

[25]See SB I:2.9,10.

[26]MS VI:92.

[27]In ancient India the students lived with the teacher and received education free of all charges.

children. Never deviate from truth. Never fail in your duty. Never neglect your welfare. Never neglect your prosperity. Never neglect study and teaching. Do not disregard your duties toward God and the ancestors. Serve the mother as a god. Serve the father as a god. Serve the teacher as a god. Serve the guest as a god. You should do such deeds as are unreproachable, and not others. You should do such virtuous deeds as we have done, and not others.[28]

A man should try to prosper in this world by the honest and efficient discharge of the duties of his station in life. Wealth or position gained by any other means is insecure and may even be harmful. Worldly success without corresponding inner development is no mark of progress; for the secret of man's strength, wisdom, freedom, and happiness is not in his external resources but in his inner nature. Wealth does not bring wisdom. Machinery does not generate moral force. Mastery over physical nature does not lead to self-mastery. Sense enjoyment does not assure health and happiness. Man's inner well-being is much more important than pomp and power. He cannot rest satisfied with the fulfillment of physical needs and cravings. Human beings live on a plane different from the subhuman.

We must not forget that man's problems are mainly psychological rather than biological. Generally speaking, the wealthy have more agonies than those who live in hardship and privation. As long as a man has moral weakness, such as jealousy, hatred, anger, fear, pride, lust, or greed, he will have trouble wherever he may be. A fortune-seeker may amass wealth huge enough to convert night into day, yet without inner light he cannot see his way in life. An aggressor may conquer territory after territory and rule over the destinies of millions of human beings, yet he remains a slave to his passions and impulses. A queen may indulge in all the comforts and luxuries of the world, yet a streak of jealousy or vanity can make her miserable for life.

Physical science may tap some multipotent or plenipotent force out of the bosom of nature, such as nuclear energy, yet it will do no good, but incalculable harm to the world, if man has not the good sense to harness it to his own service. On the human level fitness for survival depends not on physical ability nor even on intellectual attainment, but on moral and spiritual worth. It is a historical fact that any nation that tries to live in material prosperity by military power or diplomatic maneuvers declines rapidly, being subject to

[28]Tai.U. I:11.1,2.

moral breakdown. Because of inner decay it even collapses without an aggressor's blow.

4. *Hindu sages have all along recognized dharma (practice of virtue) as indispensable to secular as well as spiritual well-being.*

As noted above, Kaṇāda, the founder of Vaiśeṣika system, defines dharma as that which leads to prosperity and the attainment of the highest good. We have explained how the practice of virtue, while fulfilling the secular desires of a seeker of temporal good, develops his spiritual yearning and turns his mind from the search of the ephemeral to the search of the Eternal (Ch. IX, sec. 5). Under no circumstances should man sacrifice virtue for the sake of wealth. Moral values are far more important than the material. The former constitute the stable basis of the latter. External possessions cannot help man as much as inner resources. "Virtue protects him who protects her," says the *Mahābhārata.*[29] In storm and stress she is the best friend. A man of real worth cannot fail. He can gain wealth, position, name and fame even though he has none. On the other hand, a person may have fortune and friends, yet there is every chance of his losing them if he has no control over his emotions and temper. It is not true that honesty does not succeed. The truth is, man does not have the patience to try it. There are people in commerce, agriculture, industry, and other fields who have made themselves prosperous by fair means. The secret of their success is the influence of probity that wins the confidence of others. "Truth alone triumphs, not untruth," says the *Muṇḍaka Upaniṣad.*[30]

As we have noted, the following ten qualities have been specified by Manu under the category of virtue (dharma): contentment, forgiveness, uprightness, nonstealing, cleanliness, self-control, wisdom, knowledge, truth, and equanimity.[31] These are to be practiced by the seekers of prosperity as well as by the seekers of Supreme Good. Student or teacher, priest or soldier, monk or householder, hermit or merchant, farmer or king — theist or atheist — none desirous of his well-being should deviate from them. It is morality that maintains man's morale. Virtue strengthens, vice weakens. The practice of virtue is the one universal duty of all human beings.

[29]Mhb., Anuśāsana-Parva, IV.
[30]Mu.U. III:1.6.
[31]MS VI:92.

Whether a person believes in God or not, he must be fair in his dealings with his fellow beings. On no account should he deviate from the moral course. Principle is invigorating, while policy or expediency is enervating. "No great deed is accomplished by sagacity," says Swami Vivekananda, "but through love, devotion to truth, and superb vigor all work can be done."[32] Without virtue no corporate life is possible. There will always be conflict among individuals and among their groups, in case selfishness, pride, jealousy, deceitfulness, hatred and so forth rule within them. No security, no peace, no prosperity is attainable in the absence of social harmony. No decent life is possible where dishonesty, arrogance, and mistrust prevail.

In the pursuit of wealth, and in the pursuit of pleasure as well the seeker must adhere to the path of virtue. Otherwise he will fail in his quest. Man wants to live and be happy. For this he secures wealth and property. Self-gratification is no less strong an urge in him than self-preservation. He tries to get the utmost pleasure even from the essential needs of life — his food and drink, clothes and bed, house and furniture. Not satisfied with this, he surrounds himself with comforts and luxuries. But even these cannot make him happy unless he is in a position to enjoy them. The two essential requisites for the enjoyment of life are a sound body and a sound mind. He who is physically and mentally sick cannot relish anything. And unless a person lives with self-restraint and moderation, nothing can secure the health of the body and the mind.

A virtuous person can be happy with the bare necessities of life because his mind and body are in the normal state. By dishonest means one may gain opulence but not happiness. "He who is habitually dishonest, who earns money by falsehood, who injures others, attains no happiness in this world," says Manu.[33] His mental disquiet does not permit him to find joy anywhere. In the name of enjoyment he betakes himself to self-indulgence. Excitement is followed by exhaustion. In gratifying the senses one has to observe propriety and discretion. What is pleasant is not necessarily good. Sense-enjoyment does not guarantee physical and mental well-being. Any excess will have an unhappy reaction. So the seeker of happiness should in no way transgress virtue. From virtue arises happiness, from vice suffering.

Who can have peace of mind as long as anger, jealousy, hatred,

[32]Letter written in Bengali to Swami Ramakrishnananda, 1895.
[33]MS IV:170.

pride, fear — in short, any ill-feeling towards his fellow-being — dwells within him? "Wealth and happiness result from virtue," says the *Mahābhārata*. Hence the pursuit of wealth (artha) and the pursuit of pleasure (kāma) both should be in accord with virtue (dharma). This is the lesson enjoined by the Vedic seers on all seekers of prosperity — the followers of the way of activity (pravṛtti-mārga).[34] The way of activity being rightly pursued invariably leads to the path of renunciation (nivṛtti-mārga), the quest for Supreme Good; in other words, Liberation (mōkṣa).

5. *The predicament of the modern world: its cause and cure. The false view of progress.*

It is the disregard of the imperative need of virtue in the pursuit of wealth and pleasure that is mainly responsible for the present-day predicament of the world. Despite their unprecedented power and progress, the peoples of modern times do not succeed in strengthening the bonds of universal harmony, but are forced to prepare themselves in the name of self-defense for another global war which threatens their very existence. Neither ideological difference, nor cultural diversity, nor economic maladjustment is the primal cause of this tragic situation. There is something deeper at the root. Do not people having ideological, cultural, or religious affinity quarrel and fight among themselves? Ideological, cultural, or religious unity alone cannot solve the problem. Economic maladjustment, apparently a frequent cause of conflict, originates mainly in greed. In fact, it is the subordination of ethical values to the material, resulting in lack of moral integrity in the life of the people, which is the source of major troubles in the modern world.

With the development of physical science and technology the thought of the Western world became focused on the material plane. As a result, the inner life of man was ignored or subordinated to secular interests. Ever since Francis Bacon (1561-1626 A.D.) pointed out the utilitarian standard of knowledge, human intellect has been progressively devoted to practical ends.[35] Modern man has learned to

[34]See MS II:224, Kullūka's com.

[35]See J. B. Bury, *The Idea of Progress*, New York, Dover, 1955, pp.52-53: "The principle that the proper aim of knowledge is the amelioration of human life, to increase men's happiness and mitigate sufferings — *commodis humanis inservire* — was the guiding star of Bacon in all his intellectual labor. . . . In laying down the utilitarian view of knowledge he contributed to the creation of a new mental atmosphere in which the theory of Progress was afterwards to develop."

measure world progress and civilization in terms of material achievements. He has been taken up with the idea that he can solve all problems of life, remove all its miseries, and enrich it indefinitely only by his ingenuity in unravelling the secrets of nature and utilizing them for the invention of all possible means and devices for human needs and comforts. In the nineteenth century science became the new Messiah and techniques the way of deliverance. Dazed by the glare of "mechanical discoveries" men were dreaming of the millennium.[36]

As early as the middle of the eighteenth century, advocates of progress, beginning with Turgot (1727-1781) and Condorcet (1743-1794), were writing about "ever increasing perfection" and "indefinite improvement" of mankind on earth.[37] Some conceived progress not as a condition to be brought about by human will and endeavor, but as a settled fact, as a law of nature. "Progress is not an accident," says Herbert Spencer, "not a thing within human control, but a beneficent necessity."[38] The optimists' vision of "inevitable progress" received one rude shock after another as the baneful effects of a mechanistic and materialistic outlook on life appeared in succession in the form of greed for wealth and power, industrialism, capitalism, exploitation of the weak by the strong, mercantile colonization, imperialism, militarism, and so forth. Then followed the First World War. Still the optimists had hopes for a new and better world. Their disillusionment

[36]Cf. Lewis Mumford, *Technics and Civilization,* New York, Harcourt, Brace, 1934, p. 58: "The machine came forth as the new demiurge that was to create a new heaven and a new earth: at the least, as a new Moses that was to lead a barbarous humanity into the promised land."

[37]See Turgot's *Discourses sur l'historie,* 1750, in J.B. Bury, *Selected Essays,* p.27: "The total mass of the human race marches continually, though sometimes slowly, to an ever increasing perfection."

Alfred Tennyson, "Locksley Hall," in *The Poems of Tennyson,* Christopher Ricks, ed., London, Longmans, Green & Co., 1969, p.699:

Forward, forward let us range,
Let the great world spin forever down the
ringing grooves of change.

(Written after seeing the first opening of the railway line between Manchester and Liverpool.)

Charles Darwin, *The Origin of Species,* Vol. II, New York, D. Appleton, 1896, Ch. XV, p. 305: "And as natural selection works solely by and for the good of each being, all corporeal and mental environments will tend to progress towards perfection."

Herbert Spencer, *Social Statics,* London, John Chapman, 1851, p. 441: "And when the change at present going on is complete . . . then, none will be hindered from duly unfolding their natures: for while everyone maintains his own claims, he will respect the like claims of others. . . . And thus, perfect morality, perfect individuation, and perfect life will be simultaneously realized."

[38]Herbert Spencer, *Essays,* Vol. I, "Progress: Its Law and Cause," New York, D. Appleton, 1907, p. 60.

was all but complete when the Second World War ended in the holocaust of Hiroshima and Nagasaki.

Evidently, the optimists lost sight of some important truths. They generally identified human happiness with material prosperity.[39] It did not perhaps occur to many of them that physical comforts and pleasures do not necessarily make a man happy. Human happiness depends primarily on psychical factors rather than physical.

Many again made the assumption that man's moral development goes hand in hand with his material and intellectual advancement.[40] But this is not a fact. Not only prosperous but even highly intelligent persons are often found to be morally deficient. Neither material success nor keenness of intellect is a mark of moral growth; whereas, without moral purity, intellect does not develop into insight, but tends to rationalize, rather than reason.

Man's rational nature depends on his moral goodness more than moral goodness depends on his rational nature. The faculty of reason cannot function until the mind is more or less free from emotional involvement. It does not derive from mere intelligence, as is often assumed. To see things impersonally one has to overcome passions and propensities. In fact, rational life does not grow without the cultivation of virtue. Righteousness brightens intellect, as unrighteousness darkens it.

Then there were others among the optimists who in judging man's material achievements overlooked his moral nature. They did not perceive that material progress unrelated to the moral development of man is meaningless. Any new invention or technical device can be conducive to either man's good or evil according to the way he uses it. Progress means movement towards a desirable, salutary end. Without the ethical content it has no meaning.

A common error, to which the advocates of progress were usually subject, was the conception of good and evil as two independent

[39]Cf. Benjamin Disraeli, "The equality which is now sought by vast multitudes of men in many countries is physical and material equality. The leading principle of the new school is that there is no happiness which is not material and that every living being has a right to share in that physical welfare." (Speech at Glasgow University, November 19, 1873.)

[40]Cf. Lewis Mumford, *Values for Survival,* New York, Harcourt, Brace, 1946, p. 66: "For the last two centuries the liberal and humanitarian groups in the Western World have been governed by two leading ideas. One of them was the belief in mechanical progress, more or less openly accompanied by the conviction that there was a positive relation between material improvements and moral perfection. The other was the belief that, through the free use of the human reason, the world was ripe for a sudden transformation that would establish peace and justice forever."

existences. So they mostly cherished the hope that in course of time evil would be completely eliminated and unmixed good alone would remain. But in truth, good and evil in the relative existence are interdependent. One exists in relation to the other. With the disappearance of one the other is bound to disappear.

They are like the two sides of a sheet of paper. In eliminating one you eliminate the other; in retaining one you retain the other. If night, for instance, ceases to exist, there will be neither night nor day. If ugliness ceases to exist, there will remain neither ugliness nor beauty. So when poverty disappears, richness will vanish. With the disappearance of wrong deeds justice will vanish. To cognize light you have to cognize darkness; to cognize beauty you have to cognize ugliness; to cognize plenty you have to cognize want; to cognize pleasure you have to cognize pain; to cognize good you have to cognize evil. Absolute good or spiritual perfection is beyond relative good as well as relative evil. The Supreme Being alone is good in the absolute sense. "There is none good but one, that is, God," says Jesus Christ.[41]

6. *No scheme of life can be complete without the spiritual Ideal.*

Material life is not secure without a moral basis, and moral life is not secure without a spiritual basis. So material well-being depends finally on spiritual idealism. Essentially, morality is the attunement of the individual self to the universal, the Soul of all souls, and is therefore inseparable from spirituality. Whenever worldly glory and enjoyment become the primary objectives of life, material values gain supremacy over the moral; greed takes hold of the human mind; ethics tend to degenerate into expediency. Under this condition ethical standards can hardly prevail even as "enlightened self-interest," because man becomes too selfish to sacrifice his secular interests for the sake of the common weal.

This invariably happens when the physical order is considered to be the true type of reality and the sense-life an end in itself. All noble pursuits of man, such as arts, science, ethics, philosophy, and even religion (if it may exist then in some form), become as a matter of course subservient to the interests of sense life. The ethical ideal must guide and govern material interests dominated by sense desires, which are insatiable by nature. It cannot be determined by, or derived from them. It must be independent and stand on a solid ground

[41] Mark 10:18.

beyond them, that is, on spiritual consciousness, the sole controller of sense desire.

Without the spiritual Ideal, without God-realization or Supreme Good as the ultimate Goal, no scheme of life can be self-sufficient or safe and sound. A spiritual outlook on life is necessary not only for the attainment of the Kingdom of God, but also for the security of earthly peace and prosperity. Mere recognition of the supremacy of the spiritual Ideal, even though one may not be able to pursue it, serves as a check on one's sense desire. It is inveterate sense desire, the root of his selfishness, that makes man deviate from the moral path. Without its control no moral development is possible. But modern man, while holding to earthly prosperity and enjoyments as the supreme end of life, expects his moral nature to be free and sound enough to regulate his material interests. This is absurd. He permits his sense desire to be dominant. Thus, it has a constant tendency to overpower his reason and subvert his will and lead him astray; and yet he thinks that in practical life — social, political, or economic — his moral judgment will be intact.

Above all, the spiritual Ideal provides us with an absolute standard of values. Except Supreme Good all life-values are relative. None of them can be the ultimate objective of life. None of them can be an end in itself. They can serve best as instrumental to the highest. Without reference to the ultimate value a right scale of values cannot be framed. For all these reasons, any "this-worldly" ideal, humanistic or deistic (such as "world-affirmation," "life affirmation," "accent on life," "social duty," or the like), realistic and practical though it seems to be, is prone to lead to confusion of values and defeat its own purpose. But modern man refuses to see that it is his very love of life that makes him lose life. "He that loveth his life shall lose it; and he that hateth his life in this world shall keep it unto life eternal," says Jesus Christ.[42]

A complete scheme of life must include all the life-values, relative and absolute. Not only that; it must integrate them into a harmonious whole. This cannot be achieved without a right appraisement of the values. We have to understand their interrelation, recognize their relative importance, and determine their respective places in the plan of life. A balanced life does not rest on *equal* regard for all the aspects of life, as is usually assumed, but on *due* regard for each of them. The different aspects of life — physical, intellectual, aesthetic, and moral — have to be adjusted to the spiritual Ideal. The Vedic seers achieved

[42]John 12:25.

this by the fourfold classification of the human objectives under virtue, wealth, pleasure, and Liberation. The first three include all secular pursuits. In a wide sense, virtue (dharma) implies the internal resources, and wealth the external. A man can seek wealth in many different forms, such as property (immovable and movable), children, friends, health, beauty, fame. Pleasure can be physical, intellectual, or aesthetic. In the Vedic scheme virtue is the basic value, and Liberation, in other words Supreme Good, the ultimate value. Without a moral basis no aspect of the individual or the collective life can be safe and sound.

The point is that man must be viewed as a whole, and in the right perspective. All the aspects of life have to be taken into account and rightly appraised. Broadly speaking, human personality consists of three distinct factors, body, mind, and spirit, which are interrelated. But, rightly viewed, man is not the unity of these factors. He is embodied spirit. He is the changeless immortal self (ātman) in a changeful psychophysical garb. The real man is the luminous principle of consciousness, ever pure and free, with which the body and the mind are associated as adjuncts. The physical body is like his vehicle or dwelling house; and the mind is like an inner apparatus. Neither belongs to him intrinsically.

Man's problem is not the lack of will to live, as some modern thinkers hold, but the ignorance of the right way of living, which cannot be truly determined without knowing the Goal of life. The fulfillment of human life is not in material progress, nor intellectual achievement, nor aesthetic delight, nor moral development, but in spiritual attainment. To be free from all bondages, sufferings, and delusions man has to realize the innate perfection of his spiritual self. He must live with that end in view, attuning his entire being to that Ideal as far as he can.

CHAPTER XI

THE SPIRITUAL OUTLOOK ON LIFE. HOW IT CONJOINS THE TWO WAYS

1. *Let us recapitulate how virtue promotes spiritual awakening and sets the stage for Karma-yōga. (See Ch. IX, sec. 5, 6, 7.)*

A seeker of prosperity who recognizes that the moral and the spiritual order of the universe govern the material is naturally averse to any violation of virtue for the sake of material gain, even though he is not himself pursuing the spiritual Ideal. He has faith in the traditional moral values based on spiritual verities. His ambition does not, as a rule, turn into avidity. Whatever possessions and pleasures are desirable he tries to secure by the right performance of his duties according to his situation in life. Because of his self-composure, he is able to make the best of his wealth and position and enjoy life rightly. Affluent or not, he gets the most out of this life.

Through direct experience of well-being and felicity here and hereafter he develops, in natural course, an insight into the inherent shortcomings of all possessions and pleasures in the realm of the senses, howsoever long-lived, fine, and fascinating they may be. He sees the world as a panorama of dualities, as we have noted. He realizes that no position, no pleasure anywhere in the relative universe can satisfy his innate longing for unmixed blessing. Even the magnificence and enjoyments of the heaven-world (Svargalōka) pale into insignificance compared to Supreme Good. They are neither permanent nor flawless. He becomes convinced that "just as in this world the sense-objects gained by work come to an end, even so in other worlds do those gained by meritorious deeds."[1]

Wholly disenchanted of the glitter of the phenomenal world the seeker of secular values wants to turn away from the search for the temporal to the search for the Eternal. He tries to give up the way of activity (pravṛtti-mārga) marked by desire and betake himself to the way of renunciation (nivṛtti-mārga) marked by desirelessness. Yet he

[1]Ch.U. VIII:1.6.

cannot. The sense desires embedded in the subsoil of the mind do not permit it. He needs a preparatory measure to be able to withdraw his thoughts completely from all glories and joys achievable by work and also to develop an intense longing for the Eternal attainable through renunciation. It is said in the *Muṇḍaka Upaniṣad:*

> By thoroughly examining the sense-worlds that can be acquired by work, a seeker of Brahman must become dissatisfied with them. The self-existent One cannot be the product of work. For the knowledge of the same he should duly approach the teacher, versed in the Vedas and settled in Brahman.[2]

Before relinquishing the way of activity for the way of renunciation, the seeker of prosperity has to cultivate desirelessness by the practice of Karma-yōga; that is, by doing work with a dispassionate outlook on life. Real longing for the knowledge of Brahman cannot grow as long as the mind clings to sense objects. And without this resource, none can follow the path of renunciation with unfaltering steps. It is said in the *Bṛhadāraṇyaka Upaniṣad,* "Through the study of the Vedas, sacrificial deeds, charity, and austerity consisting in a dispassionate experience of sense-objects, the seekers of Brahman develop the desire to know It."[3]

The truth is that sense-desires do not leave a person even though he wants to leave them, being convinced of their futility. Firmly rooted in the subconscious mind they cling to him tenaciously. He has to struggle hard to get rid of them. This creates an inner conflict. On the one hand, he feels an urge to give up all secular concerns and devote himself completely to spiritual pursuits; on the other, the inveterate habits and tendencies of the mind direct him perforce to the old ruts. Even though he runs away from society he cannot fix his thoughts on God. They turn again and again to the secular affairs he leaves behind.

The seeker of prosperity is instructed not to give up his worldly activities at this stage, but to continue them while trying to make himself free from attachment by maintaining evenness of mind in success and failure, in honor and dishonor, in weal and woe. This is the practice of Karma-yōga. Śrī Kṛṣṇa says to Arjuna, "Being steadfast in yōga, O Dhananjaya, perform your actions, without attachment and with even-mindedness in success and in failure. This evenness of mind is called yōga."[4] Literally, yōga means union.

[2]Mu.U. I:2.12. [3]Br.U. IV:4.22. [4]BG II:48.

Generally, the word is used for the union of the individual self with the supreme Self, that is, the realization of God. Karma-yōga means karma as a method of God-realization. Thus, in a wide sense yōga signifies spiritual discipline.

As long as a man clings to sense-objects he cannot attain yōga, the inner composure necessary to spiritual practice. As long as he values worldly power and possessions for their own sake, his mind is liable to be attached to them, and with their gain and loss, to be swayed by hope and fear, pleasure and pain, like and dislike, pride and humiliation. But when he is able to recognize Supreme Good as the Goal of life and look upon material well-being as a means to that end, then, his mind being free from worldly attachment, it becomes possible for him to gain wealth, secure comforts, hold position, wield power, make friends, and so forth, with self-possession, without being blinded and bound. To a Karma-yōgī Supreme Good is the ultimate value. All other values are instrumental to it; thus he can view them dispassionately and manipulate them with understanding and judgment for the highest purpose. Man becomes attached to the means only when, forgetting the goal, he mistakes it for the end.

Freedom from attachment does not, however, imply indifference. No one can be indifferent to the means as long as he cares for the goal. The seeker of secular values who wakes up to the spiritual Ideal and tries to live in the world free from attachment, not permitting himself to be elated by success or depressed by failure, gradually overcomes the outgoing tendencies and develops an inwardness of the mind. Then there grows within him a natural longing for the realization of the Self and an insight into Its true nature enabling him to contemplate on It. This stage of inner development is known as *citta-śuddhi* or *sattva-śuddhi* in the terminology of Vedanta. Literally, it means the purification of the mind, the purging of sense-desires embedded in it. This, indeed, is a landmark of spiritual progress. This is the starting point of Jñāna-yōga and Bhakti-yōga as well. With the purification of the mind a Karma-yōgī of devotional type develops fervent devotion to God. His assiduous devotion turns into spontaneous devotion.

2. *Karma-yōga forms the bridge between the two ways.*

This stage of mental purification (citta-śuddhi) is the terminus of the way of activity (pravṛtti-mārga). Here the seeker of prosperity enters into the way of renunciation (nivṛtti-mārga) and turns into a seeker of Supreme Good. He becomes indrawn and passes from the active to the contemplative life. Outer activities lose their hold on him. Work is no longer indispensable to his self-development, although he may not give it up. He can even retire from the world and live a solitary life of self-resignation and meditation with the sole object of God-realization. It is said in the *Bhagavad-gītā,* "For an aspirant who wants to attain yōga activity is the way, but when he has attained yōga calmness is the way."[5] That the main purpose of his work is to prepare the mind for contemplation on spiritual Reality has been aptly expressed by Sureśvarācārya:[6] "Activities without attachment purify the mind and turn it to the inmost Self. Then, their purpose served, they disappear like clouds after the rains."[7] In fact, Karma-yōga disciplines the mind for devotion to God as well as for Self-knowledge. Śrī Kṛṣṇa says:

> One should perform work until one is dispassionate or until one has developed regard for listening to talks about Me and other devotional practices. Performing his duties and the sacrificial rites without any desire for results, a person, O Uddhava, goes neither to heaven nor to hell, unless he deviates. Becoming sinless and pure such a man attains true knowledge or perchance devotion to Me living in this very world.[8]

It is worthy of note in this connection that none can go beyond work but through work. "Not by abstaining from work does man attain freedom from work, nor by merely renouncing work does he attain perfection," declares Śrī Kṛṣṇa.[9]

Though usually included in the way of activity (pravṛtti-mārga), Karma-yōga actually forms the bridge that joins it with the way of renunciation (nivṛtti-mārga). Being intermediate between the two it serves as a connecting link. It turns the mind from the search for prosperity to the search for Supreme Good. It is preparatory to every other spiritual method that forms the way of renunciation, such as Jñāna-yōga, Bhakti-yōga, Dhyāna-yōga, and so forth. So it can be adapted to any one of them, especially to Jñāna-yōga and Bhakti-yōga, which are the principal methods of God-realization. Different types of spiritual aspirants practice Karma-yōga with different mental attitudes, an essential feature of which is equanimity.

[5]BG VI:3.

[6]One of the four leading disciples of Śaṅkarācārya, Sureśvarācārya was a celebrated author of several Vedantic treatises. Before embracing sannyāsa (monastic life) he was known as Maṇḍana Miśra. The three other disciples are Padmapāda, Hastāmalaka, and Tōṭakācārya.

[7]*Naiṣkarmya-siddhi,* 49. [8]SB XI:20.9-11. [9]BG III:4.

Karma-yōga is not mere unselfish work. It is not an ethical course. It is a spiritual discipline. None can practice this yōga or any other, until he is disillusioned of dualities and wants to go beyond the pairs of opposites that constitute the relative order. He must be prepared to direct his mind (dominated as it is by contrary tendencies acquired in the past) from the search for the relative to the search for the ultimate Good. As the stepping stone to the two principal yōgas, i.e., Bhakti-yōga (the way of devotion to God) and Jñāna-yōga (the way of Self-knowledge), Karma-yōga has a very distinct place in the lives of the spiritual aspirants.

3. *Two main types of Karma-yōgī: (1) devotional and (2) introspective.*

A Karma-yōgī of devotional type does his work as an offering to God, knowing Him to be the Supreme Master of all. All power, all beauty, all wisdom, all goodness, all greatness are His. As an ideal servant the Karma-yōgī claims nothing for himself. He resigns to the Lord all his possessions and all his actions as well. Regardless of his pain and pleasure, fortune and misfortune, he performs his duties as a caretaker, as a custodian, for the satisfaction of the Master, to whom everything really belongs. Knowing Him to be the one source of all power he regards himself as a mere instrument. He claims neither the work nor its results. To do the Lord's will is his sole aim. Surrendering himself completely to the Divine Ruler, he remains unperturbed by the varying conditions of life over which he knows he has no control. As he forsakes all claims on his work and its results, they do not react on him. That is to say, they leave no mark (saṁskāra) on his mind to produce future effects, good or evil. In this way he works out the accumulated impressions (saṁskāras) of previous actions without acquiring any new.

With regard to the practice of Karma-yōga by the devotees, Śrī Kṛṣṇa says:

> He who performs actions without attachment, resigning them to God, is untainted by their effects just as the lotus leaf is not moistened by water. Forsaking attachment the devotees work solely with body, senses, mind, and intellect, for the purification of the heart.[10]

Therefore, He instructs Arjuna to dedicate all actions to Him:

[10]BG V:10,11.

> Whatever you do, whatever you eat, whatever you offer in sacrifice, whatever you give away, whatever austerity you practice, O Son of Kuntī, do this as an offering to Me.[11] Thus shall you be free from the bondages of actions that bear good and evil results. With your mind firmly set on the yōga of renunciation you shall attain Liberation and come to Me.[12]

This is the goal that a Karma-yōgī of devotional nature attains in due course through the practice of Bhakti-yōga. When his mind is purged of all desires for the temporal through the practice of Karma-yōga, fervent devotion to God grows within him. Then his karma attended with full self-resignation is but a form of devotion.

The Karma-yōgī of introspective type, who aims at the realization of the self as Brahman (the Impersonal Absolute Being), holds his thoughts on the real nature of the self while he works. He recognizes that all actions belong to the body, the organs, and the mind, and that the self, the calm witness of all physical and mental movements, is ever at rest. He is therefore assured that, while apparently working, he does not really work. He is self-poised even when intensely active outwardly. A person regards himself as the doer simply because he identifies the self with the psychophysical complex. The body, the organs, and the mind — as well as external objects — are transformations of the guṇas of Prakṛti.[13]

[11]Cf. St. Paul's Epistles: "Whether therefore ye eat, or drink, or whatever ye do, do all to the glory of the Lord," (I Corinthians 10:31). "And whatsoever ye do, do it heartily, as to the Lord, and not unto men," (Colossians 3:23).

[12]BG IX:27,28.

[13]The three guṇas — sattva, rajas, and tamas — are the primal constituents of Prakṛti, primordial nature, *natura naturans,* from which the whole universe, physical and mental, has evolved. The self, the only immutable and intelligent entity, is ever distinct from Prakṛti and its evolutes — mind, organs, body and external objects. All changes, all movements, are in the realm of Prakṛti; the self is beyond them all. It is the very presence of the self that enables Prakṛti to function and transform. There is no awareness anywhere but in the self. Even the mind is not self-aware. It glows with the light of the luminous self.

Before the manifestation of the universe, the three guṇas remain in a state of equilibrium. They balance one another. Then Prakṛti is indiscrete and undifferentiated. As the guṇas lose their equilibrium the process of evolvement starts. From the grossest to the finest, everything in nature (physical and psychical) is composed of the three guṇas, which invariably coexist and are inseparable. But everywhere one or another of the triad predominates the other two. It is the preponderance of one or another of the guṇas in varying degrees that makes all differences in things.

The guṇas are not the attributes of Prakṛti, but its constituents — like the three strands of a rope. They may be conceived as substantive energies. Sattva is the principle of poise conducive to purity, knowledge, joy. Rajas is the principle of motivity leading to activity, desire, restlessness, or disquietude. Tamas is the principle of inertia resulting in inaction, dullness, delusion. Sattva is light, tamas heavy, rajas, medium. Sattva is represented as white, rajas as red, tamas as dark.

Activity means the occupation of the body, the organs, and the mind with the objects. The self, which is ever distinct from them all, is therefore beyond activity. On the practice of Karma-yōga by the seekers of Self-knowledge Śrī Kṛṣṇa remarks:

> All work is performed by the guṇas of prakṛti [manifest as body, organs, mind]. He whose understanding is deluded by egoism thinks "I am the doer." But, O Mighty Arjuna, he who sees the truth about the guṇas and their functions and about that which is distinct from them [that is, the Self] remains unattached, knowing that it is the guṇas [as body, organs, and mind] that associate with the guṇas [as objects].[14]

Again Śrī Kṛṣṇa says,

> "I do nothing at all," thinks the yōgī who knows the truth, for he is convinced that, in seeing, hearing, touching, smelling, tasting, in walking, breathing, and sleeping, in talking, emitting, holding, in opening and closing the eyes, it is the organs that are occupied with the sense-objects.[15]

Truly speaking, only a man of Self-knowledge can maintain such a spectator-like attitude towards all physical and mental movements, while a seeker of Self-knowledge has to cultivate it. He who thinks of himself as the doer of work naturally claims the work and its result. Consequently he has to experience its fruits, sweet and bitter, both of which create bondage. But he who forsakes the idea of the doer claims neither the work nor its result. Naturally he acquires neither merit nor demerit by his work, and has not therefore to reap its fruits. The work done creates no new bondage for him; on the contrary, it eliminates the old bondage by removing the deposits of his past actions.

4. *Work with the spirit of renunciation is the meeting point of the two ways as illustrated in the lives of the royal sages.*

After the attainment of citta-śuddhi (the standard purification of the mind), a Karma-yōgī becomes a bona fide spiritual aspirant, a seeker of Supreme Good with an inner urge, being no longer held back by sense attachment. Leaving behind the way of activity, marked by secular desire, he has entered the way of renunciation marked by desirelessness. As a follower of the way of renunciation, the seeker of Supreme Good does not necessarily give up worldly

[14]BG III:27,28.
[15]*Ibid.* V:8,9.

duties and retire into seclusion. Though free from worldly desires, he may or may not renounce the world. He may continue his worldly activities with the spirit of renunciation. It depends upon his disposition and condition of life.

As already stated, a spiritual aspirant should have internal renunciation, if not both internal and external. With regard to this type of worker, Śrī Kṛṣṇa says to Arjuna, "He who neither hates nor craves should be known as a man of constant renunciation; for, being free from the dualities, O Mighty-armed, he is easily liberated from bondage."[16] It is said in the *Muṇḍaka Upaniṣad,* "This ātman (self) cannot be attained by him who is devoid of strength, or where there is lack of vigilance, or where there is knowledge without renunciation."[17] In the opinion of Ānandagiri,[18] internal renunciation and not the conventional (monastic), is intended here. The spirit of renunciation, and not its insignia, is the essential condition for Self-knowledge.

Even after Self-realization an illumined person may continue to work for the guidance of the world. Śrī Kṛṣṇa says, "As the ignorant perform work being attached to it, O Bhārata, so should an enlightened man work, but without attachment, in order to set people on the right path."[19] But though working to all appearance, the enlightened worker does not work, being completely detached, for he is always aware of the immutable, serene Self and does not identify himself with the mind, the organs, or the body, to which actions belong. Therefore, his is only a semblance of work, as Śrī Kṛṣṇa says: "Giving up attachment to the fruit of action, ever content, and dependent on none, though engaged in work he does not work at all."[20] Commenting on this verse Śaṅkara remarks, "Finding it impracticable for some reason to give up work, an enlightened person may be engaged in work as before, free from attachment to it and its result, without any selfish end, only with the object of guiding people to the right course. Such a man does not really work."

Even some rulers of ancient India are reputed to have been illumined workers. They are called Rājarṣis, royal sages. Janaka, King of Mithila (modern Bihar), is the most famous of them. In the *Bṛhadāraṇyaka Upaniṣad* he is spoken of as the knower of Brahman:

[16]BG V:3.

[17]Mu.U. III:2.4.

[18]The great annotator on Śaṅkara's Commentaries on the *Ten Upaniṣads,* the *Brahma-sūtram,* and the *Bhagavad-gītā.*

[19]BG III:25.

[20]*Ibid.* IV:20.

" 'This is the eternal glory of a knower of Brahman — that it neither increases nor decreases through work. [Therefore] one should know the nature of that [glory] alone. Knowing it, one is not touched by evil action.'[21] Therefore he who knows it as such becomes self-controlled, calm, indrawn, enduring, and concentrated; he sees the Self in himself, and he sees all as the Self. Evil [comprising merit and demerit both] does not trouble him, but he consumes all evil. He becomes sinless, taintless, free from doubts, and a knower of Brahman. This is the domain of Brahman, O Emperor, and you have attained it," said Yājñavalkya.[22]

In the *Chāndōgya Upaniṣad* King Aśvapati is mentioned as the teacher of the Cosmic Self (Vaiśvānara Ātman). Once five great householders, who were Brāhmaṇas and well versed in the Vedas, held a discussion as to "Who the self is" and "What is Brahman." Unable to solve the problem they went to a famous Brāhmaṇa teacher, Uddālaka, who said to them as soon as they came, "Sirs, at present Aśvapati Kaikeya knows the Cosmic Self; let us all go to him." Upon their arrival the king received each of them with due respect. The next morning he offered them gifts. When they refused, the king said, "In my kingdom there is no thief, no misery, no drunkard, no man without the sacrificial fire, no ignorant person, no adulterer, and so no adulteress. I am going to perform a sacrificial rite, sirs; and as much wealth as I shall give to each priest I will give you too. Please stay, sirs." Then the Brāhmaṇas said, "We have not come for riches, O king. At this time you are the knower of the Cosmic Self. Please teach us that." "Tomorrow I will instruct you," replied the king. Early the next morning the Brāhmaṇas duly approached him with sacrificial fuel in their hands.[23] Then the king imparted to them the knowledge of the Cosmic Self.[24]

Śrīmad Bhāgavatam records the story of another royal sage, Ṛṣava. Says Śukadeva:[25]

The sage Ṛṣava was himself a free soul, an experiencer of Supreme Bliss, who had forever eradicated the whole series of evil and was pure-hearted and established in self-rule; yet he performed work to all

[21]Good as well as evil action is meant, for both are evil, being the cause of bondage.

[22]Br.U. IV:4.23.

[23]The offering is symbolic of humility, reverence, and willingness to serve, the virtues that make the pupil's mind receptive of spiritual knowledge.

[24]Ch.U.V:11.1-7

[25]The narrator of the *Bhāgavatam* to King Parīkṣit. He was the son of the sage Veda-Vyāsa and a born-free soul.

appearance like a bound man and followed the religious convention of the age to set an example to the unwise. Calm, compassionate, and even-minded, he was a friend of all and set the householders aright on the path consisting of virtue, wealth, pleasure, progeny, fame, and Liberation. What a great man does, people follow.[26]

Here Śukadeva mentions six main objectives of life, i.e., virtue, wealth, and so forth. It is to be noted that in the fourfold classification of the human objectives under virtue, wealth, pleasure, and Liberation, which we have mentioned before, progeny and fame are included in wealth.

5. *The seeker of Supreme Good has to forsake relative good as well as evil.*

We have found that it is along the path of virtue that the seeker of prosperity arrives at Karma-yōga and it is through Karma-yōga that he gains access to the way of Supreme Good. From the way of prosperity to the way of Supreme Good there is no other approach but Karma-yōga, and the only approach to Karma-yōga is virtue. Therefore, unless the seeker of prosperity follows the path of virtue he has no chance of finding the way to Supreme Good. To turn away from the search for prosperity to the quest of Supreme Good one has to realize not only the bitterness of want and misery but also the emptiness of plenty and pleasure. And without some experience of plenty and pleasure who can be convinced of their hollowness?

It has already been noticed that an unrighteous man, prosperous though he may be, cannot be happy. His cares and worries do not permit him to enjoy his possessions. Since he cannot gain the most out of his wealth or position, there is always a discontent within him. His desires, finding no satisfaction, grow from more to more. His intellect is too muddled to see through their vanity, their deceptiveness. With regard to men of demoniac nature Śrī Kṛṣṇa rightly observes:

Giving themselves up to hypocrisy, pride, and arrogance, they hold false views through delusion and act with impure resolve. Beset with innumerable cares, which will end only with death, looking on the gratification of desire as their highest goal, and feeling sure that this is all; bound by a hundred ties of hope, given up wholly to lust and wrath, they strive by unjust means to amass wealth for the satisfaction of their

[26]SB V:4.14,15.

passions. . . . Three are the gates of hell, ruinous of the self — lust, anger, and greed; therefore one should forsake them. The man who has escaped these three gates of darkness, O son of Kuntī, practices what is good for himself and thus goes to the Supreme Goal. He who discards the ordinance of the Śāstras and acts upon the impulse of desire *attains neither purity of mind, nor happiness, nor the Supreme Goal.*[27]

Then Śrī Kṛṣṇa concludes: "So let the Śāstras be your authority in determining what ought to be done and what ought not to be done. Having learnt the ordinance of the Śāstras you should do your work in the world."[28] Here it is indicated that ethical conduct must be based on the scriptural knowledge, that is, on the fundamental unity of finite selves in the Divine Being as revealed in suprasensuous experience, on which the scriptural teachings are based. It cannot rest secure on the egoistic view of life dependent on empirical knowledge. The scriptures give us, however, the guiding principles, the general rules of conduct, within the framework of which every individual has ample scope for the exercise of his understanding and judgment. It is said in the *Manu-smṛti,* "The sources of dharma are the Veda, the words and the deeds of those who know the Veda, the practice of the honest, and one's inner contentedness."[29]

In this world we are trying to solve the problem of evil by good. We are trying to overcome poverty by plenty, sickness by health, ugliness by beauty, pain by pleasure, ignorance by knowledge, vice by virtue, and so forth. But when we succeed in these efforts, we find that just as poverty creates problems so does plenty; just as sickness creates problems so does health; just as pain creates problems so does pleasure; just as ignorance creates problems so does knowledge; just as ugliness creates problems so does beauty; just as vice creates problems so does virtue; in short, evil and good as well have their peculiar problems. Indeed, life is never free from problems. We solve one problem to face another. We get out of one difficulty to find ourselves in another.

This is true not only of the life on this earth but also on any other plane of relative existence, no matter how high it may be. Just as a beggar-woman cannot conceive of the problems a queen may have, similarly, we, the denizens of this earth, cannot believe that there can be any problem in the heaven world (Svargalōka). But the entire relative existence is marked by interdependence. Wherever we turn,

[27]BG XVI:10-12, 21-23.
[28]*Ibid.* XVI:24.
[29]MS II:6.

we move from one stage of bondage to another. Bondage means dependence, freedom independence. Both evil and good bind us, the one like an iron chain and the other like a golden chain, so to speak. But the golden chain is no less strong to bind than the iron one; only its glitter hides its binding nature.

Even moral virtues are not as good as they seem to be. Kindness requires misery for its existence; justice wrong; forgiveness fault. They are good as contingent ideals, but not as the ultimate goal. For instance, medical service is desirable while there is disease; it is not an end in itself. The end is sound health where there is neither disease nor its remedy. The Supreme Good is beyond the relativity of good and evil, beyond virtue and vice, beyond duality. To attain this the aspirant has to give up relative good as well as evil. But at first he has to overcome evil by good. And then after attaining good he has to apprehend its inadequacy from actual experience before he can find the way out of relative good into the Supreme Good. As Sri Ramakrishna says, "To take out one thorn you need another. But after removing the first thorn you discard the other as well. So you remove the thorn of ignorance by means of the thorn of knowledge and then go beyond knowledge to attain Supreme Knowledge."[30]

6. *Escapism and defeatism cannot make man spiritual.*

After experiencing life's blessings here and hereafter, the virtuous alone among the seekers of prosperity can be fully convinced of their futility. Then they can freely reject even the highest glories and joys of relative existence as vanity of vanities, and seek the Supreme Good as the sole Goal. Without this exalted attitude none can enter the spiritual path. Spiritual life begins only when one is ready to discard unhesitatingly all that is perishable for the sake of the Imperishable, all that is changeful for the sake of the Changeless, all that is apparent for the sake of the Real. Neither through fear of the battle of life nor through failure in it, neither through discontent nor through despair, can a man turn away from the charms of the sense-world and be in the quest of God. Escapism or defeatism cannot make man spiritual. Neither of these can divert the habitual trend of the human mind from the sensible universe to the unseen Supreme Spirit. He who leaves the world out of fear or frustration must be lacking in the spirit of renunciation. The inflow of desires hidden within will not permit him to hold to the spiritual path. Austerity without the spirit of

[30]GSR, p.523.

renunciation is as unstable and false as the sandy bed of a subterranean stream.

The story of Naciketa in the *Kaṭha Upaniṣad* beautifully illustrates the triumphant attitude of a spiritual aspirant towards the allurements of the sense-world. In order to find the secret of death, this Brāhmaṇa boy approached Yama, the ruler of the departed spirits, for the knowledge of the Self. Then Yama to test the pupil's capacity and earnestness at first tried to dissuade him from an inquiry into this puzzling mystery of all mysteries; failing in that he offered the youth not only earthly but also heavenly possessions and enjoyments that human beings may hanker after.

Said Yama:

> Ask for sons and grandsons with a hundred years long life. Ask for plenty of cattle, horses, elephants, and gold and for vast territory and live yourself as many years as you like. . . . Ask freely for whatever objects of desire are rare in this human world. These charming celestial damsels with their chariots and lutes are not attainable by mortals. Them I present to you. Let them attend on you. Only do not ask me, O Naciketa, about the secret of death.[31]

But Naciketa stood firm, proof against temptations. Being satisfied as to the pupil's deservingness Yama imparted to him the knowledge of the Self. (See Ch. VII, sec. 7.)

7. *The yearning for Supreme Good should grow from within through progressive courses. An individual's development must be in conformity with his psychophysical constitution.*

Man is born with an inveterate tendency for sense enjoyment. Until his desires are fulfilled to a certain extent, until he has some experience of sense pleasures, he cannot see through their vanity and deceptiveness. To turn to the spiritual Ideal, to accept God, the Supreme Being, as the goal of life, he has to be disenchanted of the glamour of sense life by recurring enjoyment and suffering until his heart yearns for the attainment of the absolute Good beyond dualities. Spiritual life is not for the multitude. Only certain individuals can find real interest in it.

It is said in the *Kaṭha Upaniṣad,* "The self-existent One damaged the senses by making them turn outward. Hence they perceive the

[31]Ka.U. I:1.23, 25.

external objects and not the Self within. Rare is the wise person who, desirous of immortality, turns his eyes inward and realizes the innermost Self."[32] Deluded by the charms of sense life many do not even believe in man's survival of death, not to speak of the life eternal, all-free and perfect. So says the King of Death:

> The life beyond death does not appear to one who is of child-mentality, heedless, and under the delusion of wealth. "This world alone exists and no other," he who thinks this way comes under my sway again and again.[33]

The point is this: To follow the way of renunciation, a person has to outgrow the sense desires. One cannot seek the Eternal as the goal of life unless he is free from attachment to the temporal. Neither suppression nor overindulgence is the way. The spirit of renunciation should develop from within in due course through a well-disciplined life of experience. It cannot be imposed upon him. This is why the Vedic religion encourages men and women with worldly tendencies to seek material welfare; yet at the same time it enjoins on them certain moral and religious disciplines, which not only promote material well-being but also conduce to the development of the spiritual sense. For the worldly-minded it has even prescribed prayers and rites and ceremonies for the fulfillment of material desires. This lower form of religion however gives them a chance to turn their thoughts to God.

Without adequate preparation in worldly life a man cannot, as a rule, overcome worldliness, even though he may perchance renounce the world. One of the causes of the decline of Buddhism is considered to be undue emphasis on renunciation, that is, indiscriminate admission of its followers into the monastic order. Neither the laudation of renunciation nor the condemnation of worldly enjoyments is the way to make man spiritual. Denunciation of secular interests without proper direction to regulate them for spiritual unfoldment, may be regarded as the chief drawback of Medieval Christianity that is accountable considerably for the revolt against religion in the modern age.

The highest is not the best for all at the same time. The vast majority of human beings cannot seek Supreme Good directly, yet they can proceed towards it indirectly along the line of least resistance. They can climb to the Highest step by step through a

[32]Ka.U. II:1.1. [33]Ka.U. I:2.6.

gradation of ideals. The capabilities of men and women differ. Different ideals suit different persons, according to their levels of development. "Take man where he stands and from there give him a lift," says Swami Vivekananda.[34] In moral as well as in spiritual life a man has to rise by stages. Gradual growth is the law of life.

One distinctive feature of the Vedic religion is that, in prescribing ethical and religious disciplines, it has taken into consideration the difference in the tendencies and the capacities of individuals (adhikāri-bheda). Not only in spiritual practice but also in the cultivation of moral virtues the Vedic seers have recognized the necessity of gradation of ideals. It is better to pursue with fervor an ideal within one's capacity, than to be overawed by too high an ideal or to adopt it half-heartedly. Every individual has his own line of development in conformity with his psychophysical nature. The practice of virtue or the performance of duties should therefore be in accordance with his inborn disposition and aptitude. This is his normal way of growth. It leads to an ordered expression of his potentialities.

The following story in the *Bṛhadāraṇyaka Upaniṣad* demonstrates how different moral disciplines suit different grades of people.

Gods, men, and demons (asuras)[35] — all descendants of Prajāpati, the Progenitor Brahmā — lived with him as students practicing austerity. After a period the gods said, "Kindly instruct us, sir." Prajāpati uttered the syllable "Da," and said to them, "Have you understood?" They replied, "Yes, we have. You tell us: *Damayata* — be self-controlled." "Yes, you have understood," said Prajapati.

Then the men said, "Kindly instruct us, sir." Prajapati uttered the same syllable "Da," and said to them, "Have you understood?" They replied, "Yes, we have. You tell us: *Datta* — be charitable." "Yes, you have understood," said Prajāpati.

Then the demons (asuras) said, "Kindly instruct us, sir." Prajāpati uttered the same syllable "Da," and said to them, "Have you understood?" They replied, "Yes, we have. You tell us: *Dayadhvam* — be compassionate." "Yes, you have understood," said Prajāpati. Even today the heavenly voice thunders from the cloud: "Da! Da! Da! — Be self-controlled! Be charitable! Be compassionate!"[36]

The three moral ideals of self-control, charity, and compassion

[34]"The Ideal of a Universal Religion," CW II, p. 382.
[35]Three types of human beings — godly, human, and ungodly — are meant.
[36]Br.U. V:2.1-3.

are intended for three different types of men. They are all to be practiced by human beings according to their inner development. The cruel should practice noninjury and strive to be compassionate; the avaricious should overcome greediness by charity; and those who are free from other vices, but still have sense desires, should particularly practice inner control. In this context Śaṅkara remarks:

> Those among men who, though lacking in self-control, are possessed of other good qualities are the gods; those in whom greed prevails are men; while those who are cruel and violent are the demons (asuras). So the same human species, according to the three drawbacks — lack of self-control, greediness, and cruelty, and according to the three guṇas — sattva, rajas, and tamas,[37] are called gods, men, and demons (asuras). Therefore it is men who should learn all the three lessons.[38]

As a matter of fact, the person in whom tamas (indolence, delusion, and the like) prevails cannot lift himself directly to the level of sattva (serenity, enlightenment, and so forth). He has first to overcome tamas by rajas (activity, achievement, and so on) and then rajas by sattva. A coward must become a hero before he can be a saint. He should have the courage to uphold justice before practicing forgiveness. Otherwise, he will only make a pretense of forgiveness with vindictiveness lurking within. When he has the power to vindicate justice then he can practice forgiveness. When forgiveness becomes natural to him then it is possible for him to practice the supreme moral ideal — "Resist not evil," which means the returning of good for evil, of love for hatred, of blessing for curse, as taught by great spiritual leaders of the world, e.g., Śrī Kṛṣṇa, The Buddha, Lao Tzu, Christ. Many do not even have the power to resist evil. Before they have the power of nonresistance let them acquire the power of resistance. When they have gained the power to resist evil, then nonresistance will be a virtue; otherwise they will make a virtue of weakness.

Swami Vivekananda rightly observes:

> We must first take care to understand whether we have the power of resistance or not. Then, having the power, if we renounce it and do not resist, we are doing a grand act of love; but if we cannot resist, and yet, at the same time, try to deceive ourselves into the belief that we are actuated by motives of the highest love, we are doing the exact opposite.[39]

[37]See footnote 13. [38]Br.U. V:2.1-3, S. com. [39]CW I, p. 37.

Truly speaking, only certain individuals can develop the power of nonresistance. A nation or a society as a whole has to depend mainly on the principle of justice in internal and external affairs. It cannot dispense with government or judicature. Indeed, he who is free from the feelings of "I" and "mine," who sees the one Self in all, can actually practice nonresistance, "being friendly and compassionate to all beings."

With regard to such a person Śrī Kṛṣṇa says, "Because he sees the Lord equally present everywhere, he injures not Self by self, and thus reaches the highest Goal."[40] In the Hindu scheme of life nonresistance is strictly the creed of a Sannyāsī, who gives the assurance of fearlessness to all beings when he takes the monastic vow.[41]

[40]BG XIII:28.
[41]See Tai.Ar. X:66, appendix.

CHAPTER XII

THE ATTAINMENT OF THE HIGHEST GOOD THROUGH THE PERFORMANCE OF DUTY

The Necessity for a Spiritual Outlook on Life

1. *Duty determined by one's natural disposition, training, and condition of life is called in Hindu scriptures* svadharma, *literally, one's own religion or mode of right living. It puts each individual in his own place.*

We have seen how virtue tends to align the way of prosperity with the way of Supreme Good. The cultivation of virtue is as essential to material well-being as it is to spiritual unfoldment. It is primarily the practice of virtue that enables the seeker of prosperity to enjoy life's blessings, to realize their inherent deficiency, and to turn to something beyond, something that never fails, something that is flawless, limitless, free, and blissful. Thus, there grows within him a yearning for Supreme Good. Virtue consists principally in the right performance of duties true to one's stage and sphere of life. As noted above, a man's duty should always be in accord with his inner tendencies and capacities and his situation in life. This is what svadharma means. On this are based the four social orders (varṇas) and the four stages of the individual life (āśramas).

Svadharma makes each man great in his own place. It promotes both individual and social growth. It calls forth the best in each person by preparing him for the social function for which he is naturally endowed. It brings about complete harmony between the individual and the social life. The individual and the society are interdependent. The growth of the society depends upon the growth of the individual and the growth of the individual upon the growth of the society. Human beings cannot live without mutual help, understanding, and sympathy. From his very birth, man is dependent on his fellow beings. Unlike other living creatures, he has to develop as a social unit. He must fit into the social body as well as he can. In the interest of the society and in his own interest, every individual should be trained for those duties for which he has natural fitness. In other words, a person's place in the society should be determined by his svadharma.

In the Vedic view there are four principal types of human beings according to their inborn natures. Each type is fit for a particular social role, i.e., each has its svadharma. So from the viewpoint of svadharma there are four main classes of men in the society. Śrī Kṛṣṇa declares: "The fourfold social order has been created by Me according to the division of guṇa [inborn nature determined by guṇa] and karma (duty)."[1] The four social orders are brāhmaṇa, kṣatriya, vaiśya, and śūdra.

Some persons are born with sattva guṇa predominant in them. Their religious tendencies are remarkable. They have innate faith in God. They love truth and virtues more than wealth and pleasures. They have natural aptitudes for learning and knowledge. They can live the simplest life with the noblest ideal. They are fit to be trained as educators, philosophers, and religious teachers. By living the religious life themselves they can guide others in the path of religion. Such are the brāhmaṇas. They represent the intellectual, the cultural, and the spiritual ideals of the society. For a person to be a brāhmaṇa three things are necessary: firstly, he must be sattvika by nature; secondly, he must receive the right kind of education for its development; and thirdly, he must assume a corresponding social role. Similarly, each of the other three classes is also based on inborn nature, right training, and appropriate social function.

Next to the brāhmaṇa are the kṣatriyas. In them rajas prevails with a mixture of sattva. They are the heroic type. They understand moral values better than spiritual truths. Uprightness, valor, nobility are their principal characteristics. They can sacrifice material interests, nay, even their lives for the sake of truth and justice. They are ever ready to defend the virtuous and subdue the wicked. They are fit to be trained as rulers and warriors. No man is entitled to the use of arms unless he values righteousness more than his own life. No man has any right to take another's life in the name of justice unless he can willingly give up his own life for its sake.

Thirdly, there are the vaiśyas. Rajas with an alloy of tamas is predominant in them. They understand economic values more than the moral or the spiritual. To them life is of first importance. They are

[1] BG IV:13.

inclined to work for its preservation. They have the genius to produce and distribute the necessities and the comforts of life. They develop the material resources of a country. Rightly trained they can take care of its agriculture, commerce, arts, industries and banking.

Last of all are the śūdras. In them tamas is preponderant. They have no creative or inventive power. They lack in initiative. Such as these need others' guidance. They are fit to be employed in the service of the other three classes and to be trained for that end. They are usually the laborers.

So we see, the higher a class is, the greater are its responsibilities and its sacrifice for society. The main activities and characteristics of the four classes are thus stated in the *Bhagavad-gītā:*

> The control of the mind and the senses, austerity, purity, forbearance, straightforwardness, knowledge, realization, and faith — these are the duties of a brāhmaṇa, originating from his own nature.
>
> Prowess, courage, fortitude, ability, dauntlessness in battle, generosity, and sovereignty — these are the duties of a kṣatriya, originating from his own nature.
>
> Agriculture, cattle-rearing, and trade are the duties of a vaiśya, originating from his own nature.
>
> And work consisting of service is the duty of a śūdra, originating from his own nature.[2]

Manu-smṛti specifies the duties of the four classes:

> Study and teaching, worship and guiding worship, making and receiving gifts — these are the duties ordained for the brāhmaṇa.
>
> Protection of people, charity, worship, study, nonaddictedness to sense-enjoyments — these are in brief the duties ordained for the kṣatriya.
>
> Preservation of cattle, charity, worship, study, commerce, money-lending, agriculture — these are the duties ordained for the vaiśya.
>
> Ungrudging service to the other three classes is the main duty prescribed for the śūdra.[3]

Then again, all the classes have some duties in common. There are the moral virtues to be practiced by all. As stated in the *Śrīmad-bhāgavatam,* these are noninjury, truthfulness, nonstealing, restraint of lust, anger, and greed, and attempting to do what is agreeable and beneficial to all beings.[4]

[2]BG XVIII:42-44.
[3]MS I:88-91.
[4]SB XI:17.21.

2. *Svadharma promotes man's spiritual as well as his material well-being. It applies to all humanity. The development of the caste system.*

The practice of svadharma conduces to both the outer and the inner development of man. There is no way of combining the two other than this. By its observance one can secure material welfare and at the same time grow spiritually. Any deviation from it hampers man's development consonant with his nature, and is therefore hazardous. So Śrī Kṛṣṇa warns Arjuna and, through him, mankind:

> Better is one's dharma though imperfectly performed, than the dharma of another well performed. Better is death in the doing of one's own dharma; the dharma of another is perilous.[5]

Arjuna was a kṣatriya. As a member of the ruling class it was his svadharma to uphold justice, to quell the aggressors, to fight for the right cause. With this end in view he had come to the battlefield. But the sight of his elders, relatives, friends, and countless other human beings ranged in battle-order ready to kill one another filled him with commiseration. He wanted to give up the fight, and even to retire from the world and live on alms like a sannyāsī. Śrī Kṛṣṇa noticed it was only sentimentalism, delusion, and confusion of ideals, and not the spirit of renunciation, that prompted Arjuna to betake himself to such a course. By retiring from the world at this stage he would simply prove to be a false sannyāsī, a hypocrite. Hence the note of warning.

A few more illustrations may be necessary to bring out the full import of Śrī Kṛṣṇa's lesson. Suppose a person who is a vaiśya by nature studies theology and becomes a preacher of religion. As the commercial spirit is predominant in him, he will naturally seek material gain while performing religious duties. He will not be able to practice what he preaches. Being untrue to himself he cannot minister to the spiritual needs of others. As a mere preacher he may be successful, but spiritually he will deteriorate. It would be beneficial for him to give up the brāhmaṇa's position and take up an occupation in keeping with his vaiśya tendencies. Even if it be so that for lack of practice or sufficient training he could not perform the latter duties efficiently, still this course would help him to take up the thread of his spiritual development.

Similarly, there is danger when a kṣatriya arrogates the position of a brāhmaṇa, or a vaiśya the position of a kṣatriya. A kṣatriya will

[5]BG III:35.

bring his combative spirit into the field of religion and look for contest in some form or other. When a vaiśya takes up arms he becomes a mercenary. He can fight for self-interest and not for humanity's sake. This is why a war waged by people in whom economic or political interests are predominant always spells disaster to the world. It does not make for peace. One war leads to another. It is because none of the belligerents, including those who are on the defensive, can stand for truth and justice, even though these be their declared objectives. It is not in their nature to sacrifice material interests for moral values.

As a spiritual discipline svadharma has great significance. By its observance anyone, whether a brāhmaṇa, a kṣatriya, a vaiśya, or a śūdra, can reach the highest Goal. With his inner progress an individual, a vaiśya for instance, has not necessarily to change his occupation for a higher one, i.e., for that of a kṣatriya or a brāhmaṇa. He can perform his duties in the spirit of a Karma-yōgī, as an offering to God and continue to develop spiritually, no matter what social order he may belong to outwardly. In the practice of Karma-yōga, as we have seen, it is the mental attitude of the worker that counts rather than the nature of the work. With the inner transformation continuing, the aspirant, though there may not be any change in his outer activities or social rank, will gradually develop the spirit of renunciation and ultimately reach the Goal. About the spiritual value of svadharma Śrī Kṛṣṇa says:

> Man attains perfection by devotion to his duty. Hear from Me, O Arjuna, how perfection is attained by him who is devoted to his own duty: by worshipping Him from whom all beings proceed and by whom the whole universe is pervaded — by worshipping Him through the performance of duty a man attains perfection.[6]

The truth of this is demonstrated by the fact that there have been mystics and saints from all classes of Hindu society, from the highest to the lowest. Some of the Vedic seers such as Kavas and Mahidas were śūdras by birth.[7] The *Mahābhārata* records the words of wisdom of a hunter-sage (dharma-vyādha). In the *Rāmāyaṇa* there is the story of the scavenger-prince, Guhaka, who was a dear friend and devotee of Rāma, an incarnation of God. The saint Kavir was a weaver, Ravidas a cobbler, Sena a barber, Nama-deva of Marwar a

[6]BG XVIII:45,46.
[7]See Ai.Br. II:19 and Kau.Br. XI:3.

carder of cotton, Tukarama of Maharaṣtra a farmer, to mention just a few out of numerous instances. Among women also there have been numberless seers and sages from the Vedic time up to the present age. It reminds us of some Christian mystics and saints, who are reported to have reached God while plying their trade, such as St. Paul the tentmaker, Jacob Boehme the cobbler, John Bunyon the tinsmith.

The fourfold classification according to guṇa (inborn nature) and karma (duty) applies to all humanity. There are these four types of persons — brāhmaṇa, kṣatriya, vaiśya, and śūdra, more or less, in all countries and in all races. But they do not form distinct classes everywhere. They exist as individuals. It was in ancient India that the social order was founded strictly on the principle of svadharma. References to all these four classes are found in the Vedic literature.[8] The present hereditary caste system among the Hindus is a degenerate form of the original social plan. It would be wise to remodel it on the old basis rather than to demolish it.

The Hindu doctrine of karma traces the inborn nature of a child to its previous lives and not to heredity. In this view, parents' qualities, congenital or acquired, are not transmitted to the child. Parentage can indicate, but not determine, the child's nature. Good children are expected to be born of good parents on the ground that like attracts like.

The difficulty of ascertaining a child's inborn nature made the social order dependent to a certain extent on birth. But the old system always stressed guṇa and karma, and not birthright. The *Śrīmad-bhāgavatam* clearly states:

> The characteristics of each social order as described will alone determine what social order a person belongs to, according as they are manifest in him, even though he be born in a different order.[9]

In many cases persons born of kṣatriya families were elevated to the brāhmaṇa class or lowered to the vaiśya or the śūdra class according to their fitness.[10] Similarly, individuals born of brāhmaṇa parents were lowered to other classes because of their incapacity to live as brāhmaṇas. The Hindu society maintained its true standard by this process of elevation to a higher grade and of reduction to a lower grade. The original purpose of the social scheme was by no means to

[8] Rg.V. X:90.12; Sat.Br. V:5.4.9.
[9] SB VII:11.35.
[10] See SB V:4.13; IX:2.9,23; IX:21.19,20; and *Viṣṇu Purāṇa*.

restrict an individual to the class in which he was born or to lower him, but to raise him gradually to Brahmanhood, which was the ideal of the social life.

As long as India was able to hold to the principle of svadharma she was great both materially and spiritually. One can get glimpses of her material and spiritual greatness from her ancient literature and also from Greek, Chinese, and Arabian sources. Clear traces of her cultural expansion are still to be found in the architecture, sculpture, painting, literature, mathematics, medicine, metaphysics, and religion of most of the Asiatic countries including the Oceanic islands.

But India's prosperity at the same time drew hordes of invading races from central and northwestern Asia and even from far off Greece. For many centuries she had to fight against these aggressors. Some of them were repulsed. Some were able to enter the country as plunderers and went away with the booty. Some succeeded in getting a foothold on the soil of India and settled there. In course of time these races were assimilated into the Hindu race. This happened long before the Mohammedan rule. When such races as the Scythians, the Greeks, the Pahlavas, and the Kushans, were included in Hindu society, the Hindus acknowledged their priests as brāhmaṇas and their ruling chiefs and warriors as kṣatriyas. In this way there arose within the Hindu social polity many different groups, each with rites and customs of its own; and to maintain their cultural distinctiveness various restrictions on intermarriage and interdining were introduced.

This is how in course of time the old social order lost its original purity and flexibility and, passing through many vicissitudes, petrified into the present hereditary caste system. Professor Radhakrishnan rightly observes: "Caste was the Hindu answer to the challenge of society in which different races had to live together without merging into one."[11]

In weal and woe a distinctive trait of Hindu culture has been unity in diversity and not dull uniformity. The cultural integrity of each group has been intact throughout the ages. No attempt has been made for the standardization of diverse modes of life. Underlying all varieties of customs, manners, and conventions there has been the unity of spiritual idealism, the keynote of Hinduism, which has kept the nation alive despite all vicissitudes that mark its history.

[11]S. Radhakrishnan, *Eastern Religions and Western Thought,* 2nd ed., London, Oxford University Press, 1940, p. 373 (by permission of the Clarendon Press, Oxford).

3. *The four stages of the individual life and their duties.*

Just as the social life, according to the Hindu view, has four orders so the individual life has four stages. The four successive stages (āśramas) of the individual life are the student's life (brahmacarya), the householder's life (gārhasthya), the retired and contemplative life in the forest (vānaprastha), and the monastic life (sannyāsa). A man's svadharma depends as much on his stage of life as on his social order.

The main duties of a student, whatever social order he may belong to, are the formation of character and receiving education, religious as well as secular. In ancient India the students of the upper three classes lived a strict life of discipline with the teacher. The moral fitness of the student was an essential condition even for receiving intellectual knowledge; because, knowledge being power, there is danger in its abuse. Obedience and service to the teacher and contact with his exemplary life were the effective means to develop the student's moral nature. Moral and spiritual life do not grow without inspiration.

For intellectual development instruction may be an adequate means, but not for the moral and the spiritual. It is from living examples, and not from mere words, that one can draw inspiration. From books and talks a student may acquire lofty moral and spiritual ideas, yet they will not be implanted in his mind as ideals until he finds them exemplified in the lives of the great. Direct contact with such lives is most helpful. The greater the reverence for them the greater the inspiration. So says Lord Tennyson: "Let knowledge grow from more to more. But more of reverence in us dwell."[12]

After finishing his education a person can marry and lead the householder's life if he so desires. The householder is the mainstay of society. He is its full-fledged member, so to speak. The student, the forest-dweller, and the sannyāsī (monk) are not members of society in the same sense. The sannyāsī actually does not belong to society. He is beyond all social orders. It is especially as householders that the brāhmaṇas, the kṣatriyas, the vaiśyas, and the śūdras have specific social duties. In the other three stages of life their duties are similar.

Hindu scriptures have enjoined two special types of work on all householders. These are the *iṣṭa* and the *pūrta*.[13] The iṣṭa consists of five kinds of daily sacrifice or service: (1) service to the seers and the sages (ṛṣis) in the form of scriptural study, (2) service to the deities in

[12]Tennyson, *In Memoriam*, London, Macmillan and Co., 1905, prologue, p.2.
[13]See MS IV:226.

the form of offering oblations, (3) service to the forefathers, (4) service to humanity, and (5) service to other living creatures.[14] It is worthy of note that here the individual life is conceived as an integral part of the universal life. Man is considered to be a born debtor. He owes more to the universe than the universe owes to him. Throughout his life he should endeavor to discharge his debts to others instead of clamoring for his rights.[15] The second type of work, the pūrta, denotes humanitarian deeds, e.g., excavating water-tanks, wells, canals, etc., establishment of temples, alms-houses, rest-houses, and so forth.

In order to meditate on God and worship Him, free from the trammels of the worldly life, the householder may retire into the forest on the completion of his fiftieth year. He may either leave his wife in the care of his sons or take her with him, as the case may be. As a forest-dweller he should live in one particular place the contemplative life, practice austerities, perform certain rites, and cultivate knowledge. In the course of time, when he is convinced that without complete renunciation of all earthly ties and obligations he cannot realize the unity or the identity of the self with the Supreme Being, which is the way to Liberation, then he can be a sannyāsī (literally, a complete renouncer).

A sannyāsī is the typical follower of the way of renunciation. He does not identify himself with any particular family, society, race, or country, not even with his body or mind. He disowns everything but the Self. He is always aware of his oneness with the Supreme Spirit. God is his all-in-all. As a man of God he belongs to the whole universe. He is a friend of all. No man or society has special claim upon him. He is supersocial. His entire being aims at the attainment of Supreme Good. The nature of a sannyāsī is thus described by Śrī Kṛṣṇa:

> Alone, free from attachment, and with his senses under control, he should move in this world. All his diversions, all his delight should be in the Self; with his mind on the Self he should look upon everything with the same eyes. Taking shelter in a secluded and secure place, pure-hearted through devotion to Me, the sannyāsī should meditate on the One Self being identified with me. . . .
>
> The sage should not get vexed by people nor vex them himself. He

[14]See MS III:70.

[15]Cf. St. Paul's Epistle to the Romans, 13:7, "Render therefore to all their dues: tribute to whom tribute *is due:* custom to whom custom, fear to whom fear; honor to whom honor."

> should put up with insult and never insult anybody. For the sake of the body he should oppose none, as the animals do. The One Supreme Self dwells in all individual bodies including his own, as the moon is reflected in so many pots of water; and all bodies are made of the same material.
>
> Possessed of fortitude, he should not be dejected when he gets no food, nor be delighted when he gets any, for both are under divine control. He should try to secure food, as preservation of life is desirable; through it he can contemplate on Truth, knowing which he becomes free.[16]

The way the sannyāsīs realize Brahman has been graphically presented by the *Muṇḍaka Upaniṣad:*

> Finding the Self the seers become contented with that knowledge. Their souls attain fulfillment in the Supreme Self. Free from all desires and serene, the wise, ever meditative on the Self, reach everywhere the all-pervading Brahman and at death enter into It, the One that is all. Thoroughly convinced of the truth of Vedantic knowledge, and pure-minded through the practice of sannyāsa, the seekers, ever exerting themselves, become established in Immortal Brahman in their lifetime and at death, which is the final one, attain absolute freedom in It.[17]

Thus, by living the four stages of life successively a man can attain Liberation. This is the regular course. But everyone need not live all the consecutive stages in order to reach the Goal. There may be extraordinary students (brahmacārīs) who can live the life of a forest-dweller or a sannyāsī without going through the intermediary stage or stages, just as there may be exceptional householders who can enter into monastic life directly. As a matter of fact, there have been many such instances of extraordinary capacity. The Upaniṣads lend support to these supernormal cases:

> After completing the student's life (brahmacarya) a person should be a householder; after living the householder's life he should be a forest-dweller, and after being a forest-dweller he should be a sannyāsī. Or, it may happen that he can become a sannyāsī from the student's life or from the householder's life or from the forest-life. . . . The very day one has the spirit of renunciation one can be a sannyāsī.[18]

This view is endorsed by Śrī Kṛṣṇa:

[16]SB XI:18.20,21,31-34.
[17]Mu.U. III:2.5,6.
[18]Jab.U. 4.

> The qualified brahmacārī,[19] with his mind devoted to Me, may become a householder, or a forest-dweller, or a sannyāsī; or, he may proceed from one stage of life to another successively, but never reversely.[20]

In the process of time the old institutions of India have undergone a great change. At the present age the Hindus do not live the four orders of life (āśramas) strictly in the same way as in ancient days. The systems of brahmacarya (religious studentship) and vānaprastha (forest-life) barely exist in old forms. Most of the Hindus today, as it is everywhere, rest satisfied with the householder's life. Yet there are many men and women who repair in advanced age to holy and secluded places to live the life of devotion and meditation; and sannyāsa is still prevalent.

4. *The efficacy of svadharma for the attainment of Supreme Good.*

An important point to note in this connection is that a man can attain Supreme Good from any of these four stages of life (āśramas). Each of them is adequate to lead to the Goal, if rightly practiced. In this sense all are equally efficacious. Yet each succeeding stage (āśrama) is considered to be higher than the preceding one, because to enter it a greater advancement in life is needed than to enter the other. The fourth āśrama, sannyāsa, is the highest because no other āśrama requires such a high degree of spirituality to adopt it; and being the culmination of renunciation, it affords the greatest facilities for the attainment of the Supreme Goal. But the essential thing is the suitability of the āśramas to the varying tendencies and capacities of the seekers.

The one condition for Liberation is the complete renunciation of "I-ness" and "my-ness," culminating in whole-souled devotion to God, or in the realization of the identity of the self with the Supreme Being. The various rites and deeds, conventions and insignia of the different orders of life, have value so far as they conduce to spiritual unfoldment. Indeed, it is the one purpose of all of them. Swami Vivekananda rightly observes:

> To give an objective definition of duty is thus entirely impossible. Yet

[19]The text uses the word *dvija,* which means "twice-born." A member of any of the upper three classes of the society is so called after the purificatory rite of upanayana (investiture with the sacred cord), when he is initiated into brahmacarya āśrama (religious studentship). This is his second birth.

[20]SB XI:17.38.

there is duty from the subjective side. Any action that makes us go Godward is a good action, and is our duty; any action that makes us go downward is evil, and is not our duty.[21]

The duties of the four āśramas are so ordained that an individual, according to his psychophysical constitution, may find full scope for spiritual development in one or another of them. Some of the duties which are common to all of them are solely intended for the cultivation of the moral and the spiritual nature of the followers. These are enumerated by Śrī Kṛṣṇa as follows:

> Cleanliness, ablution, regular worship in the morning, at noon, and in the evening, straight-forwardness, visiting the holy places, repetition of the sacred word or formula, avoidance of things not to be touched or eaten and of persons not to be accosted, looking upon all beings as Myself, and control of mind, speech, and body — these, O Uddhava, are the observances meant for all the āśramas.[22]

Therefore, in order to attain Liberation it is not imperative on a brahmacārī (a celibate student) to become a householder or a forest-dweller or a sannyāsī. One may remain a lifelong (naiṣṭhika) brahmacārī and reach the Goal. Similarly, for God-realization it is not obligatory on a householder to leave the world. He has an option in this matter, as Śrī Kṛṣṇa says: "A devotee, worshipping Me through his household duties, may lead a householder's life, may retire into the forest, or, if he has progeny, may embrace sannyāsa."[23]

That a person can reach the Goal from any one of these four stages or āśramas has also been affirmed by Manu: "Of all these āśramas, one or more, being rightly pursued, according to the directions of the scriptures, lead the true follower, the seeker of Brahman, to the Supreme Goal."[24]

To sum up, the various duties of all the different orders of the social and the individual life (varṇas and āśramas) are efficacious for the attainment of Supreme Good, when performed in the spirit of worshipping the Lord. This has been very clearly stated by Śrī Kṛṣṇa:

> The worship of Me is a duty for all. He who thus worships Me constantly and exclusively, through the performance of his duties, knowing My presence in all beings, soon attains to a steadfast devotion to Me. O Uddhava, through his undying devotion he comes to Me, the Great Lord of all beings, the beginning and end of all, and so their

[21]CW I, p. 62. [22]SB XI:17.34,35. [23]SB XI:17.55. [24]MS VI:88.

> cause — Brahman. Having his mind thus purified by the performance of his duties and being aware of my Divinity he gains knowledge and realization and soon attains to Me. All this duty, consisting of specific practices, of those belonging to different social orders (varṇas) and stages of life (āśramas), if attended with devotion to Me, become supreme and conducive to Liberation.[25]

So we find that svadharma constitutes the bridge between God and the world. The fourfold division of the social and the individual life is intended to lead every human being, at whatever level of life, to Supreme Good along his own line of growth and thus to maintain the entire structure of human society in steady and progressive form.

5. *The spiritual ideal indispensable to right living. Man's sensuous outlook has to be transformed into the spiritual. The whole process is the key to his material as well as spiritual greatness.*

Thus every individual can advance towards the highest Goal, while doing his duties in life. As long as he has sense-desires he can proceed towards it indirectly, that is, through his search for material welfare. This is the way of activity, pravṛtti-mārga, characterized by desire. On this path the regulative principle of the seeker of prosperity is virtue, which directs his course and enables him through the fulfillment of his desires to realize their futility. Without the practice of virtue this insight does not grow. Each and every seeker of prosperity is not, therefore, a follower of the way of activity (pravṛtti-mārga), which is an ethical course intended to lead to the way of Supreme Good. Uncontrolled by virtue, the search for prosperity does not turn into religious discipline.

Being convinced of the blinding and binding nature of sense-desires, the seeker of prosperity tries to get rid of them by the practice of Karma-yōga, by the performance of his duties with a dispassionate attitude. When his mind is purged of them, then he can seek the Highest directly: he can make it the supreme object of his life. This is the way of renunciation, nivṛtti-mārga, characterized by desirelessness. In pursuing the way of renunciation a seeker of Supreme Good does not necessarily give up his worldly activities. It depends upon his mental constitution and situation in life. He may continue his duties (svadharma) with the spirit of renunciation, in whatever sphere of life he may be. Knowing the Divine Being to be the

[25]SB XI:18.43-47.

one Self of all, the devotee finds Him within himself and in others and gives up all egoistic thoughts and feelings. Thus, resigning himself completely to the Lord, he serves and worships Him through all his activities; finally he realizes his complete unity with Him and becomes free forever.

It has already been explained how, as a result of the practice of Karma-yōga, when the mind is adequately purified, the spiritual aspirant develops ardent longing for God-realization and gains competence for the practice of Bhakti-yogā or Jñāna-yōga proper, according to his inner attitude towards the Supreme Being. (See Ch. IX, sec.8.)

Bhakti-yōga is the path of devotion. It is the direct approach to the personal God, the Supreme Being possessed of all blessed qualities, Saguṇa Brahman. This leads to the realization of the *unity* of the individual self with the Supreme Self. Jñāna-yōga is the way of knowledge, in which reasoning rather than feeling is predominant. It is the direct approach to the All-transcendent, Impersonal Being, Nirguṇa Brahman, beyond the distinction of substance and attribute. This culminates in the realization of the *identity* of the individual self with the Supreme Self. By either of the two ways the aspirant attains complete freedom from all bondages and sufferings and gains Supreme Bliss.

Jñāna-yōga is a steep course meant for specially qualified spiritual aspirants. Bhakti-yōga is less arduous and is meant for spiritual aspirants in general. Says Śrī Kṛṣṇa in the *Bhagavad-gītā:*

> Greater is the hardship of those whose minds are set on the Indefinable, Unmanifest One. For the way to the Indefinable is difficult for them to follow who identify themselves with the body.[26]

After realizing Saguṇa Brahman by the path of devotion, the seeker can realize Nirguṇa Brahman with less difficulty. That through devotion the aspirant can realize oneness with Brahman is evident from the words of Śrī Kṛṣṇa: "By devotion he knows Me in reality, what and who I am; then having known Me in reality, he forthwith enters Me."[27]

When a Karma-yōgī gains competence for the practice of Bhakti-yōga or Jñāna-yōga, the continuation of the practice of Karma-yōga, that is to say, the performance of domestic and social duties with dispassion, is no longer indispensable to his inner development. He

[26] BG XII:5. [27] BG XVIII:55.

can give up the worldly activities and devote himself exclusively to the practice of spiritual disciplines pertaining to Bhakti-yōga or Jñāna-yōga according to the nature of the case. Or, under special circumstances, he can continue the performance of his duties, domestic and social, with higher and higher spiritual outlook relative to Saguṇa or Nirguṇa Brahman, until he reaches the Goal.

6. *Concluding Remarks.*

The whole scheme of life has been drawn up by the Vedic seers with the Ultimate Goal in view. Apparently, their purpose is to lead men and women from all levels of life to the highest end. Even from the bottom of a pit a man can proceed step by step, along proper ways, towards the mountaintop and eventually reach there. But the deeper purpose of the seers is to make man's entire life safe and sound. The Supreme Ideal is as necessary for this life as for the life beyond, as essential to the temporal life as to the spiritual. Unless directed towards the spiritual goal, life in the sense-world cannot succeed. As an end in itself it is bound to be a failure. It will collapse of its own excesses.

It is a truism that material life without the support of the moral cannot hold its own. When material well-being becomes the primary objective of life, then inveterate sense-desire, insatiable by nature, dominates human reason and will and makes all other phases of life — intellectual, aesthetic, moral, and even religious — subservient to the material. When the moral life is unsound, how can it support the material? Only the spiritual Ideal, which has control over man's sense-desire, can make his moral life secure. Then the moral life can sustain the material. The various aspects of life find right directions only when they turn towards the realization of the spiritual self, the center of human personality.

Broadly speaking, men have viewed life from two extreme positions: from the standpoint of the physical body and from the standpoint of the spiritual self. It is the inborn tendency of man to take the first. No philosopher is needed to teach him this. To take the second requires culture. Without repeated instruction and training, no one can change from the standpoint of the body to the standpoint of the spiritual self. Those who take the standpoint of the body naturally consider physical well-being and comforts to be the principal objects of life. Their feelings, thoughts, and activities tend to sense-gratification. They have, in short, a sensuous outlook on life.

Those who can take the standpoint of the spiritual self hold the realization of the true nature of the self and its unity with the Divine Being to be the Supreme Ideal. Their feelings, thoughts, and activities are directed to that end. They have a spiritual outlook on life. A man's moral nature is weakened or strengthened by the emphasis he puts on one or the other of the two ideals. It is true that between these two extremes there are other ideals, such as the pursuit of knowledge, aesthetic culture, humanitarianism, and so forth. But the seekers of these ideals also are found to be disposed to the one or the other of the two viewpoints. Whenever the sensuous outlook on life prevails, man's uncontrolled emotions motivated by the desire for sense-pleasure create many complications in his private and public life.

Little do we think that most of our present day problems, domestic, social, national, and international have their origin in the sensuous outlook predominant in the modern mind. The social, the economic, and the political troubles of the modern age are mostly symptoms of the disease and not diseases in themselves. They cannot be effectively cured simply by the readjustment of the conditions of their respective fields. As long as the disease persists the symptoms will reappear in some other form. The basic need of the world for the effective solution of its problems is a change of outlook on life. Man's sensuous outlook has to be transformed into the spiritual by progressive training. The whole process is the key to his material as well as spiritual greatness. On this depend his strength, wisdom, freedom, peace, progress, and perfectibility.

BIBLIOGRAPHY I

ENGLISH WORKS QUOTED FROM IN THIS BOOK

Bacon, Lord, "In Praise of Knowledge," in *The Works of Lord Bacon,* Vol. 1. Philadelphia: Carey and Hart, 1841.

Beck, William S., *Modern Science and the Nature of Life.* New York: Harcourt, Brace and Co., 1957.

Boss, Medard, *The Analysis of Dreams,* translated by Arnold J. Pomerans. New York: Philosophical Library, 1958.

Bury, J.B., *The Idea of Progress; An Inquiry into its Origin and Growth.* 1920; reprint ed., New York: Dover Publications, 1955.

———, *Selected Essays,* edited by Harold Temperley. 1930; reprint ed., Freeport, N.Y.: Books for Libraries Press, 1968.

Carlyle, Thomas, *On Heroes and Hero-worship and the Heroic in History.* 1935; reprint ed., London: Oxford University Press, 1963.

———, *Sartor Resartus,* edited by Archibald MacMechan. Boston: Athenaean Press, Ginn and Co., 1896.

Conklin, Edwin Grant, *Heredity and Environment in the Development of Man,* 3d ed., rev. Princeton, N.J.: Princeton University Press, 1919.

Darwin, Charles, *The Origin of Species by Means of Natural Selection,* 2 vols. New York: D. Appleton and Co., 1897.

Dasgupta, Surendranath, *A History of Indian Philosophy,* Vols. 1-5. Cambridge: At the University Press, 1932-62.

Disraeli, Benjamin, speech at Glasgow University, November 19, 1873.

Dobzhansky, Theodosius, *The Biology of Ultimate Concern,* New York: New American Library, 1967.

Eckhart, Meister, *Meister Eckhart: A Modern Translation,* Raymond Blakney, trans. and ed. New York: Harper and Brothers, 1941.

Encyclopaedia Britannica, 1948 ed., s.v. "Biology."

———, Book of the Year, 1972.

Freud, Sigmund, *Beyond the Pleasure Principle,* translated by James Strachey. New York: Liveright, 1950.

Haeckel, Ernst Heinrich, *Riddle of the Universe,* 1901, in *Outline of Great Books,* edited by J.A. Hammerton. New York: Wise and Co., 1937.

Haldane, J.S., *The Philosophical Basis of Biology.* Garden City, N.Y.: Doubleday, Doran and Co., 1931.

Head, Joseph, and Cranston, S.L., editors and compilers, *Reincarnation, An East-West Anthology.* New York: Julian Press, 1961.

Holy Bible, authorized King James Version.

Hume, David, "On the Immortality of the Soul," in *Essays.* London: George Routledge and Sons, [1900?].

Huxley, Julian, *What Dare I Think?* New York: Harper and Brothers, 1931.

Johnson, Raynor C., *The Imprisoned Splendour.* New York: Harper and Brothers, 1953.

Johnston, James, *The Essentials of Biology.* New York: Longmans, Green and Co., 1932.

Jung, C.G., "The Structure and Dynamics of the Psyche," in *The Collected Works of C. G. Yung,* Bollingen Series 20, Vol. 8, translated by R.F.C. Hull; edited by G. Adler, M. Fordham, and H. Read. New York: Princeton University Press, Pantheon Books, 1960.

Keeton, William T., *Biological Science.* New York: Norton and Co., 1967.

Lao Tzu, *Tao Te Ching,* The Texts of Taoism, Vol. 1, translated by James Legge. Sacred Books of the East, edited by F. Max Muller, Vol. 39. Oxford University Press, 1891; reprint ed., New York: Dover Publications, 1967.

Lillie, Ralph Stayner, *General Biology and Philosophy of Organisms,* Chicago: University of Chicago Press, 1945.

Livingstone, R.W., *The Greek Genius and Its Meaning to Us.* Oxford: Clarendon Press, 1924.

Mumford, Lewis, *Technics and Civilization.* New York: Harcourt, Brace and Co., 1934.

———, *Values for Survival.* New York: Harcourt, Brace and Co., 1946.

Nikhilananda, Swami, translator, *The Gospel of Sri Ramakrishna.* New York: Ramakrishna-Vivekananda Center, 1942.

Osborn, Henry Fairfeld, *The Origin and Evolution of Life.* New York: Charles Scribner's Sons, 1921.

Parker, Dorothy, *Not So Deep As A Well.* New York: Viking Press, 1938.

Plato, "Phaedrus," in *The Dialogues of Plato,* translated by Benjamin Jowett, Great Books of the Western World, Vol. 7. Chicago: Encyclopaedia Britannica, 1952.

Pope, Alexander, *Essay on Man,* The Works of Alexander Pope, Vol. 2. 1871; reprint ed., New York: Gordian Press, 1967.

Prabhavananda, Swami, *The Eternal Companion.* Hollywood: Vedanta Press, 1970.

Radhakrishnan, S., *Eastern Religions and Western Thought,* 2d ed. London: Oxford University Press, 1940.

Rhine, J.B., *The Reach of the Mind.* New York: William Sloane Associates, 1947.

Saradananda, Swami, *Sri Ramakrishna, The Great Master,* translated by Swami Jagadananda. Madras, India: Sri Ramakrishna Math, 1952.

Satprakashananda, Swami, *Methods of Knowledge: According to Advaita Vedanta.* London: George Allen and Unwin, 1965; reprint ed., Mayavati, India: Advaita Ashrama, 1974.

Schrödinger, Erwin, *What is Life? The Physical Aspect of the Living Cell.* Cambridge: The University Press, 1946.

Schubert-Soldern, Rainer, *Mechanism and Vitalism; Philosophical Aspects of Biology.* London: Burns and Oates, 1962.

Seal, Brajendranath, *Positive Sciences of the Ancient Hindus.* London: Longmans, Green and Co., 1915; reprint ed., Delhi: Moti Lal Banarsi Dass, 1958.

Sherrington, Charles, *Man on His Nature.* New York: Macmillan and Co., 1941.

Sinnott, Edmund W., *The Bridge of Life: From Matter to Spirit.* New York: Simon Schuster, 1966.

———; Dunn, L.C.; and Dobzhansky, Theodosius, *Principles of Genetics,* 5th ed. New York: McGraw-Hill Book Co., 1958.

Spencer, Herbert, "Progress, Its Law and Cause," in *Essays,* Vol. 1. New York: D. Appleton and Co., 1907.

———, *Social Statics.* London: John Chapman, 1851.

Strausbaugh, Perry D., and Weimer, Bernal K., *Elements of Biology.* New York: John Wiley and Sons, 1944.

———, ———, *General Biology.* New York: John Wiley and Sons, 1958.

Sturtevant, A.H., *A History of Genetics.* New York: Harper and Row, 1965.

Tapasyananda, Swami, *Sri Sarada Devi, The Holy Mother: (Her Life and Conversations),* conversations translated by Swami Nikhilananda. Madras, India: Sri Ramakrishna Math, 1958.

Tennyson, Alfred, *In Memoriam.* London: Macmillan and Co., 1905.

———, "Locksley Hall," in *The Poems of Tennyson,* edited by Christopher Ricks. London: Longmans, Green and Co., 1969.

Toynbee, Arnold J., "The Ancient Mediterranean View of Man," in *Man's Right to Knowledge.* New York: Columbia University Press, 1954.

Villee, Claude A., *Biology,* 4th ed. Philadelphia: W.B. Saunders Co., 1962.

Vivekananda, Swami, *The Complete Works of Swami Vivekananda,* Vols. 1-8. Mayavati, India: Advaita Ashrama, 1922-1951.

Ward, James, *Principles of Psychology.* London: Cambridge University Press, 1933.

BIBLIOGRAPHY II

SANSKRIT WORKS QUOTED FROM IN THIS BOOK

Aitareya Āraṇyaka with the com. of Sāyaṇa, ASS.

Aitareya Brāhmaṇa (Text in Punthi form).

Ātma-bōdha, The Works of Śaṅkara (new edn.) Vol. X, VVP.

Bhagavad-gītā, with the commentaries of Śaṅkara, Ānandagiri, Madhusūdana, Śrīdhara and three others, NSP, 2nd edn., 1936.

Bhāṣā-pariccheda (kārikāvalī), with the com. "Siddhānta-muktāvalī" by Viśwanātha Nyāya-pañcānana and explanatory notes "Dinakarī" and "Rāmarudrī," NSP, Revised end., 1928.

Dhammapada (Pāli Text) — one of the fifteen books of Khuddaka-nikāya of Suttapiṭaka. *The Tripiṭaka,* 41 Vols. Pali Publication Board (Bihar Government), 1956.

Brahma-sūtras of Bādarāyaṇa — with S. com. and sub-commentaries, e.g., Gōvindānanda's "Ratnaprabhā," Vācaspati's "Bhāmatī," and Ānandagiri's "Nyāya-nirṇaya," NSP, 3rd edn., 1934.

Kauṣītakī Brāhmaṇa (of the Ṛg Veda).

Kūrma Purāṇa — one of the eighteen Purāṇas (true or legendary tales expounding spiritual truths). This is one of the six dedicated to Śiva.

Mahābhārata of Kṛṣṇa-dvaipāyana Veda-vyāsa. The later of the two great Sanskrit epic poems consisting of eighteen parvas or sections. The world's longest poetical work. Eng. trans. by P. C. Ray, Bharata Press, Calcutta, 1893.

Manu-smṛti with Kullūka's com. "Manvartha-muktāvalī," NSP, 1929.

Naiṣkarmya-siddhi by Sureśvarācārya, with Jñānōttama's com. "Candrikā." Revised edn. by M. Hiriyanna, Bombay Sanskrit and Prakrit Series (38), 1925.

Pañcadaśī by Bhāratī-tīrtha Vidyāraṇya, with the commentary of Rāmakṛṣṇa, NSP, 1935.

Ṛg-Veda Saṁhitā (Text with exhaustive Index) Svadhyaya-mandala, Paradi, Surat, India.

Ṛg-Veda Saṁhitā with Sāyaṇa's com., Vols. I-V. A new critical edn. based on old unused manuscripts of the commentary. The fifth volume contains various indices to the Ṛg-Veda, Vaidika Samsodhana Mandala, Poona, India, 1933-51.

Sāṁkhya-darśana (Sāṁkhya-sūtras of Kapila) with Vijñānabhikṣu's com. "Pravacana-bhāṣya." Vacaspatya Press, Calcutta, 1936.

Sāṁkhya-kārikā of Īśvarakṛṣṇa — with Vācaspati Miśra's com. "Tattvakaumudī" and explanatory notes by Pt. Rājeśvara Śastrī Drāviḍa, CSS, 2nd edn., 1932.

Śatapatha Brāhmaṇa (Mādhyandina recension) with Vedārthaprakāśa of Sāyaṇācārya and the commentary of Hariswamin, Vols. I-V, published by Gangavishnu Shrikrishnadass, Laxmi Venkatesvara Steam Press, Kalyan, Bombay, 1940.

Śrīmad-bhāgavatam by Kṛṣṇadvaipāyana Veda-vyāsa with Śrīdhara Swāmī's com. "Bhāvārtha-dīpikā," Bangavasi Press, Calcutta, 1927. Alphabetical index to the first lines of the stanzas (14,500 approx. in 12 sections) by Ramanalal Sastri Bhagavatabhusana. Serpent Road, Ahmedabad, India, 1963.

Taittirīya Brāhmaṇa (of Kṛṣṇa Yajur-Veda), Vols. I, II, with Sāyaṇa's com., ASS.

Upaniṣads, The Ten Principal, with S. com. ("Daśopaniṣad-bhāṣyam"). Vol. I includes *Īśa, Aitareya, Kaṭha, Kena, Chāndōgya, Taittirīya, Praśna, Māṇḍūkya, Muṇḍaka;* Vol. II contains *Bṛhadāraṇyaka.* Asktekar and Co., Poona, 1927-28.

Upaniṣads, Twenty-eight (Text only). Besides the above ten includes *Śvetāśvatara, Jābāla, Kaivalya, Kauṣītakī, Muktika, Nārāyaṇa, Mahānārāyaṇa,* and others.

Upaniṣads, One Hundred and Eight, Īśa and the rest. Text only with different readings, NSP, 1938.

Vaiśeṣika-darśana (Sūtras of Kaṇāda) — with Śaṅkara Miśra's com. "Upaskāra" and Praśastapāda's exposition "Padārthadharma-saṁgraha" in two parts, CSS, 1924-1931.

Vedānta-paribhāṣā by Dharmarājā Adhvarīndra — (1) Ed. by Mm. Anantakrisna Sastri with introduction and com. "Paribhāṣā-prakāśikā." University of Calcutta. (2) with Rāmakṛṣṇa Adhvarīndra's com. "Śikhāmaṇi" and Amaladās's gloss "Maṇiprabhā," Sri Venkatesvara Press, Bombay, 1911.

Vedānta-sāra by Sadānanda Yōgīndra — with commentaries "Subōdhinī" of Nṛsiṁha Sarasvatī and "Vidvanmanōrañjinī" of Rāmatīrtha. Ed. by Col. G. A. Jacob; NSP, 1925.

Vivekacūḍāmaṇi — a masterpiece of Advaita Vedānta in poetry. *The Works of Śaṅkara* (new edn.) Vol. X, VVP.

Yōga-sūtras of Patañjali — with Vyāsa-bhāṣya, Vācaspati's "Tattvavaiśāradī" and Bhōjadeva's "Rājamārtaṇḍa." ASS, 3rd edn., 1932.

INDEX

Abiogenesis, 108
Adhikāri-bheda, 270
Advaita Vedanta, 34n
Āgāmi (prospective) karma, 139, 140, 142
Ahaṁkāra (I-ness), 80
Aitareya Upaniṣad (Ai.U.), 59n, 158n, 213
Ajātaśatru, King, 116-18, 155
Ajñāna, 37n, 181n; as causal body (blissful sheath), 64, 70, 154, 159, 161-62, 223; causes inapprehension of Real self, 37n, 130, 158, 171, 181n, 223-24; causes sense-desire, 130; experienced in deep sleep, 148, 154, 160, 161-63; freedom from, 179, 180, 181, 186, 232; limits individual self, 37; two functions of, 181n. *See also* Avidyā; Ignorance
Akāśa (ether), 52n, 123, 190
Amṛtabindu Upaniṣad 100n
Analysis of Dream, The (Boss), 166
Ānandagiri, 138n, 263
Ānandamaya kōśa (blissful sheath), 65, 66, 69-70
Annamaya kōśa (physical sheath), 66, 67
Antaḥkaraṇa. *See* Mind
Antaḥkaraṇa-vṛtti (modes of the mind), 79
Antarindriya (internal organ), 74, 78
Apāna, 60, 67, 105, 106, 156. *See also* Prāṇa
Aristotle, on dreams, 166
Arjuna, 93, 100, 192-93, 260, 277
Artha (wealth), 246, 250, 255
Āsana, 235
Āśramas (stages of life), 280-285
Ātmā-bōdha, 60n
Ātman, 48, 52-53, 161, 255; attaining, 41, 42, 70; sustains body, 50, 102-3
Avidvan (fullness of knowledge), 181
Avidyā: freedom from, 142, 236-37; veiling power of, 64, 130-31, 181n. *See also* Ajñāna; Ignorance

Bacon, Francis, 71, 250, 250n
Beck, William, 202-3
Being-Consciousness-Bliss, underlies all, 72, 119, 124, 125, 159
Being, Supreme: attaining, 47, 178, 180, 228, 234, 239, 288; attaining, brings freedom, 24, 175, 286; as consciousness in innermost self, 47, 55, 57, 58; self one with, 23, 47, 98, 154, 182, 285-86. *See also* Brahman
Beyond the Pleasure Principle (Freud), 167
Bhagavad-gītā (BG), 26n, 34n, 42n, 51, 58, 75, 82n, 83n, 92n, 93n, 98n, 100n, 101n, 134n, 138n, 176n, 179n, 184n, 188n, 189n, 191n, 193, 198n, 199n, 209n, 211n, 229, 233n, 238, 241n, 243n, 257n, 259, 260n, 261-62n, 263n, 266n, 274n, 275, 276n, 277n, 286
Bhāgavatam, Śrīmad (SB), 42n, 121, 232, 235, 264, 275
Bhakti-yōga, 230-32, 235, 237, 258, 259, 260, 261
Biogenesis, 108-9
Biological Science (Keeton), 109n, 113
Biology (Villee), 201n, 202, 203n, 207, 208
Biology of Ultimate Concern, The (Dobzhansky), 204
Birth, human, 59, 211-14
Body, causal, 49, 63-66; at death, 138, 211; forms blissful sheath, 65, 66, 69-70; medium of deep sleep experience, 63-64, 65, 151, 159, 161-62; of nature of ignorance, 64, 223
Body, gross, physical, 49, 58, 66, 103; conceived as city, 50-51, 55; control of, 40-41, 78, 81, 82, 89; death of, 36, 180, 181-82, 183; death of, does not affect real self, 199; death of, left behind, 61, 87, 138, 171, 176-77, 180, 211; distinct from mind, 72, 75, 77, 172, 199, 206, 207; endowed with consciousness, 31-33, 51, 52-53, 54, 55, 58, 198, 255; forms physical sheath, 66-67; identification with, 31, 37, 38, 39, 149, 161, 224, 233, 287; identification with, causes bondage, 24, 31, 43; identification with, causes desires, 130, 167; organs of, 50, 60, 78, 79, 150, 151-52; prāṇa animates, 61, 102-109, 123, 156, 168; not real self of man, 23, 38, 52,